Reasoning and Writing

Level E
Textbook

Siegfried Engelmann

Bonnie Grossen

SRA

A Division of The McGraw-Hill Companies

Columbus, Ohio

Cover Credits

(t) Photo Spin, (b) PhotoDisc.

SRA/McGraw-Hill

A Division of The ***McGraw·Hill*** *Companies*

Send all inquiries to:
SRA/McGraw-Hill
8787 Orion Place
Columbus, OH 43240-4027

Printed in the United States of America.

ISBN 0-02-684788-4

1 2 3 4 5 6 7 8 9 VHJ 06 05 04 03 02 01 00

Lesson 1

Part A Say the subject and the predicate for these sentences.

1. The boys were happy.
2. Those little boys were happy.
3. Those nasty little boys on the playground were happy.
4. Those nasty little boys on the playground threw stones in the air.
5. Five boys threw stones.
6. They threw large stones.
7. Their mothers became angry.
8. The mothers told the boys to stop.

Part B A good way to explain some things is with parallel sentences. Parallel sentences are very similar to each other.

- Here's a pair of parallel sentences:

  They fed sheep.
  They fed goats.

- Here's another pair of parallel sentences:

  Their house was big.
  Their garage was also big.

- You're going to write parallel sentences that have the word **also.**

They did their math homework.

Part C Look at each picture. Write a parallel sentence that uses the word **also.**

1. They cut down a large tree.

2. She wore a blue blouse.

3. The walls are dirty.

4. Squirrels were on the roof.

5. The dog was under the table.

Key

1. My brother chased a butterfly.
2. An old dog howled all night long.
3. His writing was hard to read.
4. Five red bugs got inside our tent.
5. Tom laughed at two clowns.

Lesson 2

Part A

- You can identify parts of speech without guessing when you work with regular-order sentences.
- Here are rules for most regular-order sentences:

  Rule 1: The last word of the subject is a **noun.**

  Rule 2: The first word of the predicate is a **verb.**
- All the sentences you've written follow these rules. So you can figure out a noun in the subject and the verb without guessing.

Part B

Look at each picture. Write a parallel sentence that uses the word **also.**

1. The girl's father was happy.

2. The man brushed his teeth.

3. She carried a box.

4. They had red paint.

5. A cat was in the garden.

Lesson 3

Part A

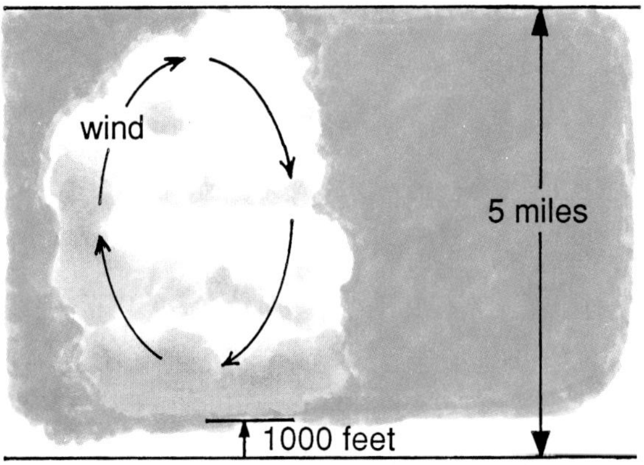

Part B

For each statement, write a parallel statement that uses the word also.

1. You can get to Greenville on Route 41.
2. You can get to Lester on Route 49.
3. Lester is 27 miles from Tintown.

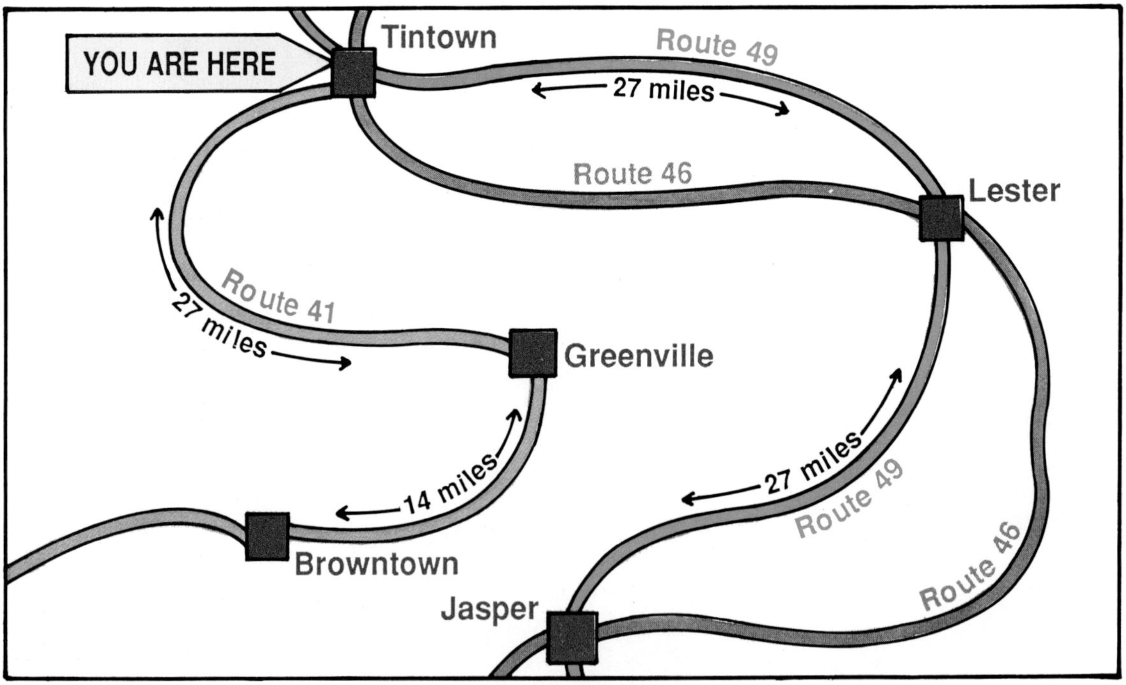

Independent Work

Part C For each item, write a parallel sentence that uses the word **also.**

1. She bought a soft drink.

2. The garage was on fire.

3. Four rabbits were in the garden.

4. Tom's shirt was soaked.

5. The Ajax Building had a broken window.

Lesson 4

Part A For each item, write **two** parallel sentences that use the word **also.**

1. Fall Creek is 14 miles from Olson.
2. The Jones family stopped in a big town.
3. The Briggs family stopped 18 miles from Dexter.

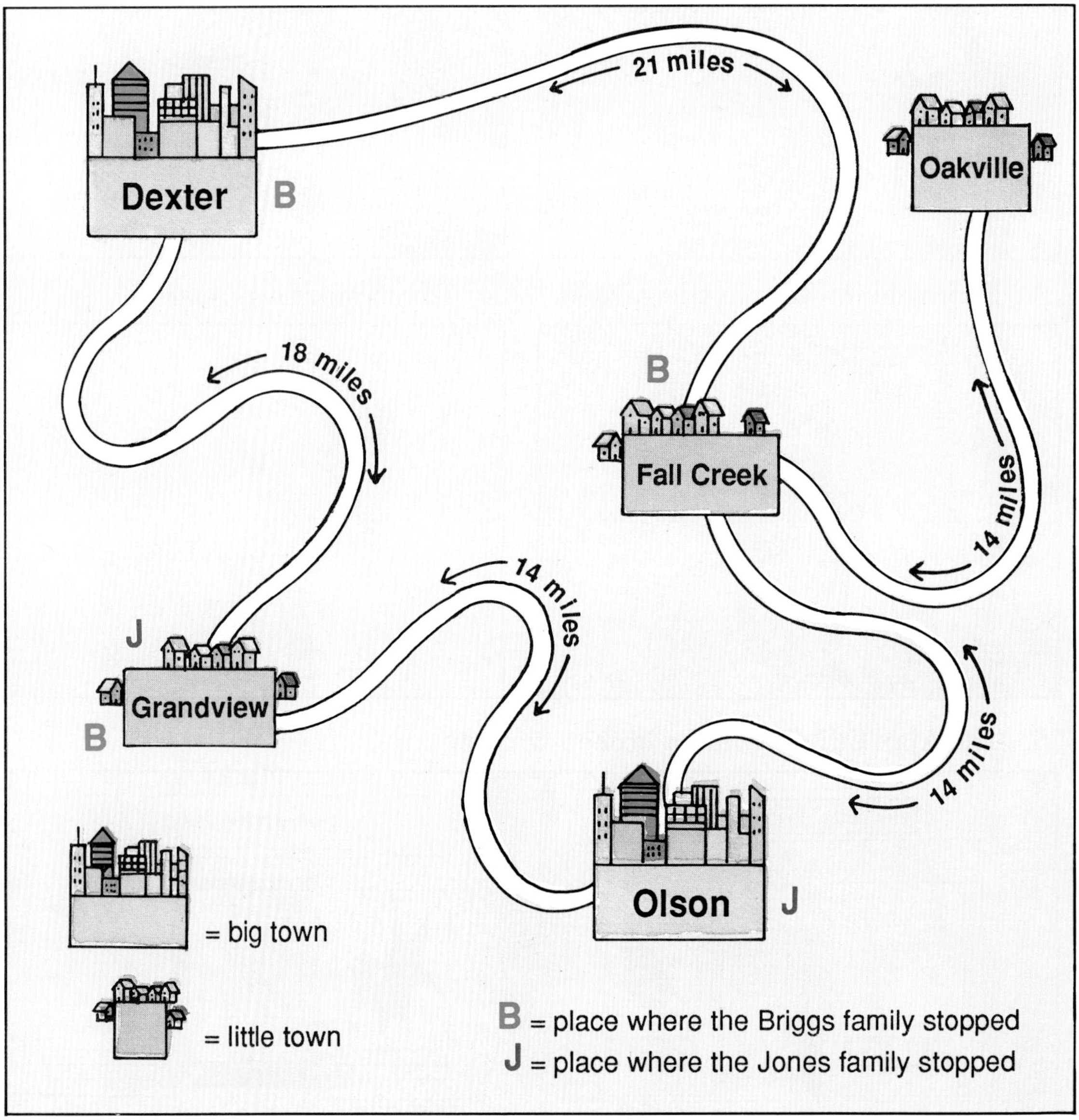

Part B

- Here's a rule for good writing:

  Good writing does not contain lots of unnecessary words. Good writing has all the words that are needed to give the reader clear ideas of what the writer is trying to present.

- Most sentences that start with the word **there** can be rewritten with fewer words.
- Here's a sentence:
  There are four students in the pool.
- Here's the same sentence written without **there:**
  Four students are in the pool.
- Here's another sentence:
  There were three colors on the card.

Part C

Rewrite these sentences so they use fewer words. Start with the thing that is named right after **there was** or **there were.**

1. There was a long line in front of the theater.
2. There were many people in the bus.
3. There is some broken glass on the street.
4. There was water in the basement.

Independent Work

Part D Write a parallel sentence for each item. Use the word **also.**

1. The girls wore straw hats.

2. The students had books.

3. He had a pet dog.

4. The girls wore striped jackets.

5. A large car was in front of the house.

Lesson 5

Part A Rewrite these sentences so they use fewer words.

1. There are many students who have ice skates.
2. There were five players on each team.
3. There were too many flies near the beach.
4. There are some birds that fly very high.

Part B For each item, write **two** parallel sentences that use the word **also.**

1. The Jones family stopped at the town of Sidney.
2. The Briggs family stopped at two towns.
3. The Briggs family stopped at places that are 8 miles apart.

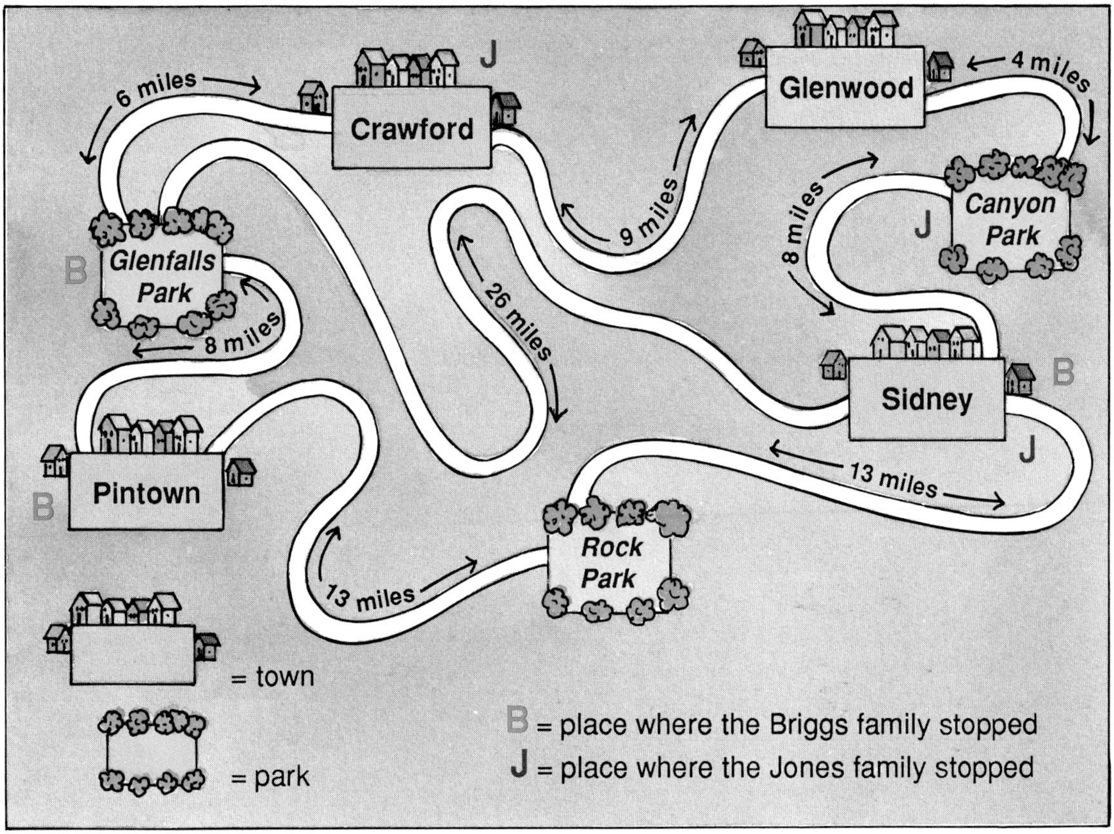

Part C

- The word **indicate** means show or tell.
- Here's a sentence:

  The weather forecast told that a storm was on the way.

- Here's a parallel sentence that uses a form of the word **indicate:**

  The weather forecast indicated that a storm was on the way.

- Remember, **indicate** means show or tell.

Part D

For each sentence, write a parallel sentence that uses **indicate, indicates** or **indicated.**

1. The map shows where the best parks are.
2. The shadows tell what time of day it is.
3. Their arguments showed that they wanted shorter recess periods.

Part E

- Not all sentences have a noun in the subject. The words **he, she, it** and **they** are not nouns.
- Here are sentences that do not have a noun in the subject:

  They were happy.
  He slipped on the ice.
  She watched the trees bend in the wind.
  It looked like a tiger.

- Remember, these words are not nouns: **he, she, it** and **they.**

Part F

The pictures show the development of the bicycle.

1813

1870

1880

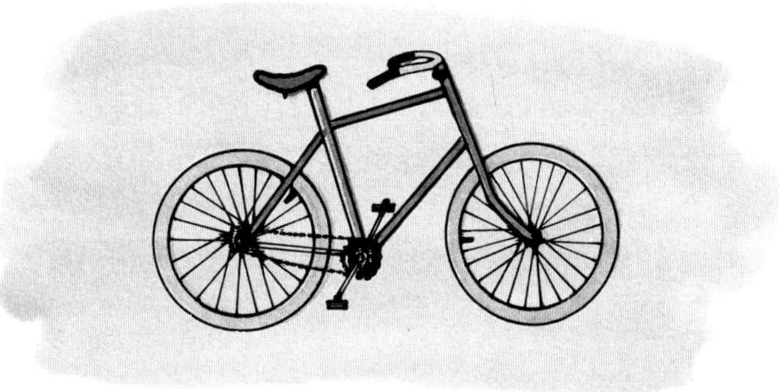

Key

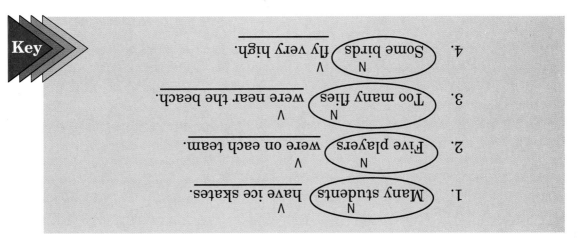

1. Many students (N) have ice skates (V).
2. Five players (N) were on each team (V).
3. Too many flies (N) were near the beach (V).
4. Some birds (N) fly very high (V).

Independent Work

Part G Write two parallel sentences for each item. Use the words shown for the item. Use **also** in the second sentence.

1. ________________followed a girl.

2. They shoveled

3. She painted

4. Mary bought

Lesson 6

Part A

Follow either the X-box or equal-box diagram to write about each statement below. Write in paragraph form.

Statements

1. Only girls go to school.
2. All adult birds can fly.
3. The first bicycle appeared before 1850.
4. Columbus landed in America before 1500.

Outline diagrams

Statement ___ indicates that ______________ ______________.	X	That statement is inaccurate. [Give fact.]
Statement ___ indicates that ______________ ______________.	=	That statement is accurate. [Give fact.]

Part B

For each statement below, write a parallel sentence that uses the word also.

The Amount of Water Used in Clover City

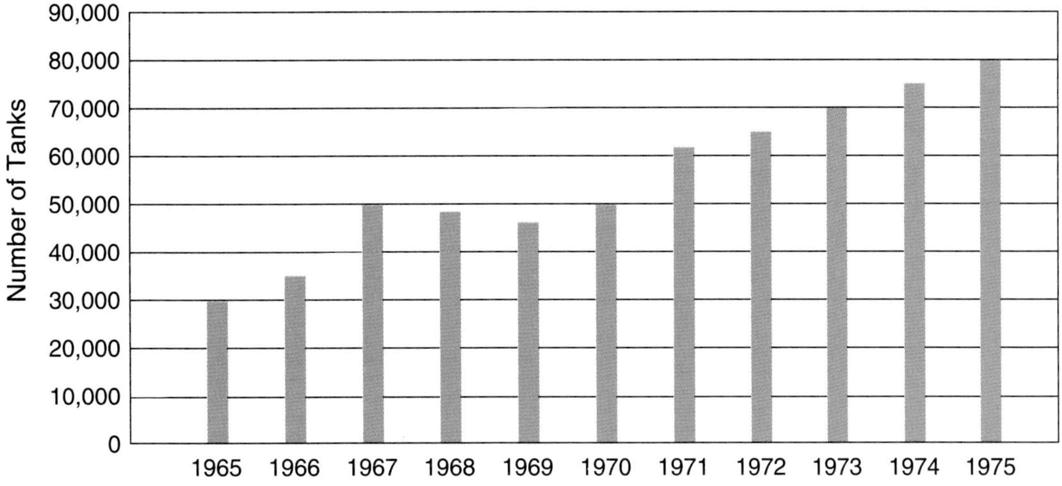

1. Clover City used 50,000 tanks of water in 1967.
2. Clover City used more than 65,000 tanks of water in 1973.
3. The amount of water decreased between 1967 and 1968.
4. Clover City used more than 50,000 tanks in 1971, 1972 and 1973.

Part C

- Some words are **contractions.** Contractions are two words made into one. Part of one word and part of another are put together.
- If a word is a contraction, **it has an apostrophe** because some of the letters from the original words are missing. If a word does not have an apostrophe, it is not a contraction.
- Here are some contractions:

isn't is a contraction for **is not**
hasn't is a contraction for **has not**
you'll is a contraction for **you will**
here's is a contraction for **here is**

Contractions

I'm ---------------- I am
it's ---------------- it is
she'd ------------- she would
they'll ------------ they will
they're ----------- they are
they've ----------- they have
we'll -------------- we will
we've ------------ we have

Part D

Sample Sentence **The workers will come home when they have finished building the barn on Mr. Jonson's farm.**

1 They will probably work there for 10 hours. 2 When they are finished with their work, the sun will be setting. 3 We will have a hot meal waiting for them. 4 We have prepared soup and a large dinner. 5 Mary said that she would fix a special dessert. 6 It is a strawberry cake with lemon filling. 7 Yum yum. 8 I am sure that the workers will love it.

Independent Work

Part E For each item, write a parallel sentence that does not have the word **there.**

1. There were four dogs in the street.
2. There is a long line in front of the theater.
3. There were some large boats on the river.
4. There are nervous people in the dentist's office.

Part F Write two parallel sentences for each item. Use the word **also** in one sentence.

1. She wore ______________________.

2. ______________________ in a tree.

Key

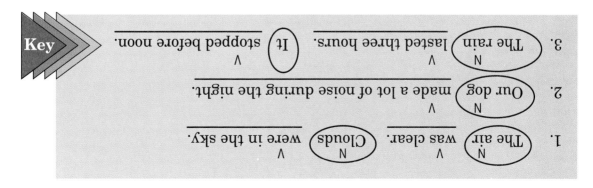

1. The air (N) was clear (V). Clouds (N) were in the sky (V).
2. Our dog (N) made a lot of noise during the night (V).
3. The rain (N) lasted three hours (V). It stopped before noon (V).

Lesson 7

Part A For each item, write **two** parallel sentences that use the word **also.**

1. The Jones family stopped in a town that is small.
2. The Jones family stopped 10 miles from Tiny Town.

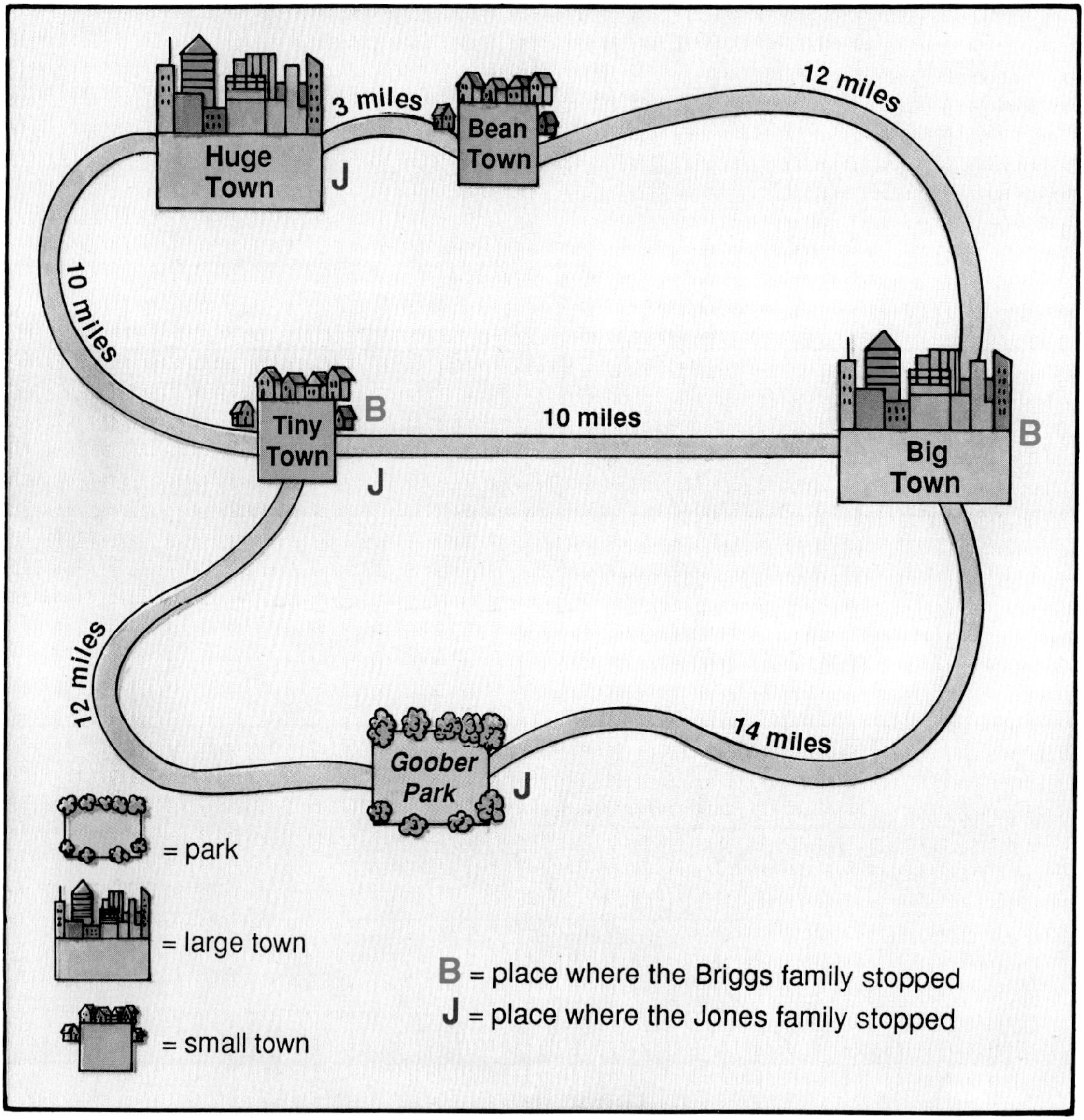

Part B Follow either the X-box or equal-box diagram to write about each statement. Write in paragraph form.

Statements

1. All vehicles have wheels.
2. Water freezes when it is between 28° and 38° Fahrenheit.
3. Cows are the only farm animals that give milk.

Outline diagrams

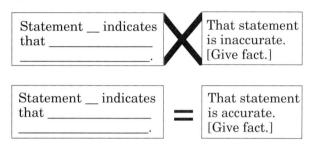

Statement __ indicates that ______________ ____________________.	X	That statement is inaccurate. [Give fact.]
Statement __ indicates that ______________ ____________________.	=	That statement is accurate. [Give fact.]

Part C Rewrite the underlined sentences so that the unclear word is clear.

1. When Jed put the lid on the jar, it broke. He threw it out and covered the jar with tinfoil.
2. Susan painted a picture of the elephant. It was enormous. When she hung it up, it covered the wall.
3. She made cookies for her children. They were small and sweet. The children waited patiently for them to cool.
4. When he put a bowl in the dishwasher, it broke. He pulled pieces of it from the dishwasher for weeks.

Part D For each sentence, rewrite the pair of words that could be combined to form a contraction. Refer to the **Reference Section** if you are unsure of how to spell the contraction.

[1] Bees fight to the death when they are attacked by wasps and other enemies. [2] Bees protect their beehive by forming a swarm and stinging the enemy. [3] The queen is their leader. [4] She does not fight. [5] She stays inside the beehive, where she is surrounded by bees who feed her and care for her. [6] They are very loyal. [7] Each bee can signal by moving its wings or by doing a dance in the air. [8] The dance may signal the other bees that it is time to attack an enemy.

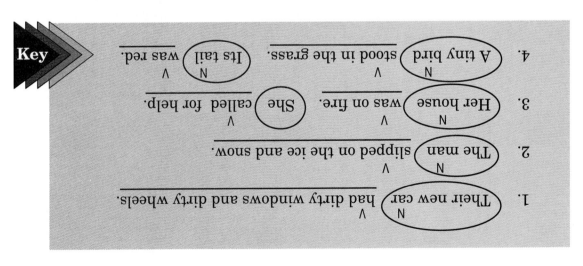

Key

1. Their new car (N) had dirty windows and dirty wheels. (V)
2. The man (N) slipped on the ice and snow. (V)
3. Her house (N) was on fire. (V) She (N) called for help. (V)
4. A tiny bird (N) stood in the grass. (V) Its tail (N) was red. (V)

Part E Follow either the X-box or equal-box diagram to write a paragraph about each statement. Look up the boxed words in the **Reference Section.**

Statements

1. Every fourth [year] is longer than 365 days.
2. The largest [mammal] is the elephant.
3. The tallest [mountain] in the world is over five miles high.

Outline diagrams

Statement __ indicates that ________________ ____________________.	X	That statement is inaccurate. [Give fact.]
Statement __ indicates that ________________ ____________________.	=	That statement is accurate. [Give fact.]

Lesson 8

Part A Say the subject and the predicate for these items.

1. Boys and girls went to school.
2. Martha and I watched birds in the distance.
3. Five ducks and seventeen dogs were in a pond.
4. No, all the girls laughed at the clown.
5. No, they were also thirsty.

Part B

- When you write a parallel sentence, you use as many words as possible from the original sentence.
- Here's a sentence: **Chickens are the only animals that are raised on farms.**
- Here are parallel sentences that start with the word **no:**

  Sentence A: **No, cows are also raised on farms.**

  Sentence B: **No, cows are also animals raised on farms.**

  Sentence C: **No, cows are also animals that are raised on farms.**
- The best parallel sentence is the sentence that uses the greatest number of words from the original sentence.
- Remember, use as many words as you can from the original sentence.

Part C For each item, write a parallel sentence that disagrees.

1. Dogs are the only domesticated animals that can be kept inside houses.
2. Ducks are the only birds you see near water.
3. The carrot is the only vegetable that is not all green.

Part D For each sentence, rewrite the pair of words that could be combined to form a contraction. Refer to the **Reference Section** if you are unsure of how to spell the contraction.

[1] Wood ducks are unusual creatures. [2] They are beautifully colored. [3] Their heads are like a rainbow of colors. [4] Wood ducks have claws that allow them to perch in trees. [5] The babies are a sight that a person would not forget. [6] You will find the babies in nests that are high above the ground. [7] When these birds are only one day old, they are ready to scramble out of their nest. [8] When these babies become hungry enough, they will leap into the air. [9] They float like a fluffy ball of feathers down to the ground, where their mother is waiting to lead them to food.

Part E Rewrite the underlined sentences so that the unclear word is clear.

1. They built a house in a the meadow. <u>It was large and green.</u> The house stood right in the middle of it.
2. The radio interfered with her homework. <u>She threw it out the window.</u> On the next day, the teacher scolded her for not turning in her assignment.
3. The bugs were getting in the peanuts. <u>I put them in the refrigerator.</u> Now I have cold bugs.
4. Two evil spies were after the letters Mr. Kelly wrote. <u>Mr. Kelly decided to destroy them.</u> They were made out of paper that burned easily.

Part F

Use the source to find accurate information. Write about each statement, using the appropriate outline diagram.

Source

The moose is the largest member of the deer family. The adult male moose is called a bull. Bulls are about six feet tall and weigh about 1400 pounds. They have a growth of skin called a *bell* that hangs from their neck. The bull's antlers may measure six feet in width. The bull's coat is not a single color. The bull's body is blackish brown. The bull's face, legs and belly are light brown.

The cow's coat is a single light-brown color. The calves are also light brown all over. Calves are born in the spring. The principal diet of the moose during the winter consists of leaves and twigs.

Statements	*Outline diagrams*		
1. A bull moose has a coat that is light brown all over.	Statement __ indicates that ______________ ______________.	X	That statement is inaccurate. [Give fact.]
2. The calf's coat resembles the cow's coat.	Statement __ indicates that ______________ ______________.	=	That statement is accurate. [Give fact.]

Independent Work

Part G

Follow either the X-box or equal-box diagram above to write about each statement below.

Statements

1. School lasts longer than three hours a day.
2. 25 plus 18 is less than 40.
3. Nickels are worth more than dimes.

Lesson 9

Part A Write complete parallel statements of disagreement.

1.

Candy is the only food that people should avoid eating before dinner.
No, ______________________ ______________________ ______________________.

2.

Skydiving is the only sport that is dangerous.
______________________ ______________________ ______________________.

3.

Wood is the only important material used to build houses.
______________________ ______________________ ______________________.

Part B

- These words are combined with other verbs to form two-word verbs:

must	could	may
should	will	might
can	would	may

Sample Sentence **They walk.**

1. Horses live a long time.
2. Some birds catch bugs.

Part C

Use the source to find accurate information. Write about each statement, using the appropriate outline diagram.

Source

The moose is the largest member of the deer family. The adult male moose is called a bull. Bulls are about six feet tall and weigh about 1400 pounds. They have a growth of skin called a *bell* that hangs from their neck. The bull's antlers may measure six feet in width. The bull's coat is not a single color. The bull's body is blackish brown. The bull's face, legs and belly are light brown.

The cow's coat is a single light-brown color. The calves are also light brown all over. Calves are born in the spring. The principal diet of the moose during the winter consists of leaves and twigs.

Statements

1. The bull moose has very large antlers.
2. The winter diet of the moose consists of leaves and mushrooms.

Outline diagrams

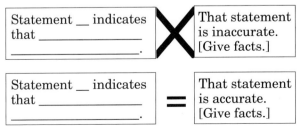

Statement __ indicates that ______________ ______________.	X	That statement is inaccurate. [Give facts.]

Statement __ indicates that ______________ ______________.	=	That statement is accurate. [Give facts.]

Part D For each sentence, rewrite the pair of words that could be combined to form a contraction. Refer to the **Reference Section** if you are unsure of how to spell the contraction.

1 Bill's job has rewards. 2 It is rewarding when Bill drives a truck into the mountains. 3 The job is not always rewarding during a flood or a forest fire. 4 Bill works as a ranger. 5 You will find Bill helping people when the valley floods. 6 Bill sometimes works all day and all night during forest fires. 7 Bill's job is hard, but he would not trade it for any other job. 8 Bill believes that he is lucky to be a ranger.

Part E Rewrite each underlined sentence so that the unclear word is clear.

1. His children played with the dogs. <u>They loved to hide behind the couch.</u> The children searched all over for them.
2. Mary wanted to plant a rose in the window box. <u>Somebody stole it.</u> She put the rose in a large pot.
3. Farmer Jones gathered eggs from his chickens. <u>They were brown.</u> He gathered them from the chickens every morning.

Independent Work

Part F For each item, write a parallel sentence that uses **also.**

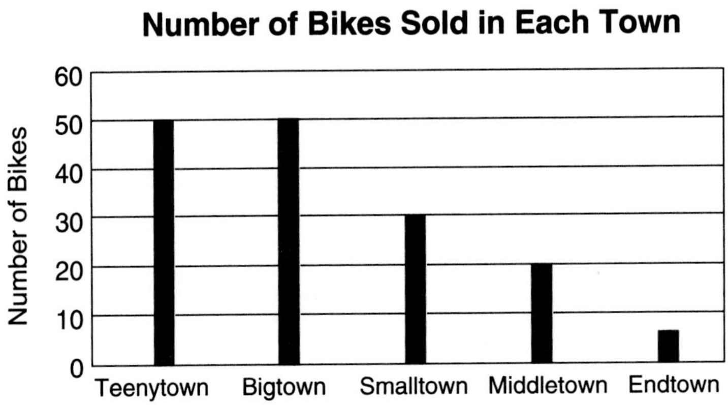

1. More than 40 bikes were sold in Bigtown.
2. Fewer than 40 bikes were sold in Middletown.

Lesson 10 – Test 1

Part A Write the items your teacher dictates. Make sure your sentences are punctuated correctly.

Part B Use the source to find accurate information. Write a paragraph about each statement, using the outline diagrams.

Source: **Dimensions of a Softball Field**

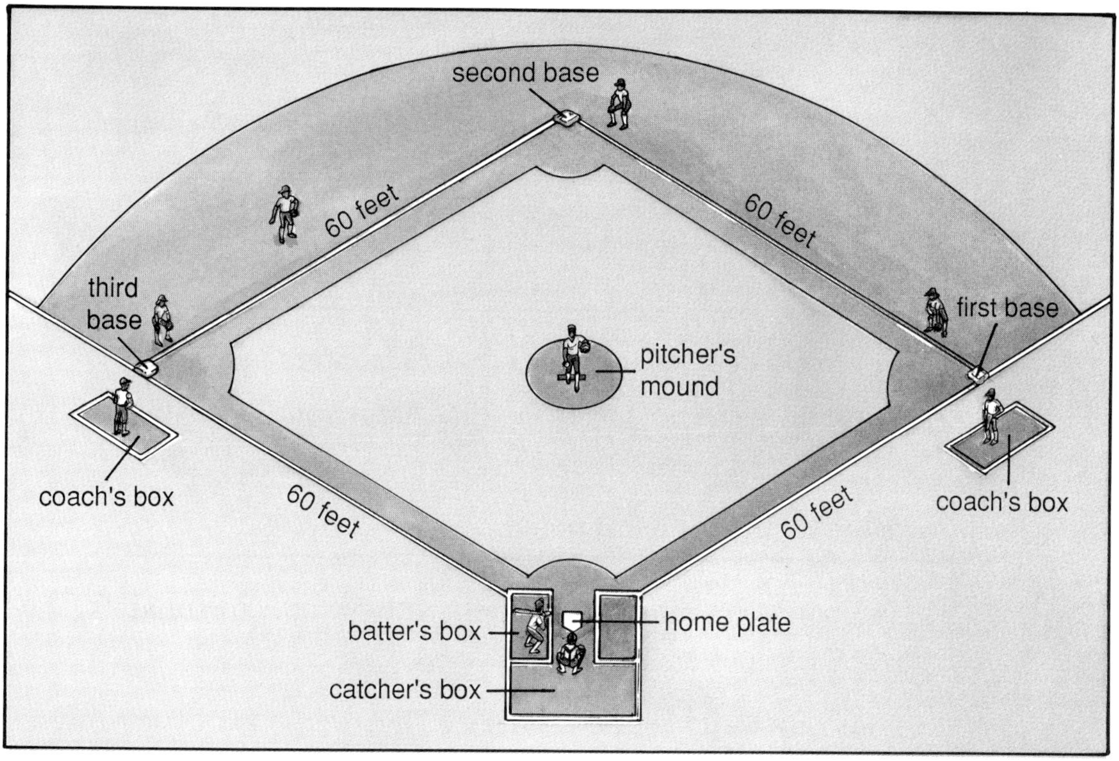

Statements

1. There's a coach's box between first base and second base.
2. If you run around the bases from home plate to second base, you will run more than 100 feet.

Outline diagrams

Statement __ indicates that ________________ ________________.	X	That statement is inaccurate. [Give fact.]
Statement __ indicates that ________________ ________________.	=	That statement is accurate. [Give fact.]

Part C Copy each sentence. Circle the subject. Underline the predicate. Write **N** above the noun in the subject and **V** above the verb.

1. Their mother was very pretty.
2. Don answered my questions.
3. Her last sentence had too many words.

Part D Write each sentence so it has as many contractions as possible.

1. The daisies are not as tall as the roses are.
2. The roses are not yellow, but they are pretty.
3. The training will help you if you are willing to work hard.

Part E Write a parallel sentence in response to each item. Begin with the word **no** and use the word **also.**

1. Hammers are the only tools that carpenters use.
2. Running is the only exercise that helps your body stay healthy.

Part F Rewrite the underlined sentences so they are clear.

1. The truck ran into the gas tank. It blew up. Fortunately, the truck was not damaged.
2. Four rats watched the children. They were ugly little things. The rats were also pretty ugly.

Lesson 11

Part A

- Here are verbs that can be used to make two-word verbs:

1. is
2. was
3. are
4. were
5. can
6. could
7. will
8. would
9. may
10. might
11. did
12. should
13. must

Part B

Rewrite these sentences with two-word verbs. Use a form of the verb shown in the sentence.

1. Jim runs every morning.
2. Those fish eat worms.

Part C

Write the number of each sentence on your paper and the contraction for each sentence.

[1] Mrs. Jones told them that they should not play in the street. [2] They looked at her, and then they went on playing. [3] They did not know what Mrs. Jones had told them. [4] They were having too much fun chasing each other and trying to bite paws or tails. [5] Suddenly, their mother appeared. [6] She told them in cat talk that they could not play in the street. [7] They listened to the mother cat, and they stayed out of the street.

Part D

Write the sentences the first person is saying. Use the word **only.**

Part E

Rewrite the underlined sentences so that the unclear word is clear.

1. Jack swung his bat at the ball. It soared into space. The coach said, "Don't let it slip out of your hands again."
2. Joe took a bus into the city. It was crowded with Christmas shoppers. The streets were so crowded that Joe had trouble finding the things he wanted to buy.
3. He made a cake for the party. It was a great success. The rest of the party wasn't very good.

Part F Source: Map of Missouri River

Statements

1. The Missouri River ends at the Gulf of Mexico.
2. The Missouri River forms the east-west boundary between two states.
3. The Missouri River empties into another river.

Outline diagrams

Statement ___ indicates ______ ______.	X	That statement is inaccurate. [Give facts.]
Statement ___ indicates ______ ______.	=	That statement is accurate. [Give facts.]

Independent Work

Part G Write parallel statements of disagreement. Start with **No, . . .**

1.

2.

3.

Lesson 12

Part A Write the sentences the first person is saying. Use the word **only.**

1.
No, secretaries and janitors are also people who work in schools.

2.
No, seals and dolphins are also mammals that live in the ocean.

3.
No, swimming every day is also a way to stay in good shape.

Part B If the sentence is correct, don't write anything. If the sentence has a wrong word, rewrite it so it has **two words** in place of the wrong word.

[1]Jan collects coins. [2]She thinks that there interesting. [3]Theirs a market for rare coins. [4]Jan has one rare coin. [5]Its an old penny with a date of 1803. [6]Some of the writing on its back side is hard to read. [7]If your interested in collecting things, look into coins. [8]They are a good way to spend your free time.

Part C

Rewrite the underlined sentences so that the unclear word is clear.

1. She put a potato in the oven, and it blew up. Pieces of it were stuck all over the oven.
2. Sally ran into Fran. She started to cry. Billy gave Fran a handkerchief to wipe away her tears.
3. She set the cake on the table. It collapsed. She'll have to buy a new table.

Part D

Source: **Diagram of a Submarine**

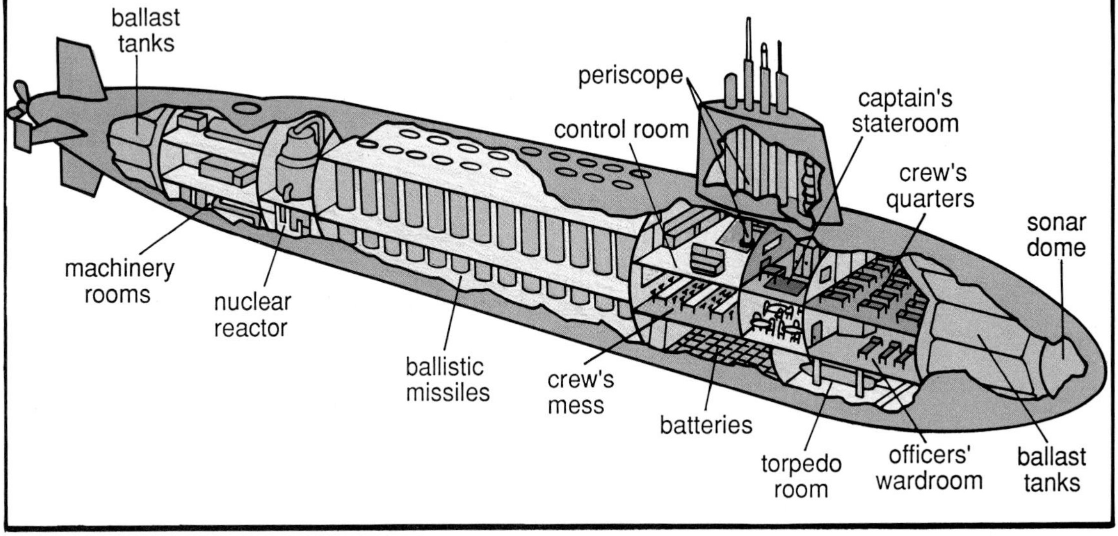

Definitions: captain's stateroom — place where the captain sleeps
officers' wardroom — place where the officers eat and sleep
crew's quarters — place where the crew sleeps
crew's mess — place where the crew eats

Statements

1. The place where the crew sleeps is in front of the place where the periscope is located.
2. The place where the crew eats is not on the same level as the captain's stateroom.

Outline diagrams

Statement __ indicates ______________ ______________.	X	That statement is inaccurate. [Give facts.]
Statement __ indicates ______________ ______________.	=	That statement is accurate. [Give facts.]

Independent Work

Part E Write the number of each sentence. Write any contractions that could be used in that sentence.

[1] Young people who live in the city should not have pets that are larger than horses. [2] Pets larger than horses are not comfortable inside houses, garages or basements. [3] They are frequently unhappy animals. [4] They make a lot of noise when they are hungry. [5] They will cost a lot to feed. [6] One young girl who kept an elephant in her house said, "I am sick and tired of feeding this elephant. [7] We do not have any room for ourselves. [8] And this elephant stinks."

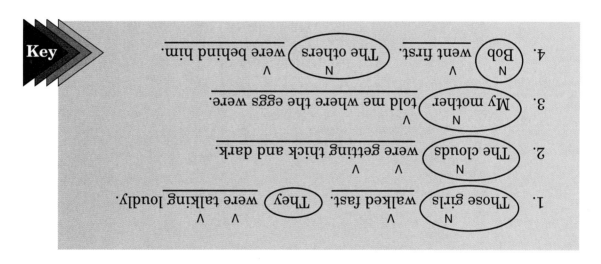

Key

1. Those girls (N) walked (V) fast. They were (V) talking (V) loudly.
2. The clouds (N) were (V) getting (V) thick and dark.
3. My mother (N) told (V) me where the eggs were.
4. Bob (N) went (V) first. The others (N) were (V) behind him.

Lesson 13

Part A

Correct the first statement in each item by writing a sentence that uses the words **no** and **only.**

1. Girls and boys played at the picnic.
   Girls played at the picnic.
2. Girls played at the picnic and in the cabin.
   Girls played at the picnic.
3. Girls played and talked at the picnic.
   Girls played at the picnic.

Part B

- Here's a rule:

  Parts of speech are the same for a statement and a parallel question that uses the same words. The subject and predicate are also the same.

- Here's a **statement** with a two-word verb:

  The girls **could walk** to school.

- Here's a **parallel question** that uses all the words in the statement:

  Could the girls **walk** to school?

- The question has the same verb words as the original statement.
- Remember, parts of speech are the same for statements and parallel questions.

Part C

Write a parallel question that uses all the words for each item.

1. That boy was running in the street.
2. My little sister can jump rope.
3. Mary should buy new shoes.

Part D

Source map: **South America**

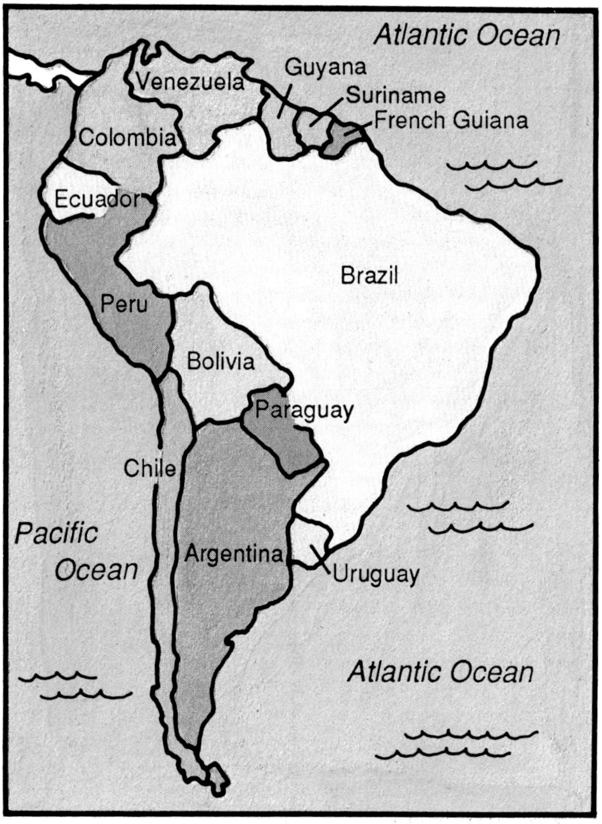

Statements

1. Brazil is the largest country in South America.
2. Bolivia is the only country in South America that does not border on an ocean.

Outline diagrams

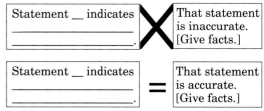

Statement __ indicates ________________________.	X	That statement is inaccurate. [Give facts.]
Statement __ indicates ________________________.	=	That statement is accurate. [Give facts.]

Source data

Country	Population (1990 est.)	Area in square miles
Argentina	32,291,000	1,065,189
Bolivia	6,730,000	424,165
Brazil	53,771,000	3,286,470
Chile	13,000,000	292,257
Colombia	32,598,000	439,735
Ecuador	10,506,000	109,483
French Guiana	94,000	43,740
Guyana	765,000	83,000
Paraguay	4,660,000	157,047
Peru	21,904,000	496,222
Suriname	408,000	63,037
Uruguay	3,002,000	68,037
Venezuela	19,753,000	352,143
Total	**299,482,000**	**6,880,525**

Part E Write a parallel sentence for the first person.

Part F If the sentence is correct, don't write anything. If the sentence has a wrong word, rewrite the sentence with **two correct words** in place of the wrong word.

1 You sweat when your working hard. 2 You will sweat more if its humid. 3 When you put mud on your hand, its pores are covered up. 4 When the pores are covered, your hand can't sweat. 5 When their not covered, sweat comes from the pores.

Independent Work

Part G Write parallel sentences of disagreement. Use the words **no** and **also.**

Part H Write any contractions that can be used in these sentences. (Don't write the sentences.)

1. You will feel proud of good work.
2. If it is done well, you can take pride in it.
3. She told me that there is a snake in the yard.
4. You are very humorous.

Lesson 14

Part A

- You've learned that when you indicate what somebody says, you use the word **that.**
- Here's something you would write:

  Statement 1 indicates *that* the moose is a large animal.
- You wouldn't write:

  Statement 1 indicates the moose is a large animal.
- You do the same thing with all ideas that are expressed as a sentence.
- Here's a sentence:

  Jan knows her mother.

  You don't need the word **that** because **her mother** is not a sentence.

  Jan knows the alphabet.

  You don't need the word **that** because **the alphabet** is not a sentence.

  Jan knows *that* winter is near.

  You need the word **that** because **winter is near** is a sentence.

Part B

Write three statements that tell about Jan's ideas.

Part C Correct the first statement in each item by writing a sentence that uses the words **no** and **only.**

1. The workers rested and talked during their break.
   The workers rested during their break.
2. The workers rested during their break.
   Some of the workers rested during their break.
3. The workers rested during their break and during the lunch hour.
   The workers rested during their break.

Part D For each statement, write a parallel question that uses all the words in the statement and no other words.

1. Your neighbors could help us.
2. Those students do know how to cook.
3. Our teacher has seen that movie.

Part E Rewrite the underlined sentences so that the unclear word is clear.

1. As the sun rose over the desert, it turned pink. The desert is so beautiful when it is that color.
2. Jerry played violin in the orchestra. It produced lovely music. He didn't want to play any other violin.
3. We got to the pond by going through a wheat field. It was full of cows. Some of them were swimming.

Part F

Statements

1. Chile is the only country in South America that borders two oceans.
2. Brazil touches the border of every other country in South America.
3. The population of French Guiana is less than 50,000.

Outline diagrams

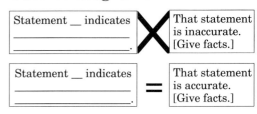

Statement __ indicates ______________ ______________. ✕ That statement is inaccurate. [Give facts.]

Statement __ indicates ______________ ______________. = That statement is accurate. [Give facts.]

Independent Work

Part G

These are statements a second person is saying. Write the parallel statement the first person said. Use the word **only.**

1.

No, tricycles are also vehicles that you can pedal.

2.

No, boots and earmuffs are also clothes that protect against cold weather.

3.

No, swans and geese are also birds that swim on ponds.

4.

No, hot-air balloons are also vehicles that can fly.

Lesson 15

Part A Write the statements that tell the ideas that Ben **believes.**

maps
his parents and grandparents
Money can make life easy.
Dogs are wonderful pets.
teachers
Ben believes

Part B Tell why these statements are false by writing a correct sentence that has the words **no** and **only.**

Sample Item
They painted the ceiling and the floor.
(The ceiling is not painted.)
No, they painted only the floor.

1. The doctor examined the children and their parents.
   (Parents did not receive examinations.)
2. The doctor examined and vaccinated the children.
   (No children received vaccinations.)
3. The doctor and the nurse examined the children.
   (The nurse did not examine the children.)

Part C Rewrite these questions as parallel statements that use all the same words.

1. Were the little bugs crawling all over your yard?
2. Is that tire losing air?
3. Was her car getting dirty?
4. Should mean dogs stay inside?

Part D If the sentence is correct, don't write anything. If the sentence has a wrong word, rewrite the sentence with **two correct words** in place of the wrong word.

[1] Rabbits are a lot of fun when their little. [2] Their paws and ears are tiny. [3] Their called bunnies. [4] A bunny wiggles its nose while it eats. [5] Sometimes bunnies make a tiny sound. [6] Its like a squeak. [7] You can't hear it unless your close to the bunny.

Part E Rewrite the underlined sentences so that the unclear word is clear.

1. My dog won't bite that mail carrier. <u>He is friendly</u>. The only people that my dog bites are unfriendly.
2. We drove a truck in the parade. <u>It was full of clowns</u>. They kept falling out of the truck.
3. She put cheese on the bread. <u>She noticed that it was covered with mold</u>. She went to the store and bought some fresh bread.

Part F

Source

Softwood Species	Common Uses
Douglas fir	Piling, plywood veneer, residential framing
Hemlock	Construction lumber, central layer of plywood panel
Eastern white pine	Containers, knotty paneling
Sugar pine	Doors, frames, window blinds
Redwood	Boards, joists, posts, outdoor furniture

Hardwood Species	Common Uses
Birch	Cabinets, cupboards, plywood veneer, doors
Black cherry	Furniture, caskets, fine veneer paneling
Mahogany	Furniture, fine veneers, paneling
Red oak	Fence posts, truck floors
Teak	Furniture, fine veneer paneling
Black walnut	Furniture, decorative paneling, cabinets

Statements

1. Douglas fir is commonly used for plywood.
2. Birch is commonly used for fence posts.
3. Black cherry and mahogany are the only woods used for paneling.

Outline diagrams

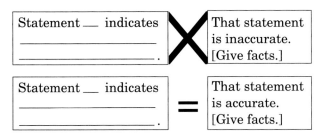

Statement ___ indicates ______________________ ______________________.	X	That statement is inaccurate. [Give facts.]
Statement ___ indicates ______________________ ______________________.	=	That statement is accurate. [Give facts.]

Independent Work

Part G Margaret states all the ideas that are listed. Some of the ideas are sentences. For **those items,** write a sentence that tells what Margaret states. Use the word **that**. Start each sentence with the words **Margaret states . . .**

1. Her name.
2. She should eat nutritious foods.
3. The order of topics.
4. The argument is contradictory.

Part H Rewrite each underlined sentence so it is clear.

1. Peg saw the mountain from the lake. <u>It was beautiful</u>. The grass was brown and flat from the snow that had just melted, but the mountain was a crisp, jagged white peak.
2. We saw Mike standing beside Phil. <u>He was wearing a red jacket</u>. Mike had on a blue jacket.

Lesson 16

Part A

- Words that come before a noun and tell about the noun are **adjectives.**
- Adjectives answer these questions:

  What kind? or **How many?** or **Which one?**

- Here's a subject: **That lazy dog** (A A N) ________.
- Here's a different subject: **Five small bugs** (A A N) ________.
- Here's a different subject: **A boy** (A N) ________.
- Remember, the words **a, an** and **the** are **always** adjectives. They answer the question **Which one?**

Part B

Copy each sentence. Circle the subject. Underline the predicate. Write **N** above the noun in the subject and **V** above each verb word. Write **A** above each adjective in the subject.

1. His oldest sister can swim fast.
2. Seven puppies barked at her.
3. An inaccurate statement was on TV.
4. The dog was chasing a cat.
5. A car ran out of gas.

Part C

Fix these run-on sentences.

1. The tree's bark is 24 inches thick and the tree weighs 2000 tons and the tree is over 3000 years old.
2. This tree is located in a national park and it is 60 miles north of Turner Mountain and people visit it every year.

Part D

Vocabulary Box

redwood half California
height building

Part E

Write responses that use the word **only.** Think about the fact in parentheses to put **only** in the right place.

1. Her brother and her sister repaired the chair.
   (Her sister did not work on the chair.)
2. Her brother repaired the chair and painted it.
   (The chair is not painted.)
3. Her brother repaired the chair and the couch.
   (The couch still needs repair.)

Part F

Irma believes all the things that are listed. For each item, write a sentence that tells what Irma believes.

Irma believes . . .

1. Three is more than two
2. Newspaper accounts
3. Her father
4. People should eat healthy food

Independent Work

Part G The passage has five contractions. Write the two words that make up each contraction.

She wasn't tired, but she had run a long distance. She told the others that she'd win the race, but nobody believed her. She was only 11 years old. All the other runners were in their teens. She didn't look like a runner, but you can't always tell how well somebody runs by looking at them. She went through the four mile course so fast that some of the runners hadn't completed half of it by the time she finished. Five years after this race she did the same thing in the Olympics. She won gold.

Part H Write a parallel sentence for what the other person must have said. Use the word **only.**

1. No, bees are also animals that fly.
2. No, a snowmobile is also a vehicle that goes through the snow.

Lesson 17

Part A

The statements in parentheses are true. Correct the first statement in each item by writing a parallel sentence that starts with **no** and uses the word **only.**

1. The wolves howled and ate at night.
   (The wolves did not eat.)
2. All the wolves howled at night.
   (Some did not howl.)
3. The wolves howled at night and in the afternoon.
   (No howling occurred in the afternoon.)

Part B

Copy each sentence. Circle the subject. Underline the predicate. Write **V** for the verb, **N** for the noun in the subject and **A** for each adjective in the subject.

1. That last statement is very misleading.
2. The first two paragraphs are long.
3. Her best work is on the wall.
4. A large branch was banging against the window.

Part C

Fix this run-on sentence.

The largest sequoia tree is named General Sherman it is 272 feet tall and it is 80 feet around and it has bark that is 24 inches thick and the tree weighs over 2000 tons it is located in Sequoia National Park.

Part D

The vocabulary box shows how to spell some important words.

Vocabulary Box

raised animals different popcorn America
wheat field Native Americans rice

Independent Work

Part E Use the X box or equal box to write about both statements.

Statements

1. The great redwood forests are in California.
2. There are only two types of corn.

Outline diagrams

Statement ___ indicates ____________ ____________.	X	That statement is inaccurate. [Give facts.]
Statement ___ indicates ____________ ____________.	=	That statement is accurate. [Give facts.]

Part F Rewrite each sentence so it has two correct words for each wrong word.

[1] When your older, you may have false teeth. [2] Your teeth will not last unless your careful. [3] Its the enamel that protects your teeth against cavities. [4] Cavities can hurt when there deep.

Part G For each statement, write a question that uses all the words in the statement. Mark the subject and predicate. Write letters for the noun in the subject and both verb words.

1. That girl will win the competition.
2. Our car was slipping in the mud.
3. Robins can make sounds that fool worms.
4. The mayor's speech has made everybody sleepy.

Key

The largest sequoia tree is named General Sherman. It is 272 feet tall. It is 80 feet around. It has bark that is 24 inches thick. The tree weighs over 2000 tons. It is located in Sequoia National Park.

Lesson 18

Part A

Passage M

Students usually go into fifth grade after fourth grade. Fifth graders are 15 years old. Young girls are shorter than boys of the same age.

- Here is a new symbol:

- Any box that has this shape is a **summary box.** It tells you to summarize. You summarize when you don't want to repeat the same thing over and over and over.
- Here's a summary about inaccuracies in a passage, followed by X-box sentences:

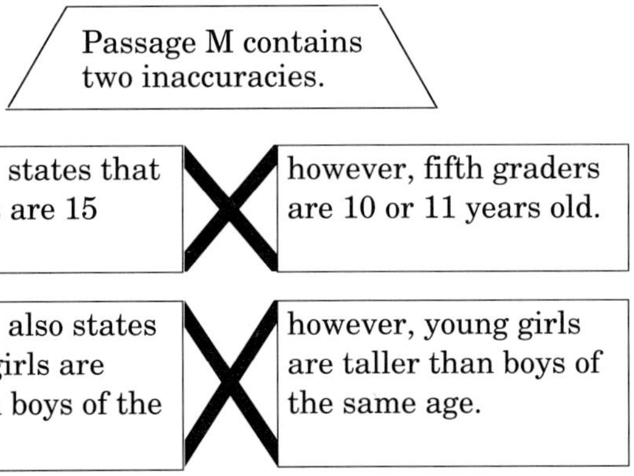
Passage M contains two inaccuracies.
The passage states that fifth graders are 15 years old;
however, fifth graders are 10 or 11 years old.
The passage also states that young girls are shorter than boys of the same age;
however, young girls are taller than boys of the same age.

- Here is the passage as you would write it without the boxes:

Passage M contains two inaccuracies. The passage states that fifth graders are 15 years old; however, fifth graders are 10 or 11 years old. The passage also states that young girls are shorter than boys of the same age; however, young girls are taller than boys of the same age.

Part B Write a paragraph that tells about the inaccuracies in passage E1. Write it like the paragraph in part A. Use the outline diagram to guide you. Refer to the source diagram for accurate information.

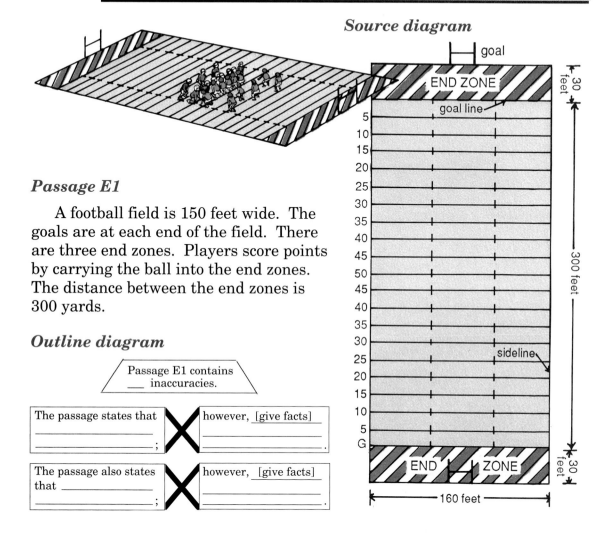

Source diagram

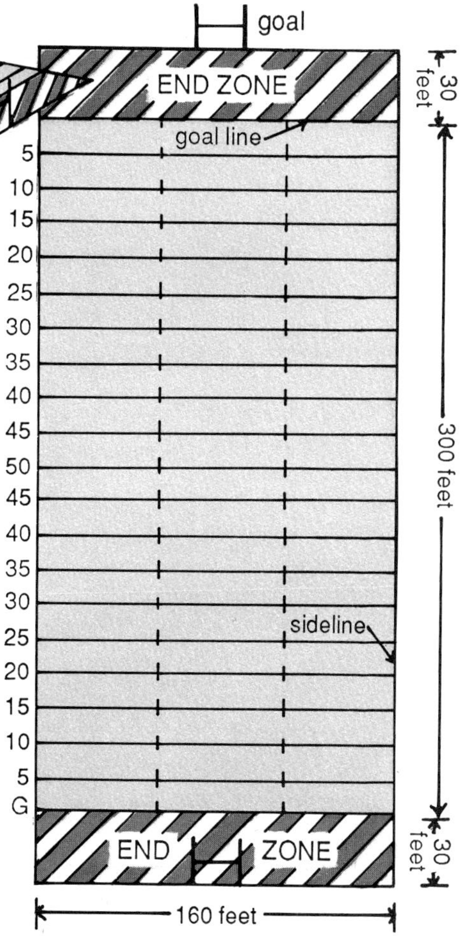

Passage E1

A football field is 150 feet wide. The goals are at each end of the field. There are three end zones. Players score points by carrying the ball into the end zones. The distance between the end zones is 300 yards.

Outline diagram

Passage E1 contains ___ inaccuracies.

The passage states that ______________________ ; however, [give facts] ______________________ .

The passage also states that ______________________ ; however, [give facts] ______________________ .

Part C Copy each sentence. Mark the parts.

1. An old goat was walking near the barn.
2. A cloud moved over the city.
3. Their only paragraph may have many mistakes.
4. His misleading comments made us angry.

Part D

- When you write clearly, you don't use the words **this** or **that** without also using a name.
- Here's an item:

  Tim jumped 12 feet. That made him the champ.

  The second sentence says, ***That* made him the champ.** That sentence doesn't name what made him the champ.
- Here's the item with the second sentence fixed up:

  Tim jumped 12 feet. That *jump* made him the champ.
- Here's another item:

  The sales decreased in March. *That* worried the owner of the company.

  The second sentence doesn't name what worried the owner.
- Here's the item with the second sentence fixed up:

  The sales decreased in March. That *decrease* worried the owner of the company.

Part E

For each item, say the second sentence with the missing noun.

1. Fran interrupted her parents. That irritated her father.
2. Dudley practiced the piano every day. That improved his skill.
3. A singer performed for the children. We recorded that.
4. Timmy requested help. Nobody paid attention to that.

Part F

Write the second sentence of each item with the missing noun.

1. Dr. Gregory concluded that all children should live on farms. That is ridiculous.
2. The company contributed $20,000 to the club. Everybody was happy about this.
3. Their teacher assigned four pages. That required a lot of work.

Independent Work

Part G The items tell things that Jan knows. For each item, write a sentence that begins with the words **Jan knows . . .**

1. More than 200 people
2. How to solve difficult math problems
3. The best way to get good grades is to work hard
4. Where to find blue seashells
5. Her mother is a good friend

Part H The second sentence in each item gives correct information. Start with the word **No,** and write sentences that have the word **only.**

1. The hounds drank from the pond.
(Some of the hounds did not drink.)
2. The hounds drank from the pond and swam in the pond.
(No hounds swam.)
3. They fixed the car and cleaned up the mess.
(They didn't clean up anything.)

Part I

For each statement, write a question that uses all the words. Mark the subject and predicate. Write letters for the noun in the subject and both verb words.

1. The workers could take hours to fix the pipe.
2. Those dark clouds are moving in our direction.
3. A hardware store would have that fixture.
4. The Jones family did stop in the town of Red Bluff.

Key

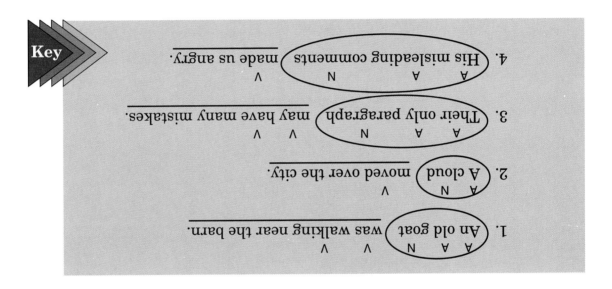

1. An old goat was walking near the barn.
2. A cloud moved over the city.
3. Their only paragraph may have many mistakes.
4. His misleading comments made us angry.

Lesson 19

Part A Write the noun for each verb.

1. confuse 2. assign 3. adjust 4. connect

Part B Use the outline diagram to critique passage E2. The source map shows you the accurate information.

Source map

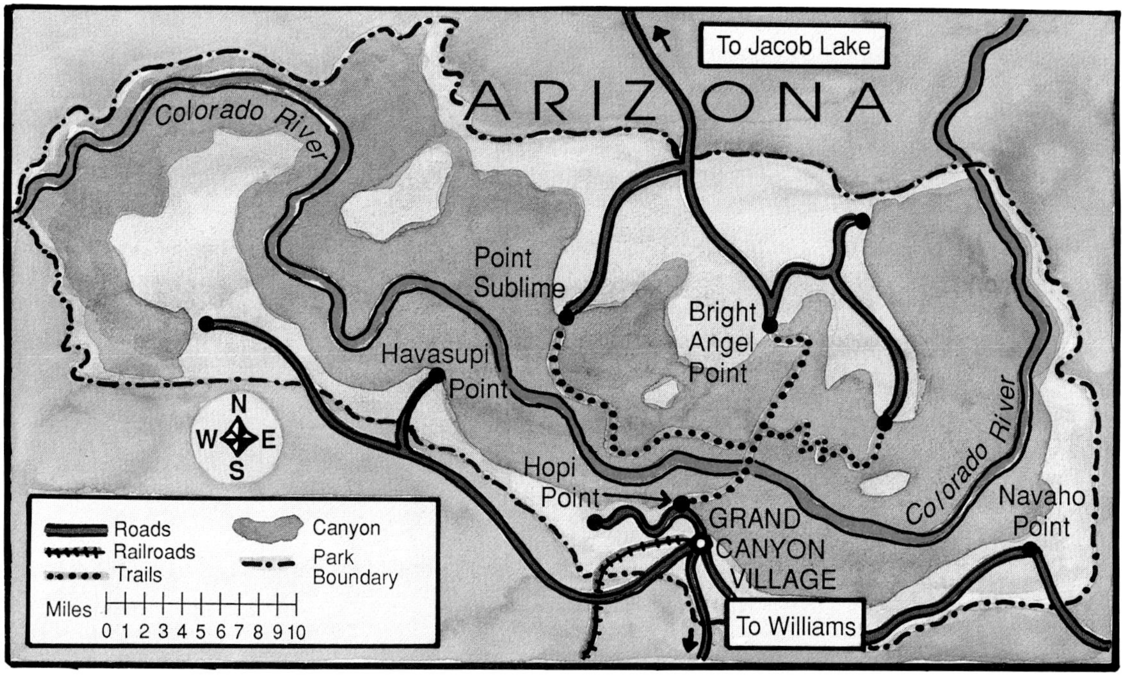

Grand Canyon National Park, Arizona

Passage E2

Grand Canyon National Park is about 55 miles wide. The Colorado River snakes through the park. There is a trail from Hopi to Bright Angel Point. Two railroad tracks are west of Grand Canyon Village. To the north of Grand Canyon National Park is Jacob Lake. The town of Williams is also north of Grand Canyon Village.

Outline diagrams

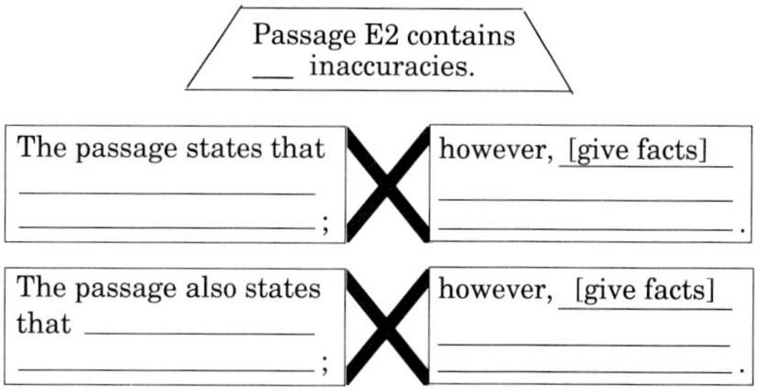

Part C Write a response to each sentence. Remember to use the words **no** and **only.**

1. The hounds chased the fox and caught the fox.
   (They did not catch the fox.)
2. All of the hounds chased the fox.
   (Some did no chasing.)
3. The hounds and the hunters chased the fox.
   (The hunters did not chase the fox.)
4. The hounds chased the fox and the rabbit.
   (There was no rabbit.)

Part D Write the second sentence of each item with the missing noun.

1. Fran discovered a secret door. That excited her.
2. Elisa adjusted her rearview mirror. That helped her see better.
3. The teacher criticized Tom's work. He felt embarassed about this.
4. The ad stated that Burpo cars were best. Nobody believed that.

Part E Move part of the predicate to the front of the sentence and put a comma after it.

Sample Item

Three girls ate popcorn during the entire movie.

During the entire movie, three girls ate popcorn.

1. A dog followed us as we went home.
2. The ground was soaked after the rainstorm.

Part F

Move part of the predicate to the front of the sentence and put a comma after it.

1. We will go home when the work is finished.
2. We caught a lot of fish at the pond.
3. He would buy a bike if he had enough money.
4. The campers sang songs as the sun set.

Independent Work

Part G

Write about each statement. Use the appropriate outline diagram.

Statements

1. The bull moose is smaller than an adult deer.
2. The bull moose has something hanging from its neck.

Outline diagrams

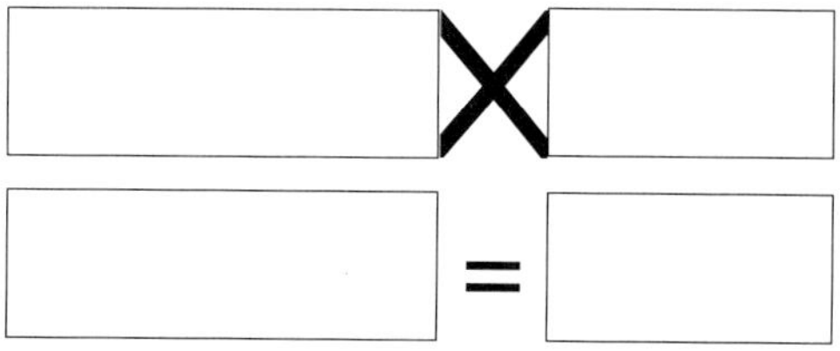

Part H

Fix this passage.

The most common language in the world is Chinese and it is spoken by 68% of the world population and English is spoken by only 10% of the world population.

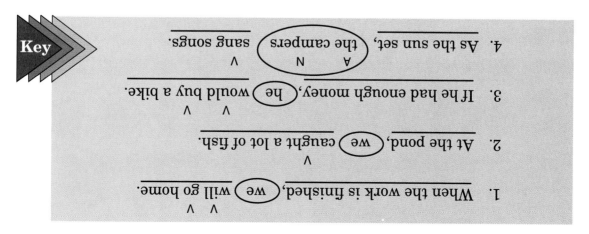

Key

1. When the work is finished, (we) will go home.
2. At the pond, (we) caught a lot of fish.
3. If he had enough money, (he) would buy a bike.
4. As the sun set, (the campers) sang songs.

Lesson 20 — Test 2

Part A Contractions in these sentences are not spelled properly. Rewrite each sentence so it has **no** contractions.

1. There mad because your late.
2. Its cold outside, but the car has its heater running.
3. Their angry because your late.

Part B Rewrite each statement as a parallel question.
Circle the subject; underline the predicate.
Write **N** above the noun and **A** above each adjective in the subject. Write **V** above each verb word.

1. The morning air can feel cold.
2. Our dog would get the paper every day.
3. Our best friend is planning a trip.

Part C Write a parallel response to each sentence. Use the words **no** and **only.**

1. The men and the women argued loudly.
   (The women were not arguing.)
2. They found old bottles and an old chest.
   (They didn't find any bottles.)

Part D Fix this passage.

You should have seen that tree and it was a redwood and redwood trees are the tallest trees in the world.

Part E Write a paragraph about each statement. Follow the appropriate outline diagram.

Source

Softwood Species	Common Uses
Douglas fir	Piling, plywood veneer, residential framing
Hemlock	Construction lumber, central layer of plywood panel
Eastern white pine	Containers, knotty paneling
Sugar pine	Doors, frames, window blinds
Redwood	Boards, joists, posts, outdoor furniture

Hardwood Species	Common Uses
Birch	Cabinets, cupboards, plywood veneer, doors
Black cherry	Furniture, caskets, fine veneer paneling
Mahogany	Furniture, fine veneers, paneling
Red oak	Fence posts, truck floors
Teak	Furniture, fine veneer paneling
Black walnut	Furniture, decorative paneling, cabinets

Statements

1. Pines are hardwoods.
2. Birch has many uses.
3. Black walnut is used for firewood.

Outline diagrams

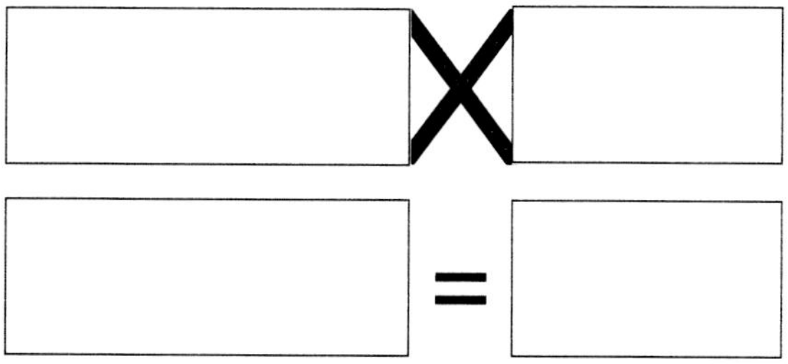

Lesson 21

Part A Write a paragraph that tells about the inaccuracies in passage E3. Use the outline diagram to guide you. Refer to the source diagram for accurate information.

Passage E3

Before telephones were invented, Morse code was used to send messages over long distances. The person sending the message would press a key down to make a signal. Morse code has dots and dashes. To send a dot, the sender holds the key down for a very short period. To send a dash, the sender holds the key down for a longer period.

To send the word **man,** the sender would send the combination of dots and dashes for the letters **m**, **a**, **n**:

m is ■ ■
a is ● ■
n is ■ ■ ●

The next group of dots and dashes spells the word **eggs:**

e is ●
g is ■ ■ ●
g is ■ ■ ●
s is ● ●

A sender sends the word **not** at the end of the message.

n is ■ ●
o is ■ ■ ■
t is ■

Source

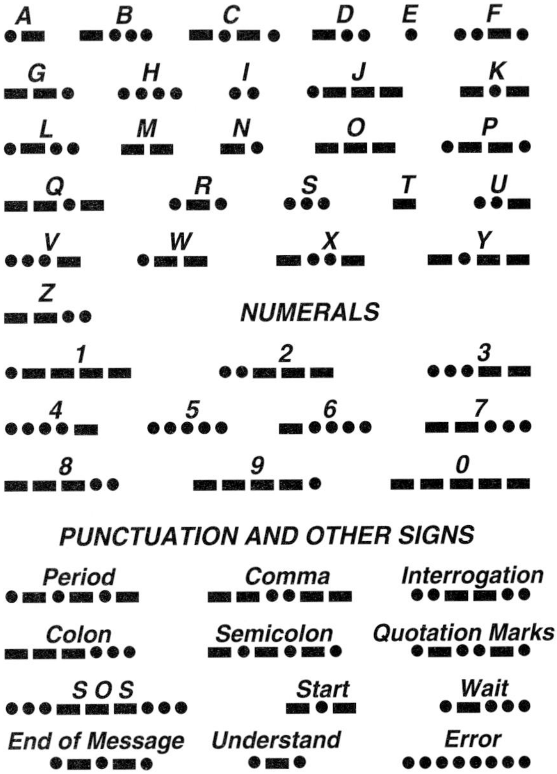

Outline diagram

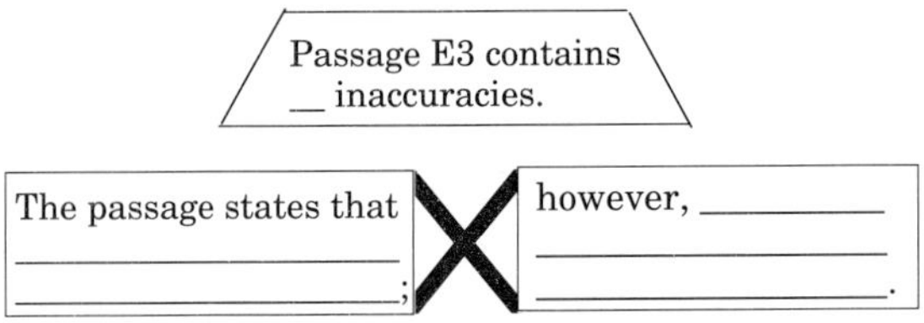

Passage E3 contains __ inaccuracies.
The passage states that ________________;
however, ________________.

Part B

- Some words are more general than other words. More general words tell about more things. More specific words tell about fewer things.
- Here are two words:

  buildings **garages**

- **Buildings** is more general because it tells about garages and other things that are not garages.
- Here are two other words:

  girls **people**

- **People** is more general because the word can be used to tell about girls and other persons.

Part C

For each item, write the word that is more general.

1. vehicles .... trucks
2. girls .... females
3. tools .... hammers
4. clothing .... hats
5. fish .... goldfish
6. boys .... children

Part D

For each item, copy only the more general statement.

1. They drove a vehicle.
   They drove a truck.
2. She worked at Tina's Burger Palace.
   She worked at a restaurant.
3. You should eat fish.
   You should eat perch.
4. Children should not play with sharp objects.
   Children should not play with knives.
5. Keep valuable things in a bank.
   Keep valuable things in a safe place.

Part E Write the second sentence with the missing noun.

1. They argued for two hours. Nothing was gained by that.
2. He stated that Zappo costs less. That was misleading.
3. They requested help. Nobody listened to that.

Part F Rewrite each sentence so it begins with part of the predicate. Label the subject, the predicate, the noun in the subject and the verb.

1. The last person left the meeting just before midnight.
2. My mom went to the store early in the morning.
3. Their cat walked along the ledge without looking down.

Part G Write the question that uses all the words. Label the subject, predicate, the noun and adjectives in the subject, and the verb words.

1. A sentence could have a short subject.
2. The old car does run well.
3. His last test will cover 20 lessons.
4. Their favorite entertainer is coming to town.

Independent Work

Part H Edit this passage. Write sentences that are not runs-ons and that do not have inappropriate words.

there dog was all black and their cat was the same color she made a loud purring noise when you petted her Are cat is not black and he don't make a loud purring noise.

Part I Rewrite the underlined sentence. Replace the unclear word.

1. The clowns in the picture had stripes on their umbrellas. Don didn't like the way they looked. He drew umbrellas that did not have stripes.
2. Martha got good grades from all of her teachers. She was very happy with them. They were the best grades she'd ever received.
3. Beth talked with Marge yesterday. She was on her way to class. Marge was sitting outside the office.

Lesson 22

Part A

For each sentence, write a question. Label the subject, the predicate, the noun and adjectives in the subject, and the verb words.

1. An adjective could be in a question.
2. Her sentences are getting better.
3. The other workers were loading trucks.
4. His brother is watching her.
5. A music class will give a performance.

Part B

Rewrite the second sentence so the meaning of **this** or **that** is clear. Use the verb-noun list in the Reference Section if you need to.

1. The clowns will entertain the children. This will create a lot of laughter.
2. The committee concluded that Ted should receive a raise in pay. All the people on the committee agreed with that.
3. They explored the entire island. That led to a lot of interesting discoveries.
4. Our whole family gathers every spring. That lasts for a weekend.

Part C

Vocabulary Box

human	size	flea
inches	fields	record

Part D

For each item, write the word that is more general.

1. ball .... basketball
2. furniture .... couch
3. move .... run
4. water .... liquid
5. container .... basket

Part E

For each item, write the sentence that is more general.

1. All buildings have walls.
   All restaurants have walls.
2. Beagles make good pets.
   Dogs make good pets.
3. She has fancy necklaces.
   She has fancy jewelry.
4. Hobbies are fun.
   Stamp collecting is fun.
5. They liked to watch basketball games.
   They liked to watch sporting events.

Part F

Rewrite the sentences so they begin with part of the predicate. Circle the subject and underline the predicate. Write the letter for the noun and adjectives in the subject and for the verb.

1. Their roof leaked during the rainstorm.
2. A young fox followed the bird without making a sound.
3. Our door blew shut after she walked outside.
4. The sun came out just before lunch time.

Independent Work

Part G Edit this passage. Write sentences that are not run-ons and that do not have inappropriate words.

They've ants in they're kitchen and there going to hire Bug Busters to make sure their kitchen don't have no bugs. Its going to be a big job.

Part H For each item, write a parallel response that starts with the word **no** and uses the word **also.**

1. Wise old men are the only people who are smart.
2. The only way Mary can get a good workout is by riding a bike fast.
3. The only way you can lose weight is by eating less.

Part I Rewrite each sentence so it does not have the word **there.**

1. There were four birds standing near the water.
2. There was a large boulder in the middle of the stream.
3. There is a kite far above the trees.

Key

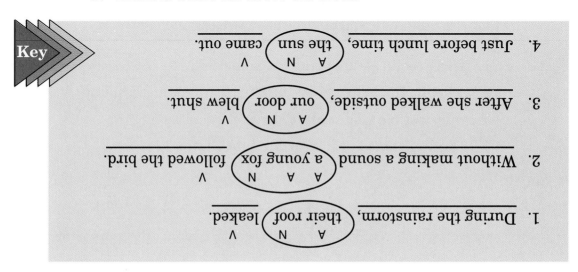

1. During the rainstorm, their roof (A N) leaked. (V)
2. Without making a sound a young fox (A A N) followed the bird. (V)
3. After she walked outside, our door (A N) blew shut. (V)
4. Just before lunch time, the sun (A N) came out. (V)

Lesson 23

Part A

Rewrite each sentence so it begins with a part of the predicate. Label the subject, the predicate, the noun and adjectives in the subject, and the verb word.

1. Four dogs barked when the car started.
2. Our roof leaks when the rain blows from the south.
3. My class went to a farm last week.

Part B

Vocabulary Box

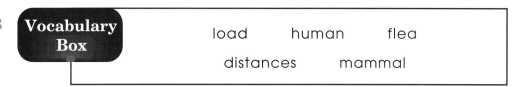

load human flea
distances mammal

Part C

Some sentences are unclear because words that tell where or when are in the wrong place.

- Here's a sentence:

They studied the history of birds in 1975.

- That sentence has two meanings. The two pictures show two meanings.

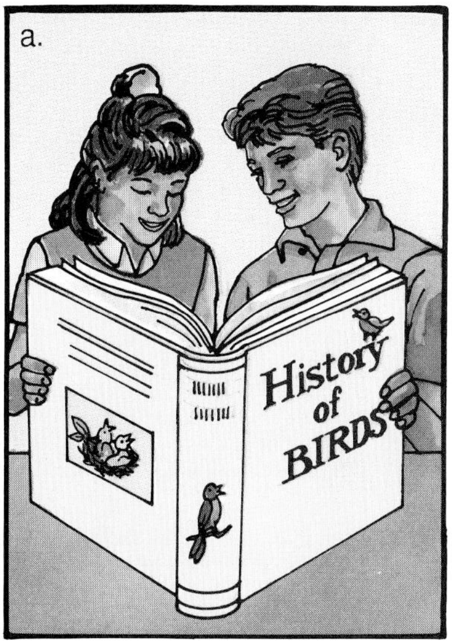

Part D Each sentence has more than one meaning. Write the more specific meaning for the second picture.

1. They discussed their future in the kitchen.

2. Mark went to a meeting on fishing with four friends.

3. We watched the rockets take off from our couch.

Part E Write the part of speech for the missing word. Then write each sentence with a word in place of the blank.

1. (A big _____) delivered packages.
2. (A _____ bulldog) growled at us.
3. (Mary) _____ her brother.
4. _____ (the rain) ruin our party?

Part F Rewrite the sentences so they are correct.

1. They could of gone with us.
2. He don't know nothing.
3. She should of gave that paper to him.

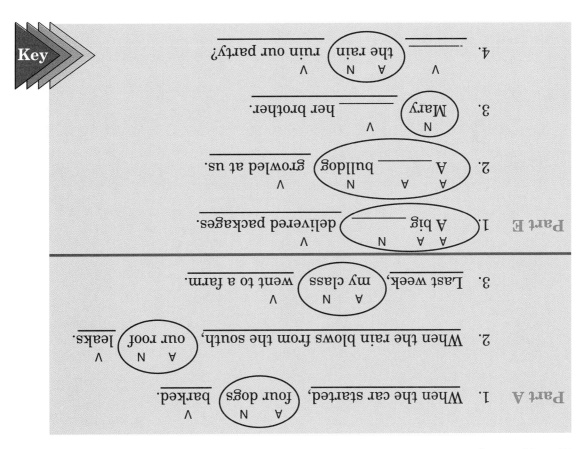

Key

Part A

1. When the car started, (four dogs) barked. (A N V)
2. When the rain blows from the south, (our roof) leaks. (A N V)
3. Last week, (my class) went to a farm. (A N V)

Part E

1. (A big _____) delivered packages. (A A N V)
2. (A _____ bulldog) growled at us. (A A N V)
3. (Mary) _____ her brother. (N V)
4. _____ (the rain) ruin our party? (V A N V)

Independent Work

Part G Edit this passage. Write sentences that are not run-ons and that do not have inappropriate words.

The best way to keep you're heart in good shape is to run and that'll make your heart beat faster and it'll beat more than 90 times per minute.

Part H Rewrite the second sentence so the meaning of **that** is clear. Use your verb-noun list if you need to.

1. The mechanic adjusted the clutch. That made the car operate better.
2. My doctor has a scale in the waiting room. A lot of people use that.
3. Uncle Henry connected the electrical wires. That caused all the fuses to blow.
4. Mr. Davis observed birds carefully. That showed how much the birds eat.

Lesson 24

Part A Use the facts to tell what is wrong with statements 1 and 2. Follow the X-box diagram.

Sample Item

Jerry, Ginger and Julie went to the store.
Fact: Julie stayed home.

The statement indicates that Jerry, Ginger and Julie went to the store;	X	however, that statement is inaccurate. [Tell why.]

Statement __ indicates ______________________ ______________________;	X	however, that statement is inaccurate. [Tell why.]

1. Fran's brother swept and washed the garage floor.
   Fact: The garage floor was not washed.
2. Three types of ducks and two types of geese flew down from Canada.
   Fact: One type of geese was from Canada.

Part B Rewrite each sentence with a word in place of the blank. Label the subject and the predicate, the noun and adjectives in the subject, and the verb words.

1. Did the boys _____ that car?
2. His _____ statement was inaccurate.
3. Their little _____ started howling.
4. _____ only question had five answers.

Part C Write just the second sentence for each item making the word **that** clear by adding the correct noun.

1. Terry requested information. We sent that the next day.
2. We listened to the lecture. That was boring.
3. They put a huge crate in the elevator. That took up a lot of space.

Part D Each sentence has more than one meaning. Write the more specific meaning for the second picture.

1. He bought a tool for cleaning his furnace at the store.

2. They watched thousands of geese flying from their yard.

3. Mary knows how birds communicate on the phone.

Independent Work

Part E For each sentence, write two parallel sentences.

1. Hatfield borders on the McNerd River.
2. Hopstown is more than 10 miles from Bowman.
3. Jasper is 14 miles from Hamburg.

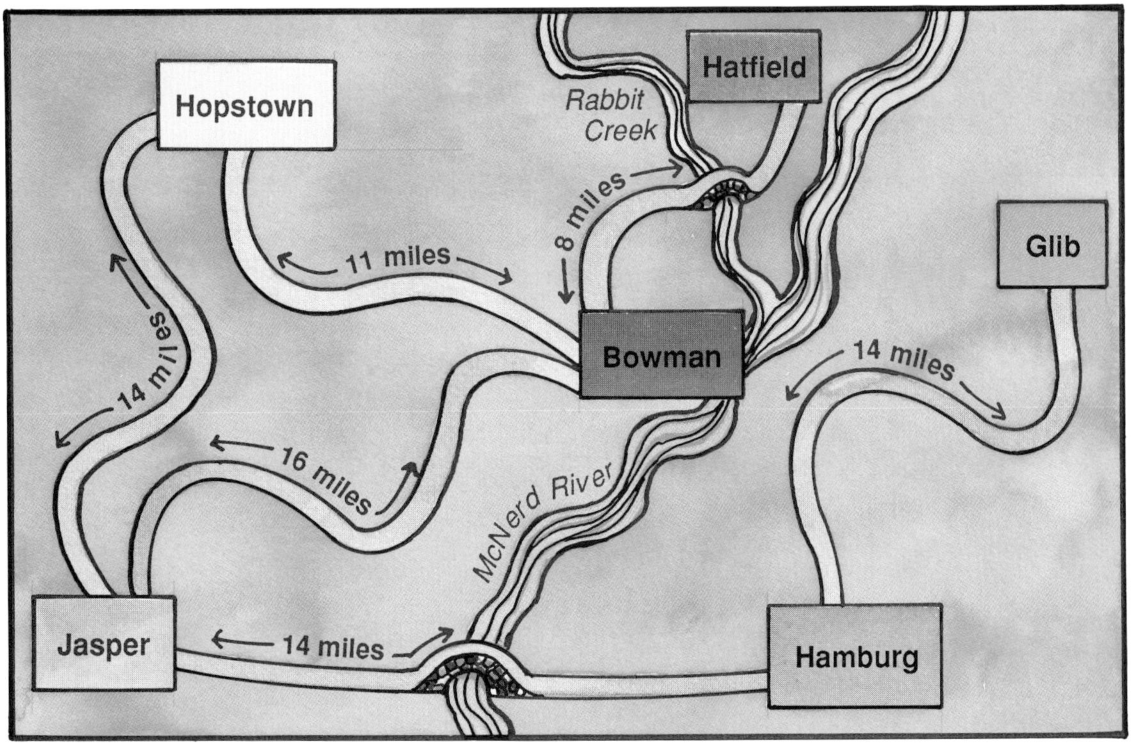

Part F Write a response to each sentence. Remember to use the words **only** and **no.**

1. All the students finished their work.
   (Some did not finish.)
2. The students and their teachers went on a trip.
   (The teachers did not go on the trip.)
3. The students finished their work and went on a trip.
   (No one went on a trip.)

Part G Rewrite each sentence so it begins with part of the predicate. Remember the comma. Then circle the subject and underline the whole predicate. Write **N** above the noun in the subject. Write **V** above each verb word.

1. Six boys walked to the fishing hole in the morning.
2. Our committee will meet with the mayor on Tuesday evening.
3. The house burned during the night.
4. The wind got stronger as the day got hotter.

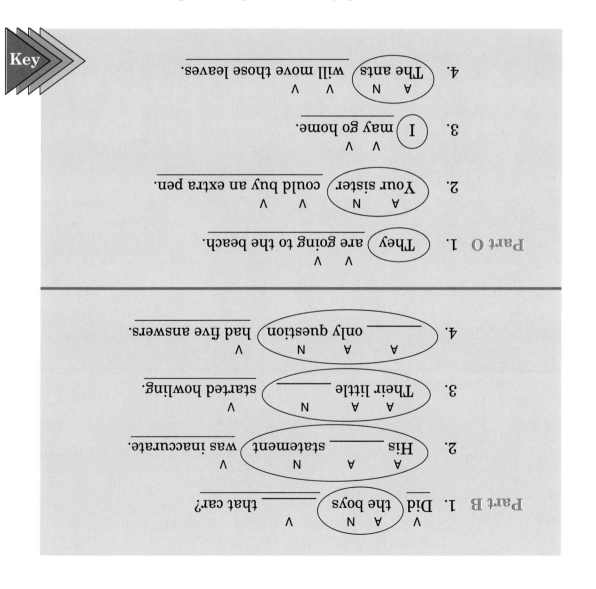

Key

Part B

1. Did the boys ______ that car?
2. His ______ statement was inaccurate.
3. Their little ______ started howling.
4. ______ only question had five answers.

Part O

1. They are going to the beach.
2. Your sister could buy an extra pen.
3. I may go home.
4. The ants will move those leaves.

Lesson 25

Part A Copy the sentence in each item that is more general. Underline the part of the sentence that makes it more general and write three things that show why that part is more general.

1. The boys crowded into the bus.
   The people crowded into the bus.
2. Pets should stay out of the street.
   Cats should stay out of the street.
3. The containers were full.
   The jars were full.
4. They walked into the kitchen.
   They walked into the room.

Part B Use the outline diagram to write about the main inaccuracy in Tina's account.

Tina's account

I completed three major jobs on Saturday morning. The first job was washing four sweaters and hanging them out to dry. The next job was cleaning the closet in my room. That job took nearly two hours. The last job I did on Saturday morning was helping my stupid brother fix a stupid flat tire on his stupid bike. So you can see that I was very busy all morning.

Source: **Facts about What Tina Did on Saturday**

Time	Activity
9:18 – 9:26	ate breakfast
9:30 – 9:45	washed sweaters and hung them out
9:50 – 11:35	cleaned closet
12:00 – 12:20	ate lunch
12:30 – 1:00	talked on phone
1:00 – 1:45	helped brother fix tire
2:00 – 3:30	went riding with brother

Outline diagram

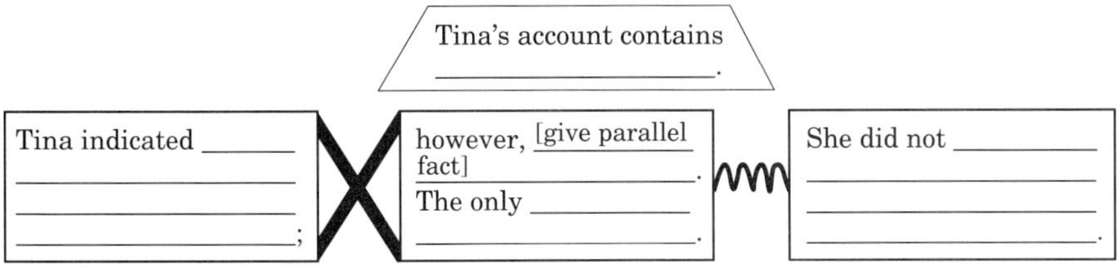
Tina's account contains ________.
Tina indicated ________;
however, [give parallel fact] ________.
The only ________.
She did not ________.

Part C First write about the general meaning of each sentence. Then write the more specific meaning.

1. They learned about arguing in school.

2. Mr. Briggs told how he worked on 18 bridges yesterday.

3. They discussed the new freeway in the library.

Part D Write the parallel statement for each question. Mark the subject and the predicate and label the noun and adjectives in the subject and both verb words.

1. Can all those clowns fit in that tiny car?
2. Are the younger children doing well in school?
3. Have the birds eaten all the food?
4. Should those cats sleep on the porch?

Part E Write the second sentence with the correct noun after **that.** The missing noun may be related to the verb or to some other word in the sentence.

1. They studied in the library. That was very quiet.
2. They studied in the library. That helped them prepare for the test.
3. We received an invitation to her party. That surprised us.
4. We received an invitation to her party. That is going to be held next week.

Independent Work

Part F Edit this passage. Write sentences that are not run-ons and that do not have inappropriate words.

Mark should of told us he was sick and he could of called us and he don't think of other people sometimes. We waited their for an hour and he don't show up.

Part G Write a parallel response to each sentence. Begin with the word **no** and use the word **also.**

1. Turtles are the only animals that lay eggs.
2. You can fish only in rivers.

Part H Rewrite each sentence so it begins with part of the predicate. Circle the subject in each sentence and underline the whole predicate. Write **N** above the noun in the subject. Write **V** above each verb word.

1. Fifteen students went to lunch after finishing the math assignment.
2. One student will receive a special award next week.
3. The magician swallowed fire without flinching.
4. We walked home after the movie.

Lesson 26

Part A Rewrite these questions as statements.

1. Have all the puppies had lunch?
2. Do the clouds indicate rain?
3. Can the sled dogs pull the sled?

Part B Rewrite the second sentence so its meaning is clear.

1. Our teacher reminded us to do our homework. That helped me remember.
2. They put fertilizer on the field. That helps the plants grow.
3. They practiced in the classroom. That made them ready for the talent show.

Part C Write the part of speech for each blank. Then write sentences with words for the blanks.

1. The ____ bunnies played in the grass.
2. Did that turtle ____ under water?
3. That ____ will fall on our car.
4. Last winter ____ beautiful.
5. ____ her brother finish his work?

Part D Use the outline diagram to write about the inaccuracy in the Clipper advertisement.

Source: **An Advertisement for Clipper Boats**

If you buy a brand new Clipper boat right now, you'll save four ways.
First, you'll save $10 on the windshield.
You'll save more than $500 on the engine.
You'll save $200 on the custom seats.
And you'll save $10 on the owner's manual.
Remember, when you buy a Clipper, you get clipped.
Clipper

Facts

These things are reduced in price:

windshield ....reduced $10

custom seats ....reduced $200

owner's manual ....reduced $10

Outline diagram

The Clipper ad contains ____________________.

The ad indicates ____________________ ____________________ ____________________;

however, [give parallel fact] ____________________. The only items you'll save on are ____________.

You will not ____________________ ____________________ ____________________.

Part E Fix these unclear sentences by moving the confusing part to the beginning of the sentence. Put a comma after the part you move.

1. Mr. Briggs told how he worked on 18 bridges yesterday.
2. We watched thousands of geese take off from our yard.
3. Mary learned how birds communicate during the last month.
4. He bought a tool for cleaning his furnace at the store.

Independent Work

Part F Rewrite the second sentence so its meaning is clear.

1. Carl collects stamps from foreign countries. Some of them are small. England is very small.
2. We loaned five books to the boys. They were in great shape. By next week, they will probably have bent pages.
3. My uncle loves to go out with little Billy. He rides a tricycle. Little Billy also has a tricycle.
4. That woman has a kitten in her coat pocket. It is light colored. The coat pocket is black.

Part G Rewrite this passage. Fix up all mistakes.

Are house has a leak in the roof and every time their's a heavy rain, we have'ta put a bucket in our kitchen so it'll catch the water. We have'ta keep emptying the bucket and my brother says that we should of used a bigger bucket.

Part H

Copy the sentence that is more general. Underline the part of the sentence that makes it more general, and write three things that show why that part is more general.

1. George trains lions.
   George trains animals.
2. You should eat vegetables.
   You should eat carrots.

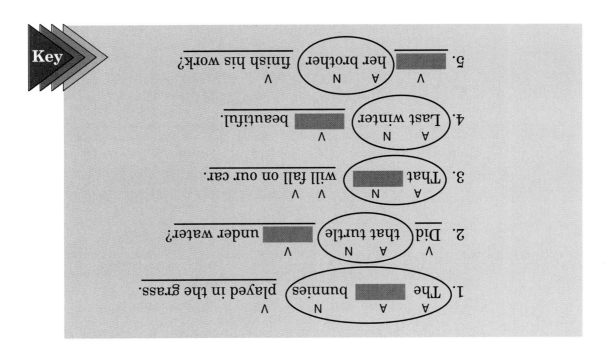

Key

1. The ___ bunnies played in the grass.
2. Did that turtle ___ under water?
3. That ___ will fall on our car.
4. Last winter ___ beautiful.
5. ___ her brother finish his work?

Lesson 27

Part A

Copy the sentence that is more general. Underline the part of the sentence that makes is more general, and write three things that show why that part is more general.

1. They went into a church.
   They went into a building.
2. The meal was delicious.
   The breakfast was delicious.
3. He received a communication.
   He received a Morse code message.
4. We heard a dog fight in the alley.
   We heard a disturbance in the alley.

Part B

- You've worked with nouns and adjectives in the subject. Sentences may also have nouns and adjectives in the predicate.
- The nouns name things. The adjectives come just before the nouns.

Part C

These sentences have nouns in the predicate. The nouns in the predicate are boldfaced. Copy the sentences. Mark the subject and predicate and label all of the nouns, adjectives and verb words.

1. A cat sat on a small black **pillow.**
2. That woman chops **wood.**
3. His longest jump was 18 **feet.**
4. John was reading **books.**

Part D The picture shows the more general meaning for each sentence. Write the more specific meaning for each picture. Then rewrite the original sentence so it doesn't have that meaning.

1. They discussed the farm animals they saw in school.

2. We read about the man who discovered America last year.

3. I found a book about repairing bikes in our basement.

Part E Rewrite the second sentence in each item so its meaning is clear. You may either change the words or change the order of the words to make the sentence clear.

1. Martha put a penny on the stove. Fortunately, it was cold.
2. Bill accidentally got water on his paper. This ruined his day.
3. She made sure that all the pencils had good erasers. She knew that the students would use them a lot.
4. Tim warned his little brother about going in the street. That didn't work well.

Part F Rewrite these questions as statements. Then circle the subject, underline the predicate and write **V** above each verb.

1. Would they buy those baskets?
2. Are you having fun?
3. Did George complete his homework assignment?

Independent Work

Part G Write the second sentence so its meaning is clear.

1. Jan arranged the flowers very carefully. She was proud of that.
2. She judged his weight to be 150 pounds. That was not accurate.
3. The doctor took time to explain the problem. That gave us important information.
4. The crew extended the parking lot 40 feet. That made it possible to park buses in the lot.

Part H Edit this passage. Write sentences that are not run-ons and that do not have inappropriate words.

They must of had a big party at Judy's house and about 20 cars were on there street and lot's of music was coming from they're house. My brother's friend went to the party and he told us that their going to have another one in April.

Part I Rewrite these sentences so they don't use the word **there.**

1. There are four climbers on the side of that mountain.
2. There was a young girl who lived in the town of Freedom.
3. There were six dogs trying to catch a squirrel.

Part J Rewrite these sentences so they begin with part of the predicate. Circle the subject, underline the predicate, and label the noun in the subject and the verb word.

1. Our car stopped between the towns of Glick and Glump.
2. The show began just before the thunder started booming.
3. Dan hummed his favorite song during the entire dinner.

Lesson 28

Part A

- Some sentences are called **commands** or **directions.** They tell somebody what to do.
- These sentences are strange because they don't have a subject. The first word is usually a verb. It is capitalized.
- Here are sentences that are directions:

  Turn the corner.

  Put the dog outside.

  Stop making so much noise.

  Turn your paper over and copy the problems.

Part B

Follow these directions and make two figures as different from each other as possible.

- Make a square.
- Make a **J** in the square.
- Make a **V** just above the square.

Part C

- Subjects with more than one word have a noun. The noun is usually the last word of the subject.
- Sometimes predicates have nouns, too.
- Nouns name persons, places or things. These are nouns:

Tommy	**brother**	**city**
argument	**dream**	**building**

- These are not nouns:

  handsome **quickly** **over** **handy**

- Remember, if it's the name of a person, a place or a thing, it's a noun.
- Sometimes, the last word in the sentence is a noun. Here's a sentence of that type:

  Fran drank the water.

- **Water** is the name of a thing, so **water** is a noun.

Part D Write the number of each sentence and write the nouns that are in that sentence.

1. John stood next to the house.
2. Yoko moved quickly.
3. My friends were quiet.
4. Susie had a bad dream.
5. The truck hauled seven large logs.

Part E

- Some claims are **inaccurate.** They're false.
- Other claims are **misleading.** They're true, but they're right on the edge of being false. They give a false impression, but they are not really false.
- Here are two pillows:

Dandy

$19\frac{1}{2}$ ounces

Floppo

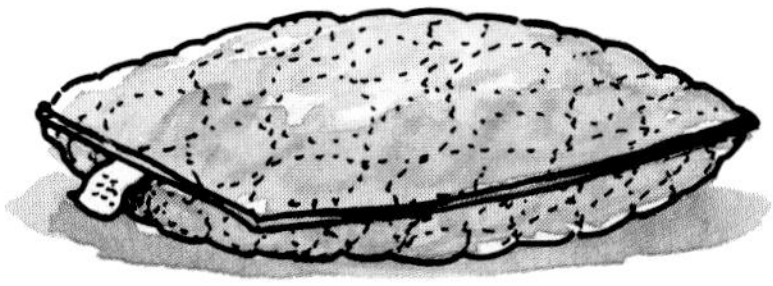

19 ounces

- This claim is inaccurate:
  Dandy pillows weigh a lot more than Floppo pillows.
- This claim is inaccurate:
  Dandy pillows are lighter than Floppo pillows.
- This claim is **true,** but **misleading:**
  Floppo pillows are lighter than Dandy pillows.
- This claim is **true** and **not misleading:**
  Floppo pillows are slightly lighter than Dandy pillows.
- This claim is true, not misleading and **very specific:**
  Floppo pillows are 1/2 ounce lighter than Dandy pillows.
- Remember, claims that are true but that refer to very small differences may be misleading.

Part F Label the statements **true** or **false.** Then indicate which of the true statements are misleading.

Bumpo
2700 pounds

Sinko
2702 pounds

Statements

1. Bumpo weighs two pounds less than Sinko.
2. Bumpo and Sinko weigh the same amount.
3. Bumpo weighs less than Sinko.
4. Sinko weighs a lot more than Bumpo.
5. Sinko weighs two pounds less than Bumpo.

Part G For each item, rewrite the second sentence so its meaning is clear.

1. The river had one high bank. It almost dried up in the summer.
2. The mechanic adjusted the brakes on Mr. Bill's bike. That made the bike stop more smoothly.
3. The nurse gave Martha a shot. She didn't cry.
4. Those dogs chase mice. They live behind our kitchen wall.

Part H Use the vocabulary box to help you spell some important words correctly.

Vocabulary Box

McKinley Alaska North Pole
boundary Canada North America
sea level peak

Independent Work

Part I Rewrite the second sentence so its meaning is clear.

1. The students in Ms. Green's classroom spent time preparing for the test. That paid off.
2. The general wanted to destroy the factories. That seemed unnecessary.
3. We wanted to expand our argument. That would allow us to draw more powerful conclusions.

Part J Write parallel statements for these questions. Use all the words.

1. Can David run as fast as Julie?
2. Were you considering all the possibilities?
3. Should young kittens go far from their mother?

Part K Write a paragraph that tells about the inaccuracies in the passage. Use the outline diagram to guide you. Refer to the source map for accurate information.

Source map: **Alaska**

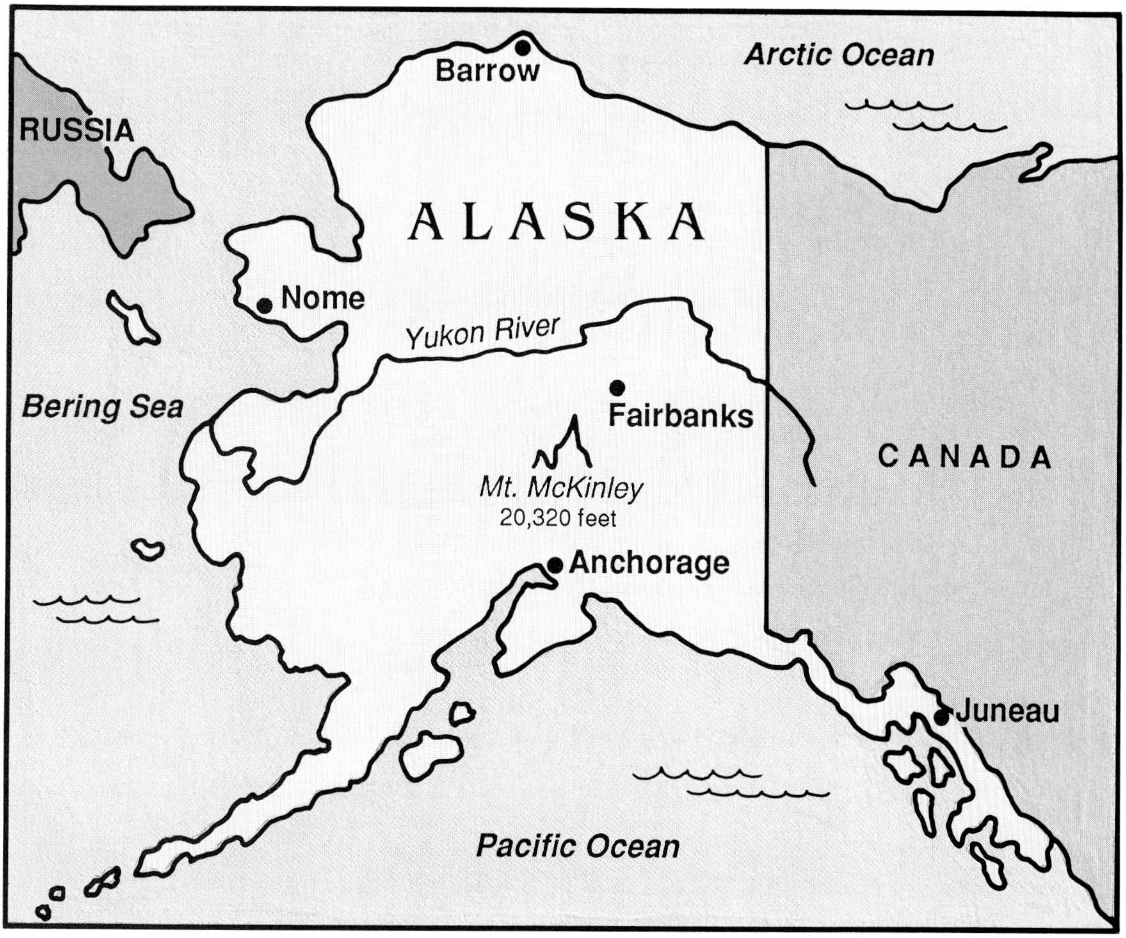

Passage

Alaska is the largest state in the United States. Alaska borders on Canada and Norway. The highest mountain in North America is in Alaska. That mountain is Mt. McKinley. It is 30,200 feet high. The town that is farthest north in Alaska is Barrow. The city that is farthest south is Juneau.

Outline diagram

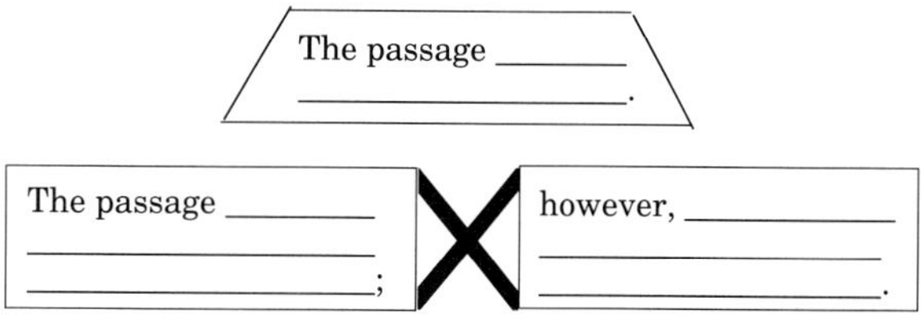

Lesson 29

Part A

For each item, copy the sentence that is more general. Underline the part of the sentence that makes it more general, and name three things that show why that part is more general.

1. I have read that document.
   I have read that magazine.
2. She lived in North America.
   She lived in Nebraska.
3. We had lots of quarters.
   We had lots of currency.
4. They went to a birthday party.
   They went to a gathering.

Part B

Follow the directions and make two figures that are as different as possible.

- Make a rectangle that is about three inches wide.
- Make a **B** just outside the lower corner.
- Make a **T** on the top line.

Part C

Label the claims **true** or **false.** Then indicate which of the true statements are misleading.

Claims

1. A gallon of Creamo covers a larger area than a gallon of A-1 covers.
2. A gallon of A-1 covers the same area that a gallon of Creamo covers.
3. A gallon of Creamo covers 450 square feet.
4. A gallon of Creamo covers 5 square feet more than a gallon of A-1 covers.
5. A gallon of Creamo covers a much larger area than a gallon of A-1 covers.
6. A gallon of Creamo covers more than 325 square feet.

Covers 350 square feet

Covers 345 square feet

Part D **Vocabulary Box**

treasure buried island

pounds inches cube

Part E For each sentence, write the more specific meaning for the picture. Then rewrite the original sentence so it is clear and has only one meaning.

1. We listened to the professor's account about capturing elephants in our classroom.

2. We saw a movie about a terrible war last night.

3. We asked him how much his sister grew yesterday.

Part F Write the number of each sentence. Then list all the **nouns** in the sentence.

Sample Items

A. The girls were talking.

B. We saw a tree falling.

C. The mud was soft.

D. A frog was in the mud.

1. That little boy drives tractors.
2. His song echoed loudly.
3. The advertisement contained a misleading claim.
4. George ate two carrots.
5. The girls were running.

Independent Work

Part G Rewrite the second sentence in each item so its meaning is clear.

1. The tallest building was on a hill. It was green during most of the year.
2. Baby Amy bit Clare's finger. That hurt.
3. Baby Amy bit Clare's finger. She didn't have any teeth.
4. The music came from an old radio. It filled the room.
5. The music came from an old radio. That made us want to dance.

Part H Rewrite these statements as questions. Label the verb words and the noun and adjectives in the subject.

1. Those children should stay in their yard.
2. That demonstration will win first prize.
3. Some monkeys can hang by their tail.

Part I Write the general meaning and more specific meaning for each picture. Then make the original sentence clear.

They discussed why birds migrate on Monday.

Lesson 30 – Test 3

Part A Use the vocabulary box to help you spell some important words correctly.

Vocabulary Box

Devil's Angel waterfall
United States Venezuela thousand

Part B Write the second sentence with the missing noun after **that.** The missing noun may be related to the verb or to some other word in the sentence.

1. Ginger's swimming improved. That pleased her coach very much.
2. Ginger's swimming improved. That took place every morning at 7:30.
3. Jenny requested 40 dollars from her father. She needed that to buy athletic equipment.
4. Jenny requested 40 dollars from her father. That was the third one he had received since May.

Part C For each item, copy the more general statement. Underline the part of the sentence that makes it more general, and write three things that show why it's more general.

1. She could not find that letter.
   She could not find that document.
2. The settlers moved across the United States.
   The settlers moved across North America.
3. They attended a lot of activities.
   They attended a lot of dancing classes.

Part D For each sentence, write the more specific meaning for the picture. Then rewrite the original sentence so it is clear and has only one meaning.

1. Fred told how he completed college before lunch.

2. Fred told how he completed college in Fran's backyard.

Part E Rewrite each question as a statement. Use all the words. Circle the subject, underline the predicate, write **V** above each verb word. Label the noun and any adjectives in the subject. Do not label nouns or adjectives in the predicate.

1. Could your mother pick us up after school?
2. Were the older girls having fun during the rainstorm?
3. Did George complete his homework assignment?

Partner Activity

Pick one silly sentence. With your partner, make a picture that shows the **unintended** meaning.

1. We saw rockets take off from our couch.
2. They discussed farm animals on their way to school.
3. They argued about the new freeway in the library.
4. Mary learned how birds communicate on the phone.

Lesson 31

Part A

- You've worked with pairs of sentences that are the same except for one part. That part makes one of the sentences more general than the other sentence.
- For each pair of sentences you've worked with, you can make a **deduction.**
- Here are the rules for making deductions:
  - ✔ Write the more general sentence first.
  - ✔ Skip a line. Write **Therefore, comma,** and the more specific sentence.
  - ✔ Underline the part of each sentence that makes it more general or more specific.
  - ✔ Make up a middle sentence by combining the underlined parts.
  - ✔ Start the middle sentence with the more specific part.

Part B

Follow the instructions in part A to write a complete deduction for each of these items.

1. All humans need air.
   All grandmothers need air.
2. Fran Johnson studies.
   All students study.

Part C

- You can test words to see if they are nouns by putting the adjective **the** in front of them.
- If the two words name some **thing,** the second word is a **noun.**
- If the two words don't name some **thing** or don't make sense, the second word is **not a noun.** For example:

  the houses
  - **Houses** is a noun.

  the arguments
  - **Arguments** is a noun.

  the always
  - **Always** is not a noun.

Part D Write **the** in front of each word. If the word is a noun, write **N** above it.

1. beautiful
2. only
3. claims
4. relatives
5. misleading
6. inaccuracy
7. silent

Part E Follow the directions and make two figures that are quite different from each other.

- Make a square.
- Draw a **diagonal line** from the upper corner to the lower corner.
- Make an **R** in the upper triangle.

Part F Here is a Spuddo ad and some accurate facts. Read the facts and check the ad for inaccuracies and misleading claims.

Source: **Spuddo Ad**

A *Spuddo* bike weighs less than a Yusha.
A *Spuddo* bike costs less than a Yusha.
Standard equipment includes a 15-speed gearbox, a rear fender and racing stripes.

Facts

- Weight of Spuddo: 22 pounds
- Cost of Spuddo: $210.99
- Weight of Yusha: 44 pounds
- Cost of Yusha: $211.00
- Standard equipment: 15-speed gearbox, racing stripes
- Additional equipment available: headlight, rear fender, heavy-duty tires

Part G Follow the outline diagram to write a paragraph about the inaccuracy and misleading claim that you found in the Spuddo ad in part F. Use proper paragraph form.

The Spuddo ad contains
_______________ and a
claim that is misleading.

The ad claims ______	however, that claim ___
________________	________________.
________________	_____ only _________
________________;	________________.

Part H Answer the question for each sentence.

1. What was in the garage?
   a. The bats in the garage heard a noise.
   b. The bats heard a noise in the garage.
2. What came from Mexico?
   a. An old man delivered a package from Mexico.
   b. An old man from Mexico delivered a package.
3. What was in New York?
   a. A company in New York sent a price list to its customers.
   b. A company sent a price list to its customers in New York.

Independent Work

Part I Copy these sentences. Circle the subject; underline the predicate. Write a letter to show the part of speech for **every word.**

1. Our cats chased the little mouse.
2. His last painting showed an incredible rainbow.
3. That paper had the best score.
4. My favorite uncle called the doctor.

Part J Edit this passage. If a sentence is unclear, move part of it to make it clear.

Our teacher told us about dinosaurs on a field trip. We visited a place that had dinosaur bones and they were all around and we talked about them and discussed the past. That was interesting. Our teacher said that some dinosaurs ate plants on the bus.

Key

1. the beautiful
2. the only
3. the claims N
4. the relatives N
5. the misleading
6. the inaccuracy N
7. the silent

Lesson 32

Part A

- For every noun, there's a more general word that's called a **pronoun.**
- For the word **boys,** the pronoun is **they.**
- For the word **car,** the pronoun is **it.**
- For the word **James,** the pronoun is **he.**
- Sample sentence:

  Elephants eat grass.
- Here's the sentence with pronouns:

  They eat it.

Part B Rewrite each sentence so it has no nouns, only pronouns.

Pronouns: **he she it they him her them**

1. George is watching birds.
2. Fred and Carlos build houses.
3. Sand flew at Mary.
4. Dad chased Kevin.

Part C Write directions for drawing this picture.

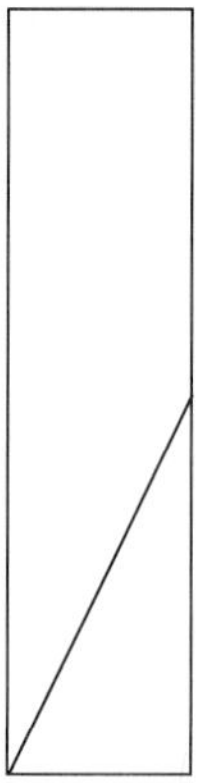

H

Part D

Write either **reasonable** or **unreasonable** to describe each statement below.

1. In my house, I'm going to build a doorway that's about six and a half yards high.
2. Our car gets about 25 miles to the gallon in the city.
3. John's big brother must be nine feet tall.
4. If you stand on top of that mountain, you can see halfway across the United States and Canada.
5. She works late each night so she can get home sooner.
6. The campers went on a four-mile hike.

Part E

Write a complete deduction for each item.

1. All vertebrates have a liver.
   All lizards have a liver.
2. All plants grow.
   All living things grow.

Part F

Answer the question for each sentence.

1. What was near the river?
   a. People near the river saw three planes.
   b. People saw three planes near the river.
2. What was under the maple tree?
   a. The squirrels watched a crow under the maple tree.
   b. The squirrels under the maple tree watched a crow.

Part G Here is an ad and some accurate facts. Follow the outline diagram to write a paragraph describing the ad's inaccuracies and misleading claim.

Source: **Posho Ad**

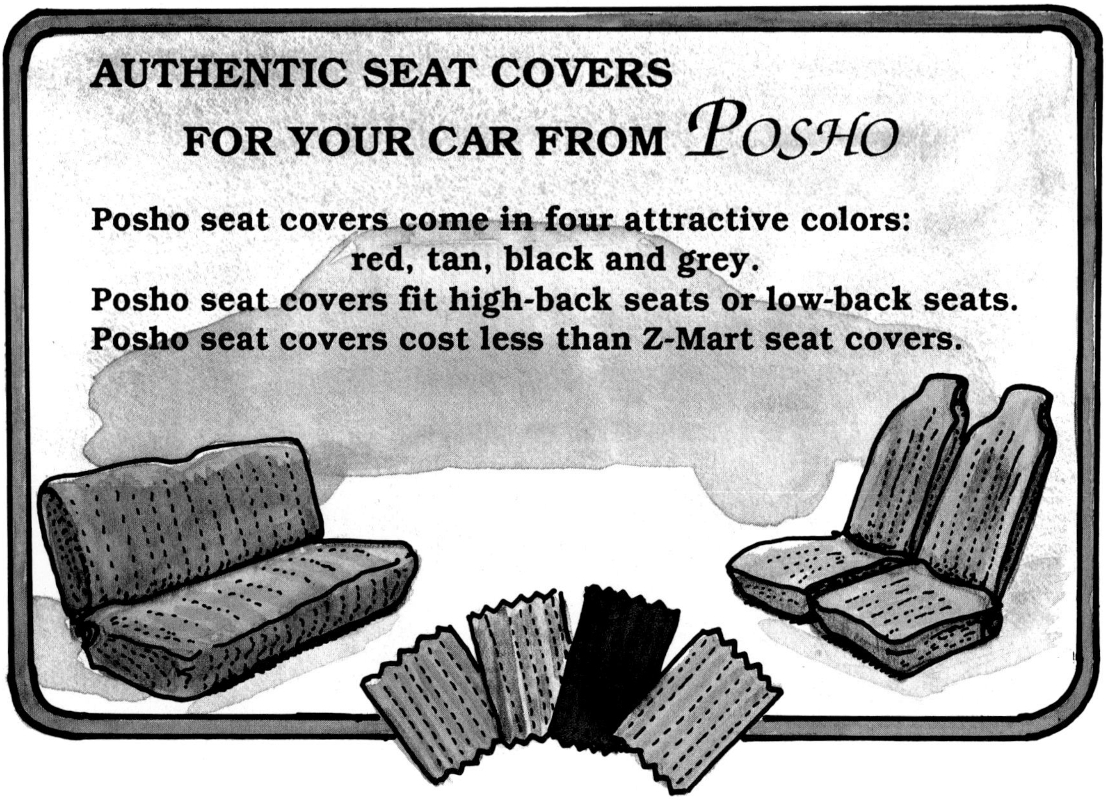

AUTHENTIC SEAT COVERS
FOR YOUR CAR FROM POSHO
Posho seat covers come in four attractive colors:
red, tan, black and grey.
Posho seat covers fit high-back seats or low-back seats.
Posho seat covers cost less than Z-Mart seat covers.

Facts

- Colors: tan, grey, black
- Fits: low-back seats only
- Cost of seat covers: $7.99 each
- Cost of Z-Mart seat covers: $16.00 a pair

Outline diagram

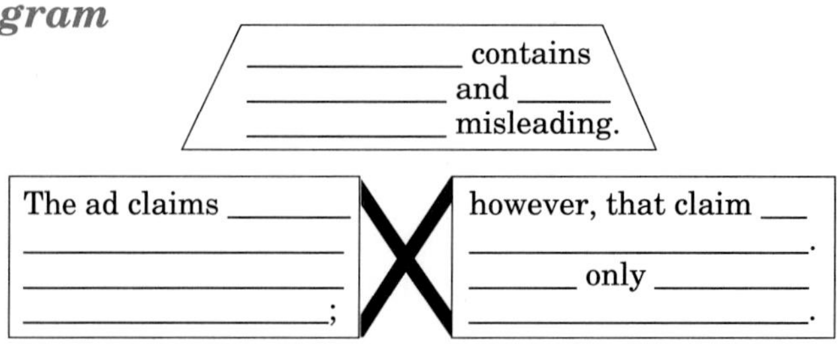

Independent Work

Part H Follow the outline diagram to write about the problems in Tim's account. Make sure that your sentences are clear.

Accurate source

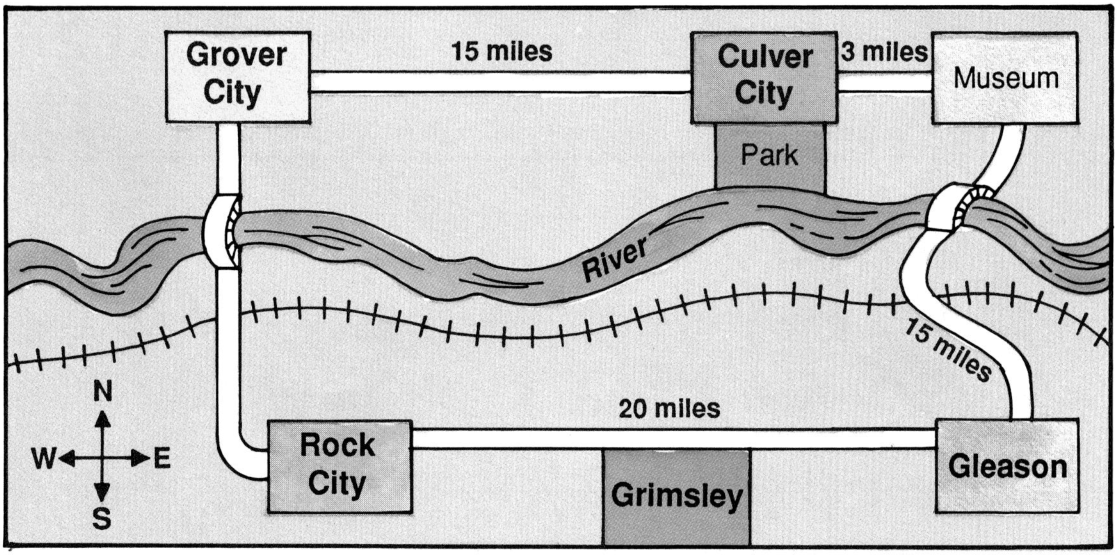

Tim's account

We left Grover City in the morning and drove about 8 miles to Culver City.

We had breakfast in a park just outside Culver City. The park was right on the river.

After breakfast, we drove south 3 miles to the museum. We looked at a lot of old boats.

Then we went south again about 15 miles to the town of Gleason. My cousin lives there, and we visited with her for a while. We had lunch with her.

Then we drove about 20 miles west to the town of Grimsley. We bought some stuff there. Then we drove back to Grover City.

Outline diagram

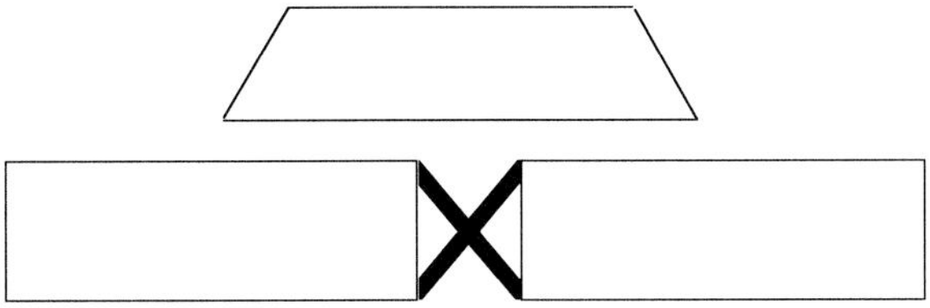

Part I

Rewrite each sentence so it begins with part of the predicate. Circle the subject and underline the entire predicate.

1. That wall will fall if a stiff wind starts blowing.
2. Our neighbors had a baby on Sunday.
3. The children played ball in an empty lot.
4. The new manager will quit unless the store changes its policies.

Part J

Write the in front of each word. Then write N over the word if it is a noun.

1. fast   2. runner   3. wishful   4. milk

Key

First set:

- Make a rectangle that is one-half inch wide and two inches high.
- Make a diagonal line from the lower left corner to the middle of the right side.
- Make an **H** just below the middle of the figure.

Second set:

- Make a rectangle that is two inches high and one-half inch wide.
- Make a diagonal line from the middle of the right side to the lower left corner.
- Make an **H** just under the middle of the bottom line.

Lesson 33

Part A Follow the outline diagram to explain what the second statement would have to say to be consistent with the first statement.

Item A: **1. The teacher gave everybody a high grade in writing.**
2. 90% of the class got an F in writing.

Statement 2 contradicts statement 1.

If the teacher ______________ ______________, statement 2 would indicate that ______________.

However, statement 2 indicates that ______________ ______________.

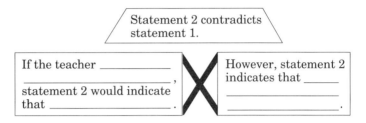

Item B: **1. Mr. Jones left work at 5 p.m.**
2. When he got home, it was 4:45 p.m.

Statement 2 contradicts statement 1.

If ______________ ______________, statement 2 would indicate that ______________.

However, statement 2 indicates that ______________ ______________.

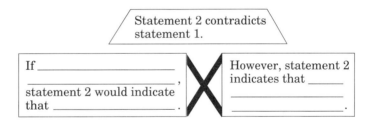

Part B For each item, write **reasonable** or **unreasonable.**

1. We went to the zoo and saw thousands of elephants.
2. Fred must drink five gallons of orange juice every day.
3. My work will improve if I just put more effort into doing well.
4. John has so many trading cards that they fill his room.
5. Terry's youngest sister is seven years younger than Terry.
6. Mrs. Jones is 33 years old, and her oldest daughter must be 40 years old.

Part C The statements below tell about the sales of Bumpo cars. Graph E2 shows accurate information. Write **true** or **false** for each statement. Then write **misleading** for each true statement that gives a false impression.

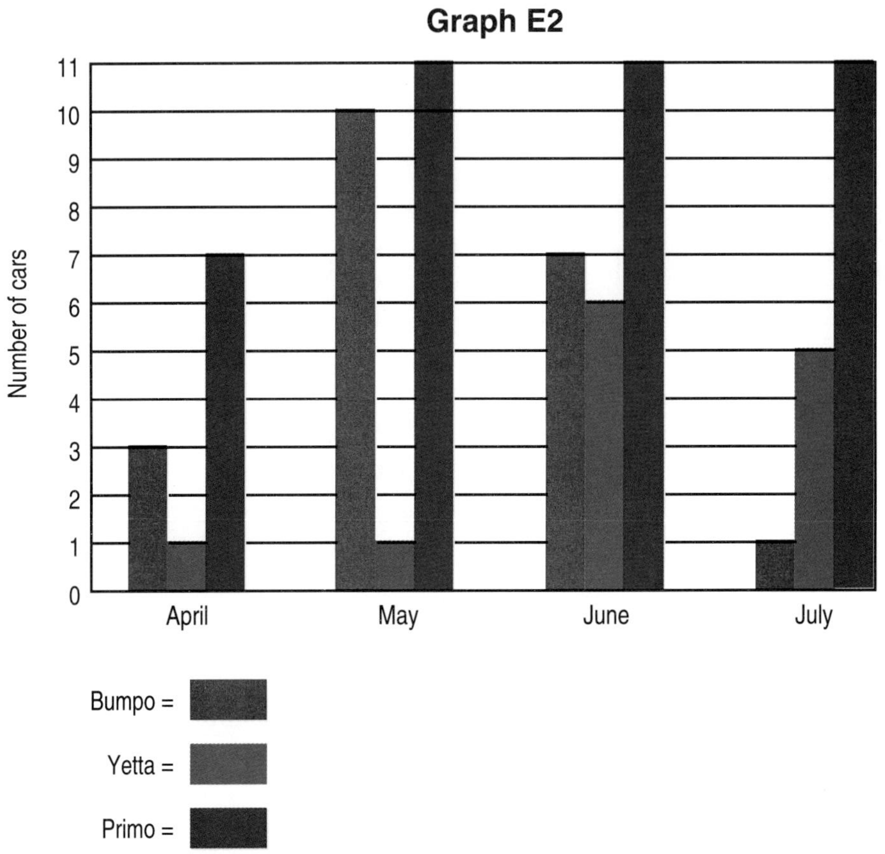

1. Bumpo sold nearly as many cars in April as in May.
2. In April, Bumpo sold three times as many cars as Yetta sold.
3. In April, Primo sold only four more cars than Bumpo sold.
4. In June, Bumpo sold as many cars as Primo sold.
5. In June, Bumpo sold many more cars than Yetta sold.
6. Primo sold more cars than Bumpo or Yetta sold.

Part D

Rewrite each sentence so it ends with a pronoun.

1. We looked at old photo albums.
2. We watched them run around a barn.
3. We were walking behind a yellow pony cart.
4. We watched James crawl under the old boards.
5. We hated those boring arguments.

Part E

- Here's a symbol for **Source:**

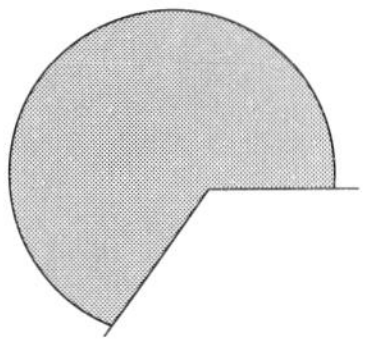

- Your source is a graph or a table or a map that gives you **accurate information.** A source circle behind a summary box tells you **to name your source.**

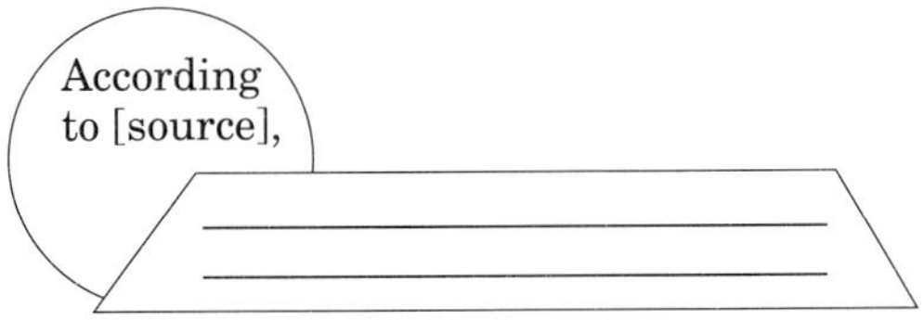

- If you got your facts from a source labeled Graph E7, you'd start your summary sentence with these words:

According to Graph E7, ________ .

Part F Here is Bryan's account and a graph that shows accurate facts. Check Bryan's account for inaccuracies. Follow the outline diagram to write a paragraph about the inaccuracies. Use proper paragraph form.

Graph E3: Tons of Flour Used in River City

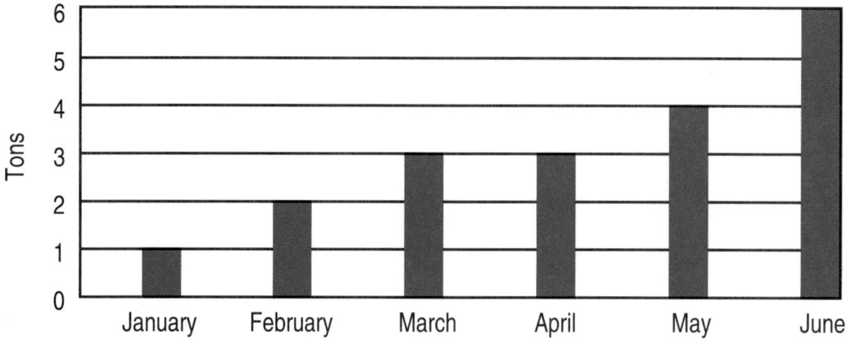

Bryan's account

River City used between one ton and six tons of flour each month from January through June. In March, River City used three tons of flour. In April, River City used four tons of flour. In June, River City used three tons more flour than it used in May.

Outline diagram

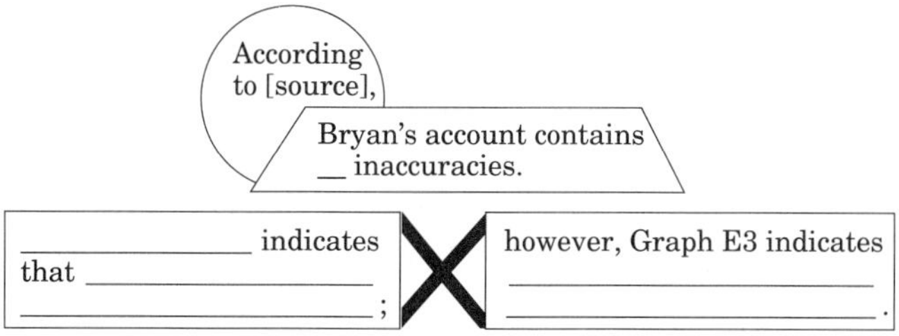

Part G Write **the** in front of each word to test if it is a noun. Write **N** above each noun.

1. day
2. brother
3. glad
4. always
5. garden
6. failure

Independent Work

Part H Write directions that are specific enough so that a person could follow them and make this figure. Your directions should have three sentences. Start each sentence with the word **Make** or **Draw.** In your first sentence, tell about the main thing the person should make.

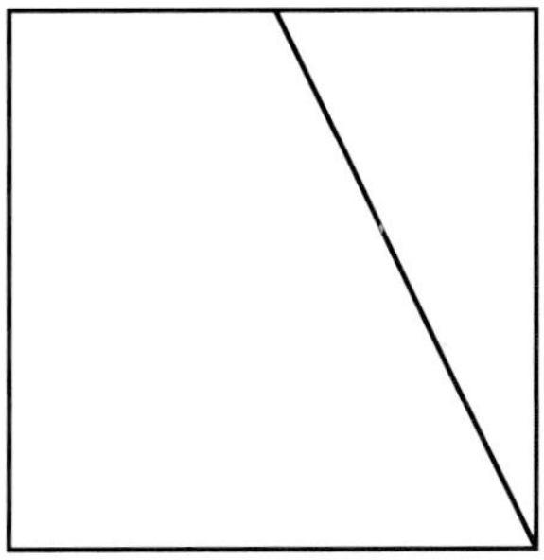

Part I Answer the question for each statement.

1. What is next to our house?
   a. The car next to our house cast a long shadow.
   b. The car cast a long shadow next to our house.
2. What was in the woods?
   a. The dogs barked at a raccoon in the woods.
   b. The dogs in the woods barked at a raccoon.
3. What was in the kitchen?
   a. The woman in the kitchen called to her neighbor.
   b. The woman called to her neighbor in the kitchen.
4. What was near Mr. Taylor's house?
   a. The oak tree dropped acorns near Mr. Taylor's house.
   b. The oak tree near Mr. Taylor's house dropped acorns.

Part J Rewrite each sentence so it is clear. *Optional:* Make a picture that shows your favorite unclear sentence.

1. Ginger told me about her sister's marriage on the telephone.
2. My brother described how tigers hunt after school.
3. Mr. Briggs indicated that he would help us fix the garage in a long letter.
4. We discussed ways we could help unfortunate children on our back porch.
5. We watched the planes fly over the river from our front porch.

Key

1. the day (N)
2. the brother (N)
3. the glad
4. the always
5. the garden (N)
6. the failure (N)

Lesson 34

Part A All of the statements are true. Write **misleading** for each statement that gives a false impression.

1. In April, Bumpo sold twice as many cars as Hambo sold.
2. During the four-month period, Bumpo sold more cars than Hambo sold.
3. Bumpo sold more cars in July than in April.

Car Sales in Freetown

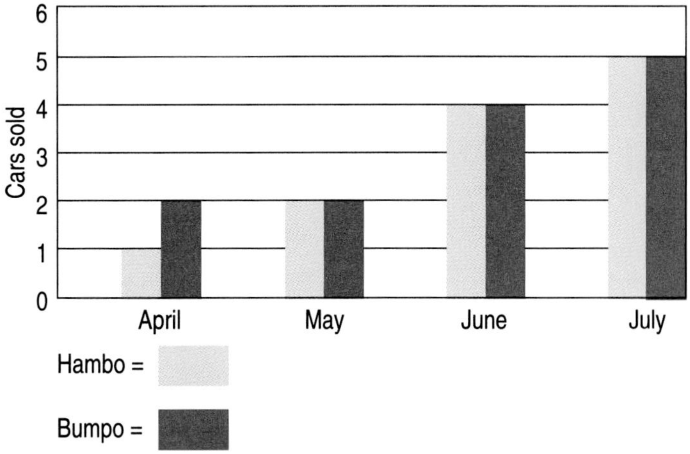

Part B Here is Tony's account of his spending habits and a graph showing accurate information about his spending. Follow the outline diagram to write a paragraph about the inaccuracies in Tony's account.

Tony's account

I earn $2,440 each month. I save $300 every month. I pay about the same amount for food as I do for rent. My auto expenses are $350 each month. My entertainment expenses are $200 each month. My last expense is taxes.

Graph E4: Tony's Monthly Expenses

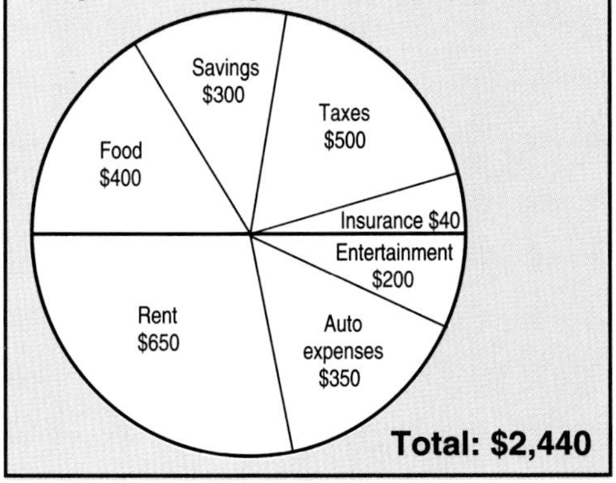

Outline diagram

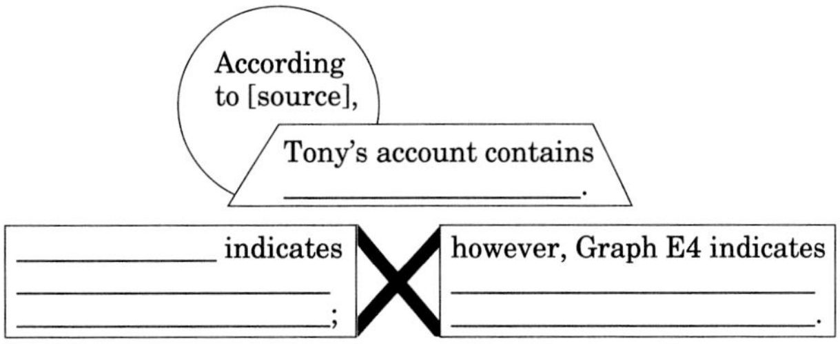

Part C Write a complete deduction for each item.

1. You can trust Bob.
   You can trust all your close friends.
2. Liquids flow.
   Water flows.
3. You should try to do all jobs well.
   You should try to do schoolwork well.

Part D Each pair of sentences has a part that is the same. Write what that part refers to.

1. What does **with a long tail** refer to?
   a. A cat with a long tail jumped at a kite.
   b. A cat jumped at a kite with a long tail.
2. What does **carrying a large sack** refer to?
   a. A yellow truck almost hit a man carrying a large sack.
   b. A yellow truck carrying a large sack almost hit a man.

Part E Follow the outline diagram to tell about the contradiction in each item.

Item A: 1. The shortest man was taller than any of the women.
2. One man was two inches shorter than Ms. Brown.

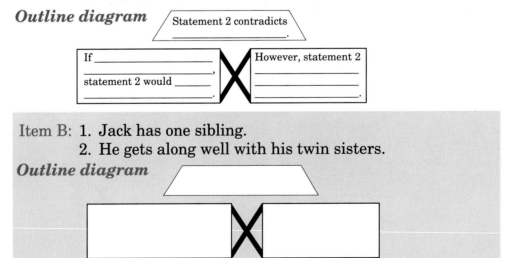

Outline diagram

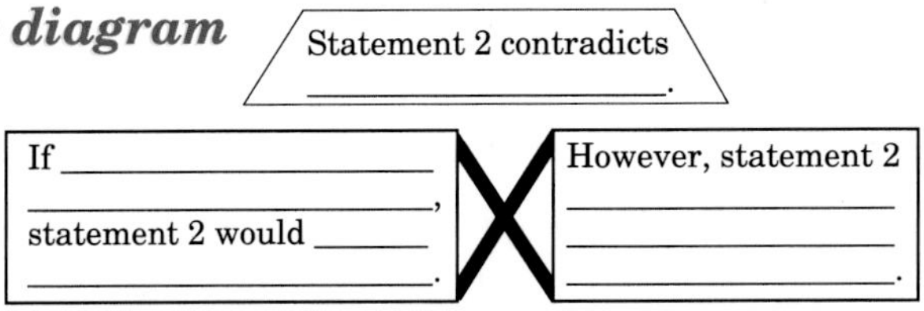

Statement 2 contradicts ____________.
If ____________ ____________, statement 2 would ____________ ____________.
However, statement 2 ____________ ____________ ____________.

Item B: 1. Jack has one sibling.
2. He gets along well with his twin sisters.

Outline diagram

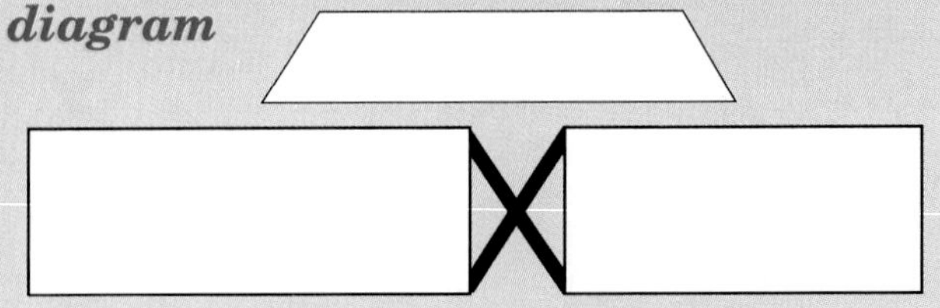

Part F

- For some directions, you use the words **horizontal, vertical** and **diagonal.**
- **Horizontal** is flat like the horizon.
- **Vertical** is straight up and down.

Part G

Write directions for making this figure.

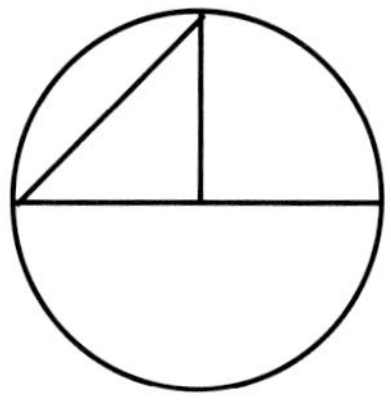

Independent Work

Part H

Copy each sentence. Circle the subject, underline the predicate and label the parts of speech for every word in the sentence.

1. Both boys loved the national park.
2. George was watching his favorite movie.
3. My three best friends celebrated my birthday.
4. Their largest pumpkin filled her wagon.

Part I

Rewrite each sentence in part H so it has a pronoun in place of each noun and its adjectives.

Part J Edit this passage. In some sentences, you may need to move part of the predicate.

There was a beautiful bird in our backyard and we didn't know what kind it was it's head was bright red it's eyes were orange. We told my mother about the bird in the kitchen. She indicated that some woodpeckers were building they're nest nearby. She said that their getting ready to lay eggs.

Part K Write **reasonable** or **unreasonable** to tell about each statement.

1. Our new car gets 234 miles per gallon.
2. Mr. Briggs has a car that weighs just about one ton.
3. Tim's oldest brother is over 3 meters tall.
4. Our garage door is 84 inches high.
5. Jill can run over 10 miles per hour.

Key

First set:

- Make a circle that is about one inch in diameter.
- Make a horizontal line through the center of the circle.
- Make a vertical line from the center of the circle to the upper edge.
- Make a diagonal line from the left end of the horizontal line to the top of the vertical line.

Second set:

- Make a circle that is about one inch wide.
- Make a horizontal line through the middle.
- Make a vertical line from the top of the circle to the horizontal line.
- Make a diagonal line from the top of the circle to the left end of the horizontal line.

Lesson 35

Part A Write a complete deduction for each item.

1. You should be polite to grandmothers.
   You should be polite to older people.
2. All monkeys have lungs.
   All mammals have lungs.
3. All birds lay eggs.
   Penguins lay eggs.

Part B Each pair of sentences has a part that is the same. Write what that part refers to.

1. What occurred **in the morning**?
   a. The hike had some difficult moments in the morning.
   b. The hike in the morning had some difficult moments.
2. What occurred **in April**?
   a. The vacation in April had a long rainy period.
   b. The vacation had a long rainy period in April.

Part C Follow the outline diagram to write about the contradictions between the map and the statements.

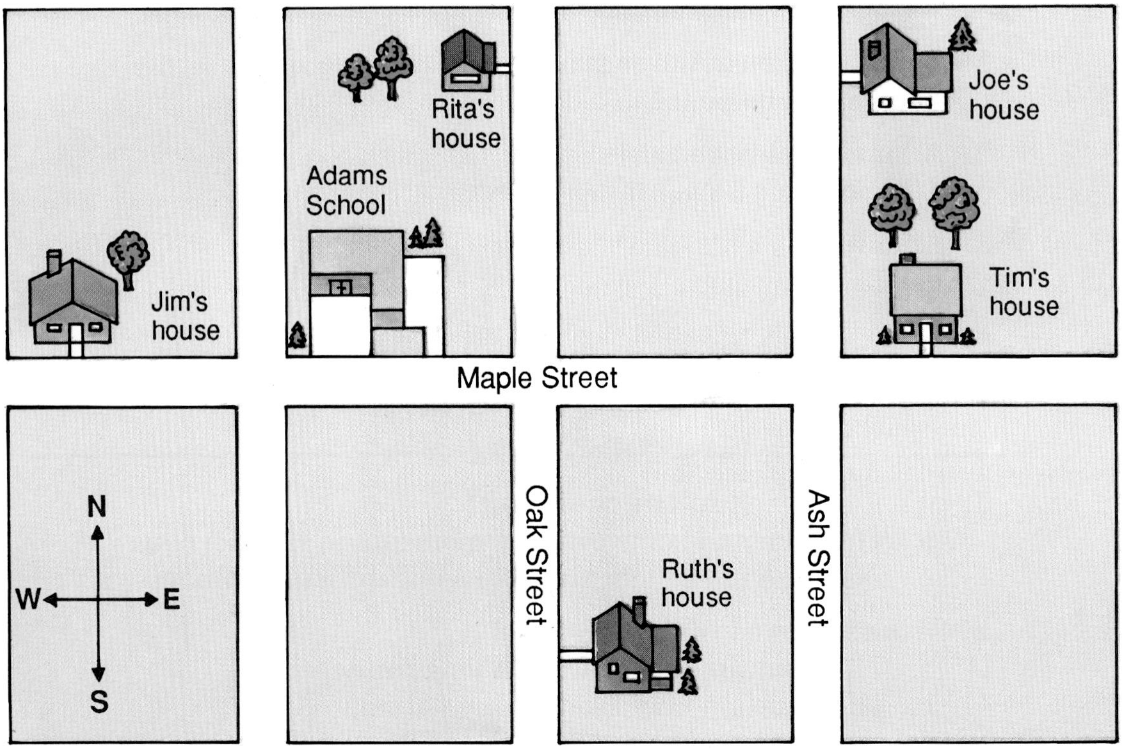

Statement 1: Rita gets to Adams School by walking south on Oak Street.

Statement 2: Rita's house is farther from school than Joe's house is.

Outline diagram

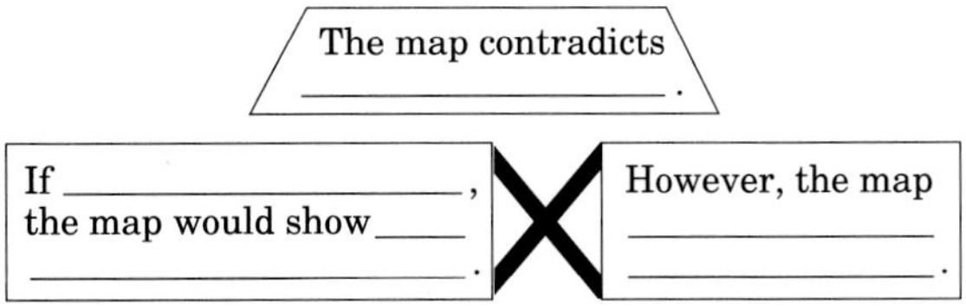

Part D Copy each sentence. Circle the subject and underline the predicate. Write **P** over every pronoun, **N** over every noun, **A** over every adjective and **V** over every verb.

1. They were arguing about the assignment.
2. He was looking at them.
3. They looked under three red rocks.

Part E Follow the outline diagram to write about the misleading impression in Rod's account.

Rod Vernon's account

I can't believe that my neighbors, the Jacksons, did the nasty things they did. My dog, Herman, is usually on a leash, but once in a while, he goes out by himself. When this happens, he may run into the Jacksons' yard.

Last week, Herman dug a hole in the Jackson's yard. And you would not believe the fuss they made about it. They called the police. They tried to get me arrested. They wanted to take Herman away and lock him up. All that fuss for digging one hole in their backyard! I can't believe that the Jacksons could be so unreasonable.

Police report

Thursday, 7:45 p.m., at 1230 Devine Street.

Don and Donna Jackson claim that a dog owned by Rod Vernon dug the hole in their backyard. Rod Vernon did not deny that the dog named Herman had been let out and may have dug the hole. The hole measured 12 feet wide and 5 feet deep. There was a pile of dirt on one side that was over 6 feet high.

Outline diagram

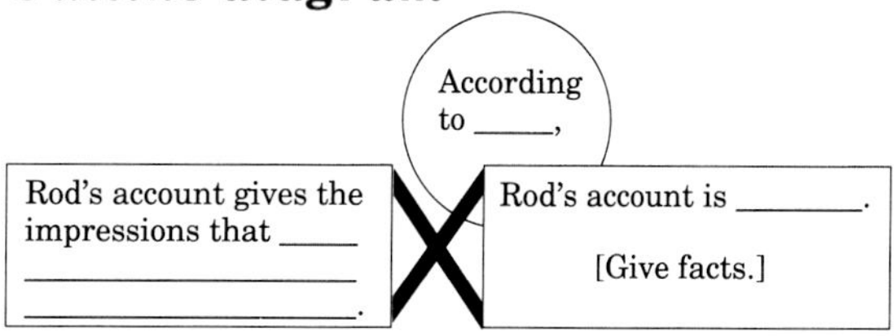
According to ______,
Rod's account gives the impressions that ______ ______ ______.
Rod's account is ______.
[Give facts.]

Part F **Sample Items**

A. Children love to play.
Little boys are children.

B. Orange juice is a fruit juice.
All fruit juice is good for you.

Write the item number and the conclusion. Don't write the whole deduction.

1. All animals need oxygen.
A sponge is an animal.
2. Dishes are household items.
Household items wear out.
3. All documents have symbols on them.
A report card is a document.

Independent Work

Part G Write directions for making each figure. Start each sentence with the word **Make** or **Draw.**

Figure 1

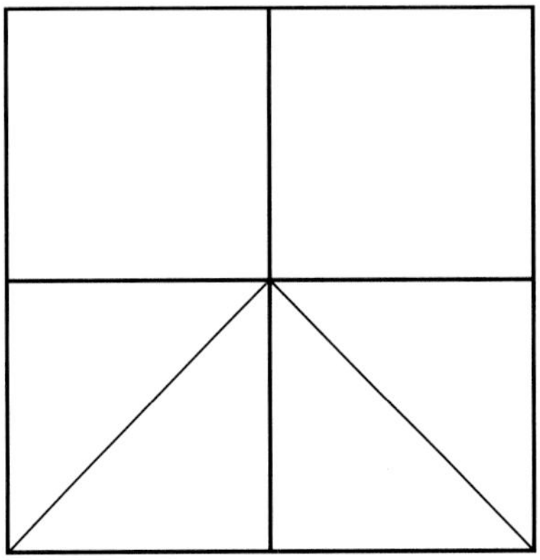

Figure 2

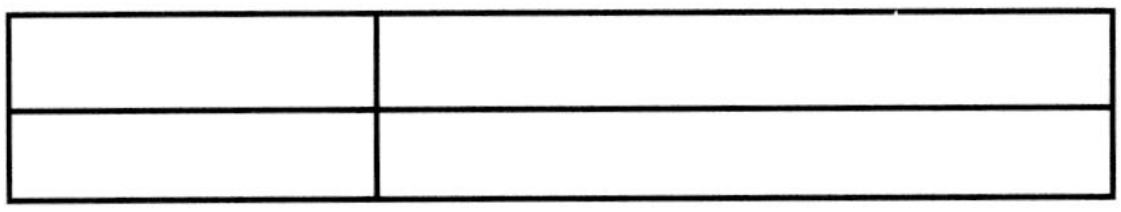

Part H Write **reasonable** or **unreasonable** for each item.

1. We picked two large baskets of apples from the big apple tree in our backyard.
2. Our puppy eats five pounds of dog food every day.
3. My mother is 61 inches tall.
4. We saw a huge redwood tree that was over 400 years old.
5. My dad and I painted the entire kitchen in 25 minutes.
6. My uncle climbed a mountain that was over two miles high.

Lesson 36

Part A

Read each passage. Use **context** to figure out what each boldface word means and answer the questions.

1. Water will **inundate** the room if the tank bursts. Everything will get wet. The floor will be covered with water. The water will even flow down the stairs and **inundate** the basement.

   Questions

   a. What part of speech is *inundate?*

   b. What does *inundate* probably mean?

2. It took them 14 hours to climb to the top of the peak. The **arduous** climb left everybody exhausted.

   Jill said, "I've never worked that hard."

   "Yes," Andy replied. "This was the most **arduous** job I've done in a long time."

   Questions

   a. What part of speech is *arduous?*

   b. What does *arduous* probably mean?

Part B Rewrite the directions so they are specific and clear.

Directions for going from X to Z:

- Turn at the dirt road.
- Go past the white house. Turn at the paved road.
- Stop at the third house.

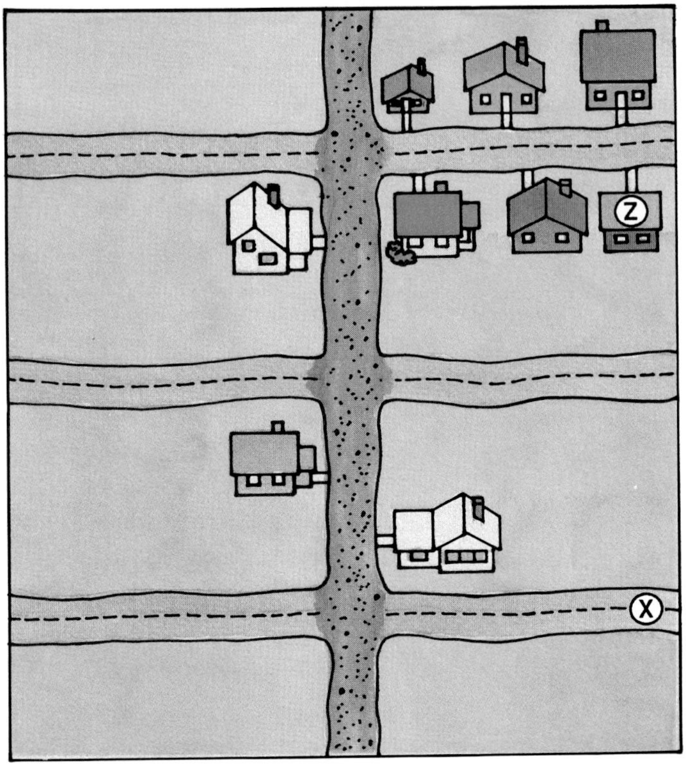

Part C **Sample Item**

All the roads in Nebraska will need repair within four years.
Route 20 is a road in Nebraska.

Write only the conclusion for these deductions. Remember, the more specific subject is the subject of your conclusion.

1. All parts of Africa are suffering from a terrible drought.
   Sudan is a part of Africa.
2. Japan is an industrial country.
   All industrial countries have factories.
3. All whales are mammals.
   All mammals breathe air.
4. All winners will receive a blue ribbon.
   Fran and Ginger are winners.

Part D For each sentence, write what was between the rivers. Then list the pictures the sentence could describe.

1. The city between the rivers had a large business district.
2. The city had a large business district between the rivers.

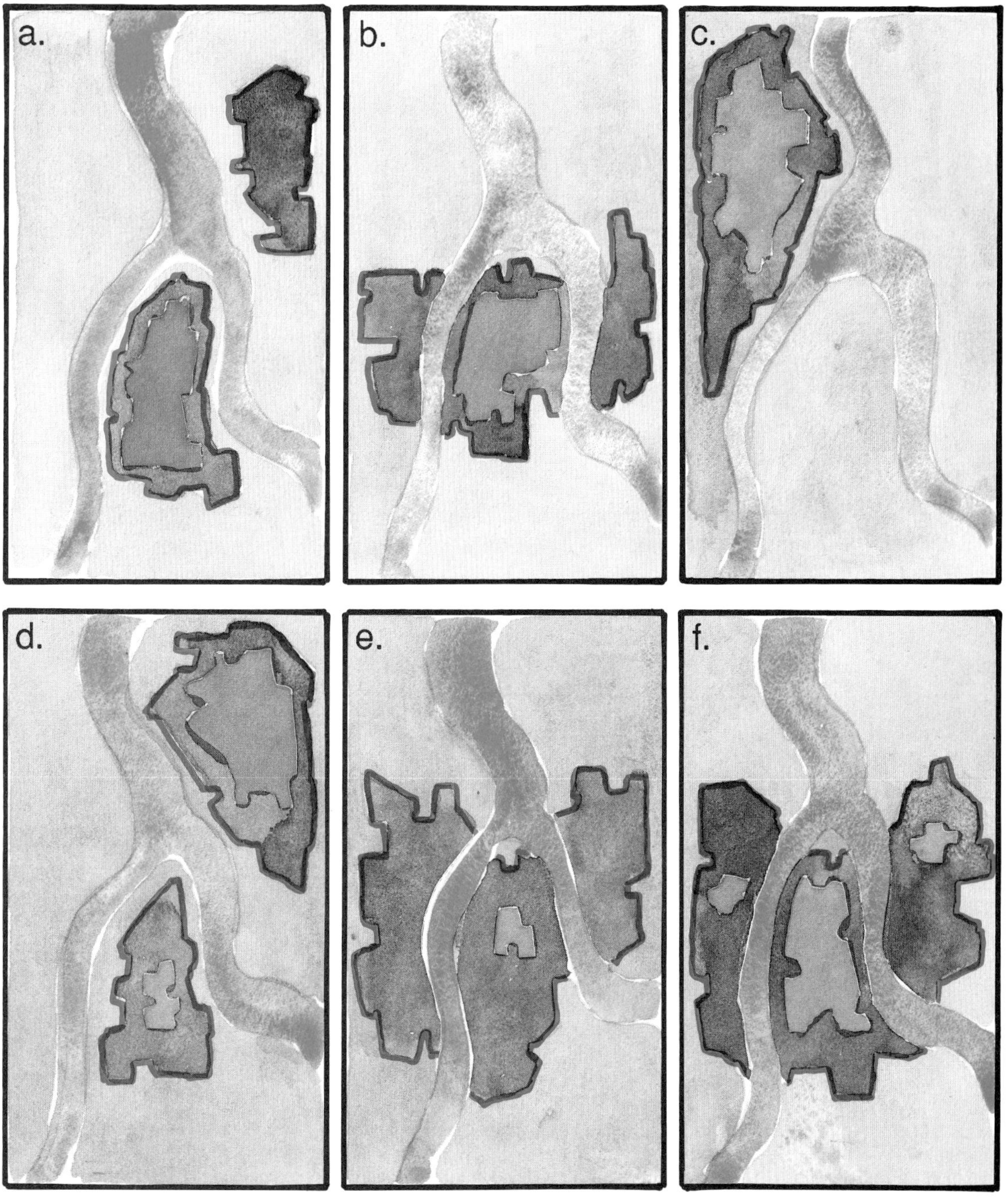

Part E For each sentence, write what was next to the farm. Then list the pictures the sentence could describe.

1. The forest next to the farm had a grove of maples.
2. The forest had a grove of maples next to the farm.

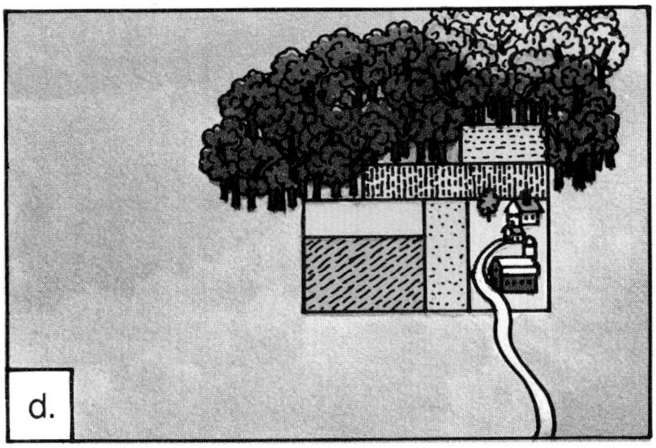

Part F Write **N** or **P** to indicate the part of speech of the last word in each sentence.

1. An old woman sat on it.
2. The birds moved from tree to tree.
3. Our neighbors installed a new garage door.
4. The dog chased them.
5. The lifeguard stood in it.
6. The wall was covered with ugly designs.
7. A little girl sat next to her.

Part G

Rewrite the sentences so they end in at least one adjective and a noun. Write the sentences so they tell about the picture.

1. An old woman sat on it.
2. The dog chased them.
3. The lifeguard stood in it.
4. A little girl sat next to her.

Independent Work

Part H Follow the outline diagram. Write a summary sentence, and then write about each inaccuracy in the ad.

Nemo Ad

Nemo tires are less expensive than any other major brand. *

Nemo tires are guaranteed for 50,000 miles.

If a **Nemo** tire goes flat, **Nemo** will send somebody out to fix it and charge you nothing.

* When you buy a full set of **Nemos, Nemo** will mount them free.

Source: **Table E1: Major Brand Tires**

Tires	Cost per tire	Guaranteed for	Cost of mounting	Cost of roadside service
Nemo	$45.50	50,000 miles	no cost	$25
Brand A	$42.50	50,000 miles	$5 each tire	no charge
Brand X	$51.17	70,000 miles	no cost	no charge

Outline diagram

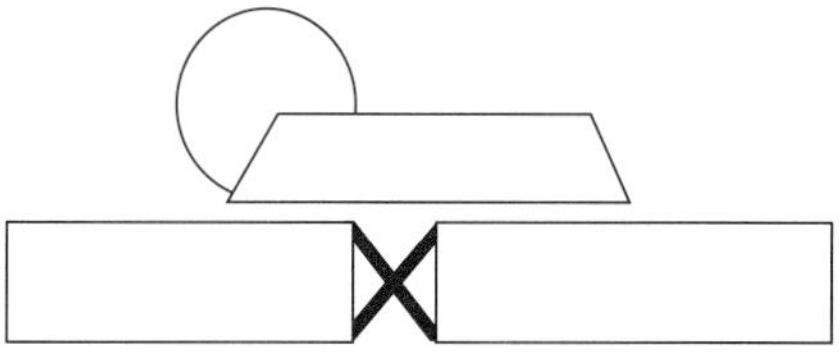

Part I For some items, the second sentence contradicts the first sentence. Write **contradictory** or **possible** to tell about the second sentence in each item.

1. The girl had five pets. Three were turtles; two were cats; one was a dog.
2. Jenny rushed home from school at 3:05. She arrived home at 3:18.
3. As the sun came up, Ted drove west. The sun was in his eyes.
4. On Monday, Ms. Green had no money. On Tuesday, she had $350.
5. On Monday, Mr. Jones had no money. On Monday, he gave his brother $200.

Lesson 37

Part A

Rewrite each sentence so it uses the word **inundate** or **arduous.** Use the words correctly so your sentences make sense.

1. Thousands of letters flooded the radio station.
2. They began a very difficult journey.
3. It took days of hard work to clean up the flooded town.

Part B

Sample Item

They loved **it.**
Four girls loved **the party.**

Rewrite each sentence so it has a noun and an adjective in place of each pronoun.

1. They looked at it.
2. She kept smelling it.
3. He walked around it.

Part C The map and the statements contradict each other. We don't know if the map is accurate or the statements are accurate. Follow the outline diagram to write about the contradictions.

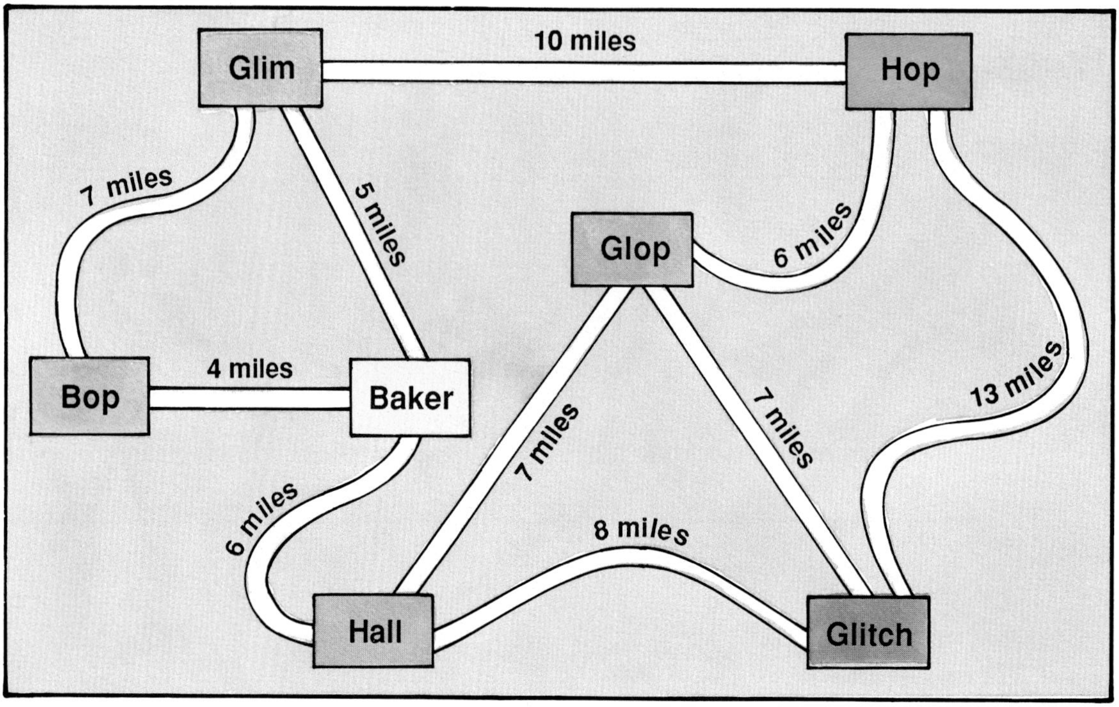

Statement 1: Three towns are the same distance from Glop.

Statement 2: Roads lead from Baker to the four closest towns.

Outline diagram

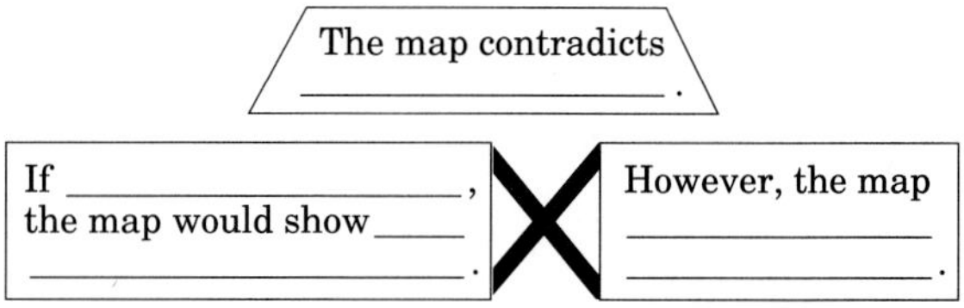

The map contradicts ________.
If ________, the map would show ________.
However, the map ________.

Part D For each item, write these sentences and the missing middle sentence to make a complete deduction.

1. Ducks have feathers.
   Birds have feathers.
2. Things that float on water are less dense than water.
   Oil is less dense than water.
3. Insects have six legs.
   Flies have six legs.

Part E

For each sentence, write what is near the river. Then list the pictures the sentence could describe.

1. People saw three planes near the river.
2. People near the river saw three planes.

Part F

For each sentence, write who was sitting in a chair. Then list the pictures the sentence could describe.

1. The man who was sitting in a chair talked to a woman.
2. The man talked to a woman who was sitting in a chair.

Independent Work

Part G Follow the outline diagram. Write a summary sentence, and then write about each inaccuracy in the graph.

Source: **Map E3**

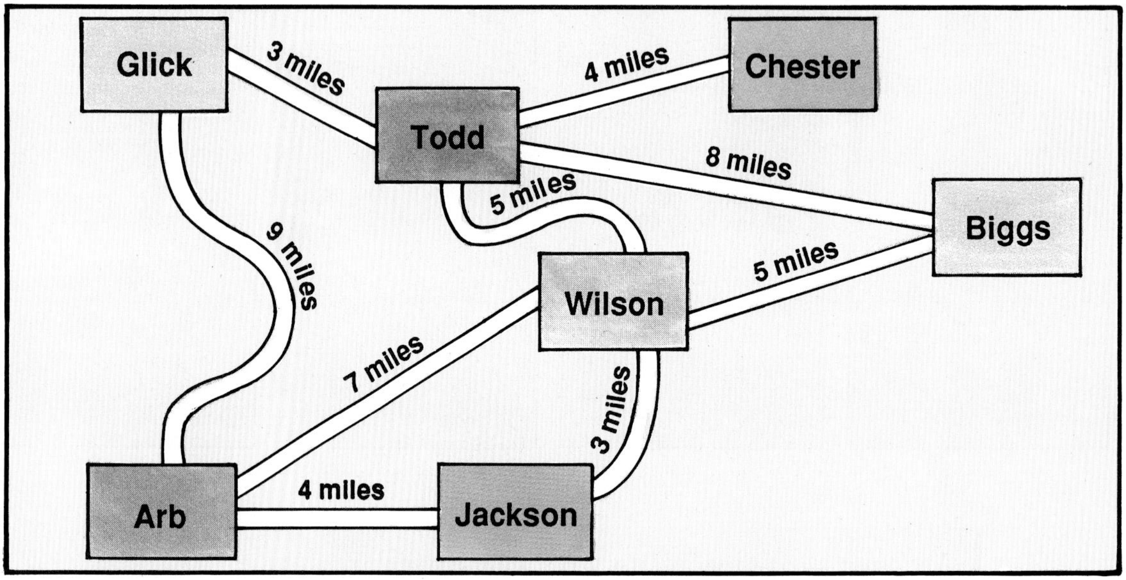

A Graph of Distances

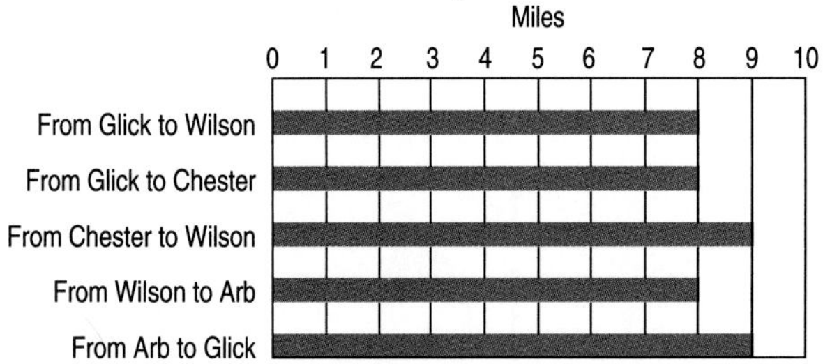

Outline diagram

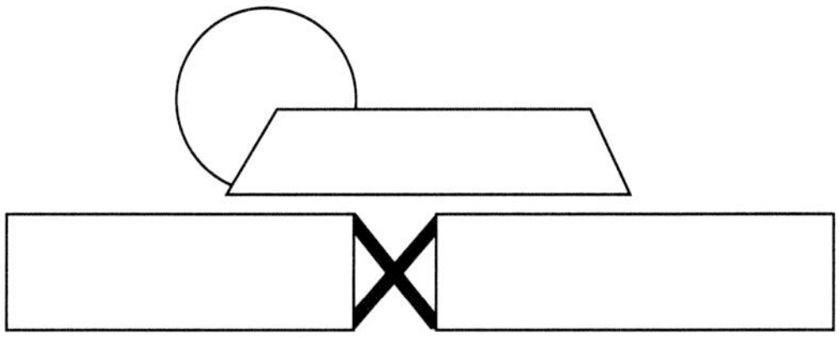

Part H Copy each sentence. Circle the subject and underline the predicate. Label every word as a part of speech: noun, pronoun, verb, adjective.

1. Six tired workers left the factory.
2. Wild dogs were chasing a young fox.
3. She gave Tim her new book.

Lesson 38

Part A Check the paragraph you wrote about Map E3.

Part B

- For some directions, you use the words **horizontal, vertical** and **diagonal.**
- **Horizontal** is flat like the horizon.
- **Vertical** is straight up and down.

Part C Write directions for making this figure. Tell about the biggest part first. Write at least four sentences.

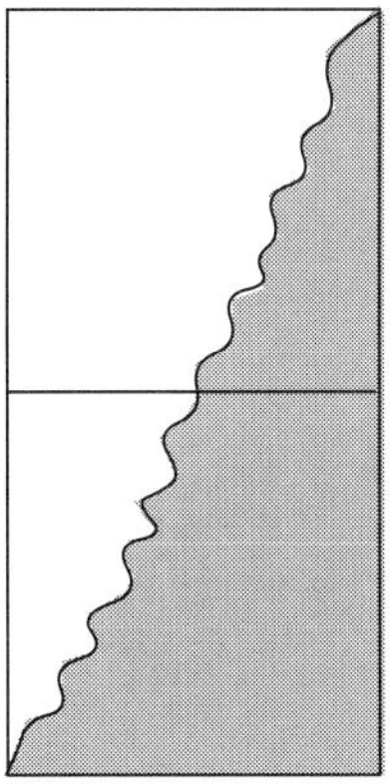

Part D Write **N** or **P** to indicate the part of speech for the last word in each sentence.

1. Big Bill pulled a wagon full of them.
2. Four girls wore the same kind of bathing suit.
3. Jane and her sister played with it.
4. Margo and Terry pushed it.
5. Tiffany's kite got caught in a tree.
6. Henry carried them.
7. The men loved to play horseshoes.

Part E Rewrite the sentences so they end in two adjectives and a noun. Write the sentences so they tell about the picture.

1. Big Bill pulled a wagon full of them.
2. Jane and her sister played with it.
3. Margo and Terry pushed it.
4. Henry carried them.

Part F Follow the outline diagram to write about the misleading impression in Matt's account.

Matt's account

I can't believe how silly some people are. The people in our neighborhood are always complaining about walking across the railroad tracks. There's always a train going by, and they have to wait a long time before they can get across. There's a shopping mall on the other side of the tracks, and people could easily walk there, but walking across those railroad tracks is a serious problem.

So I offered a serious solution. Why not build a footbridge over the tracks? Everybody could get together, donate their time and some material, and we could build a footbridge.

What did the neighbors say when I told them about my solution? They said, "You're nuts."

Well, I happen to think that my solution makes a lot of sense.

Engineer's report

The bridge would have to be at least 30 feet high, 8 feet wide and 200 feet long. The materials would cost around $200,000. The steel beams would be the most expensive items. Installing the bridge would cost another $300,000 in labor and equipment.

Outline diagram

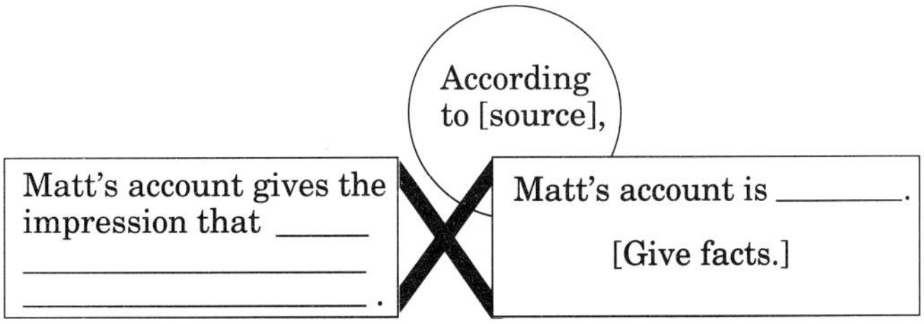
According to [source],
Matt's account gives the impression that ______ ______ ______.
Matt's account is ______.
[Give facts.]

Part G Rewrite the sentence so it tells about each picture. Add the words **in the yard.**

The children saw a shovel.

Part H Read the passage. Use **context** to figure out what the boldface word means and answer the questions.

The general said, "We will **expunge** the enemy. When we are finished, there will be no enemy. There will be no city either, because we will also **expunge** the city."

Questions

a. What part of speech is *expunge?*

b. What does *expunge* probably mean?

Independent Work

Part I Edit this passage so it is clear and has no mistakes.

Martha met a group of mountain climbers and he were resting. The climbers told her that they had climbed all morning as they drank hot chocolate. Their going to the top of the mountain. She said that its a long hike.

Part J Rewrite each sentence so it uses one of the new vocabulary words you've learned.

1. The homework that Mrs. Frankle assigned was too difficult for some students.
2. Water from the broken pipe was flooding our kitchen.

Part K Write directions for making this figure. Copy the first sentence and write three more sentences. You can use the adjectives **outer** and **inner.**

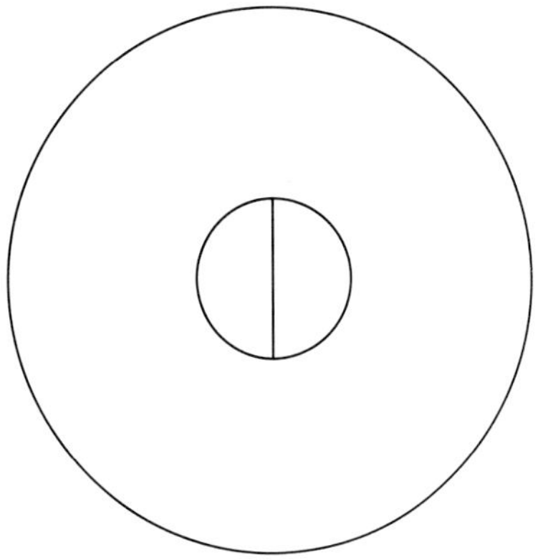

1. Make two circles that have the same center.
2.
3.
4.

Key

First set:

- Make a rectangle that is one inch wide and two inches high.
- Make a wavy diagonal line from the upper right corner to the lower left corner.
- Shade the area below the wavy line.
- Make a horizontal line through the middle of the rectangle.

Second set:

- Draw a rectangle that is two inches high and one inch wide.
- Draw a wavy line from the lower left corner to the upper right corner.
- Shade in everything to the right of the wavy line.
- Draw a horizontal line through the center of the rectangle.

Lesson 39

Part A Rewrite each sentence so it uses one of the new vocabulary words you've learned.

1. They tried to get rid of an ink spot.
2. This work is far too difficult for children.
3. Sid got rid of all the ants that were in his house.
4. Water from the broken dam flooded River City.

Part B Use the vocabulary box to help spell some difficult words.

Vocabulary Box

sequoia Sierra General Nevada
Sherman Fresno weigh
National California

Part C

- Descriptions that are too general lead to confusion because they tell about more than one object or event.
- Here's a set of objects:

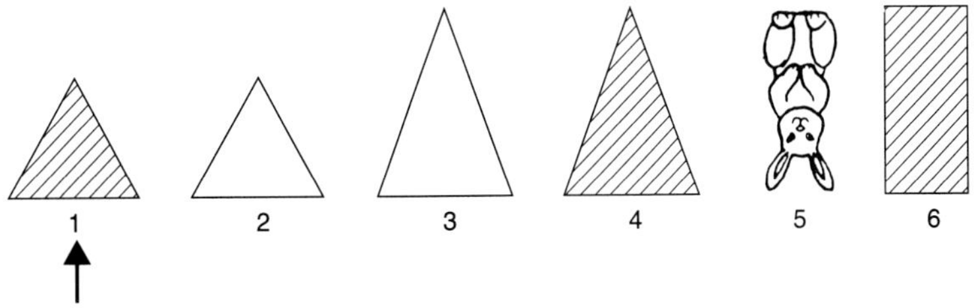

- The arrow shows the object the description is supposed to tell about.
- Here's a description that is too general:

The object has three sides.

- That tells about the arrowed object, but it also tells about three other objects.

- Here's a description that is less general:

  The object has three sides. The object is striped.

- That description tells about the arrowed object, but it also tells about the fourth object.
- You can fix up the description by adding something that is true about the arrowed object but not true about the fourth object.

Part D Write a description for each arrowed object by following the directions below the set.

Set A

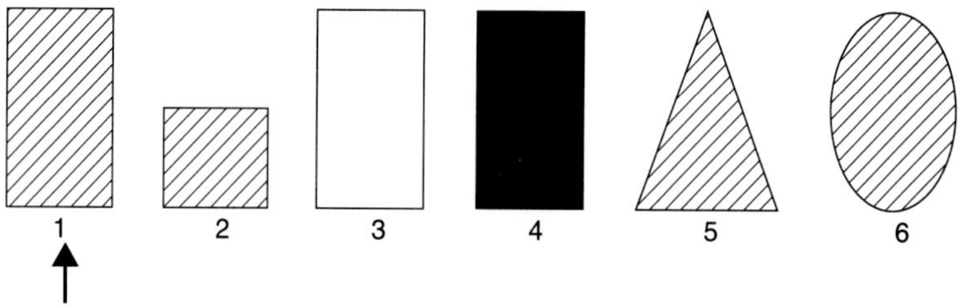

- Write a sentence that rules out the third and fourth objects.
- Write a sentence the rules out the second object.
- Write a sentence that rules out the fifth and sixth objects.

Set B

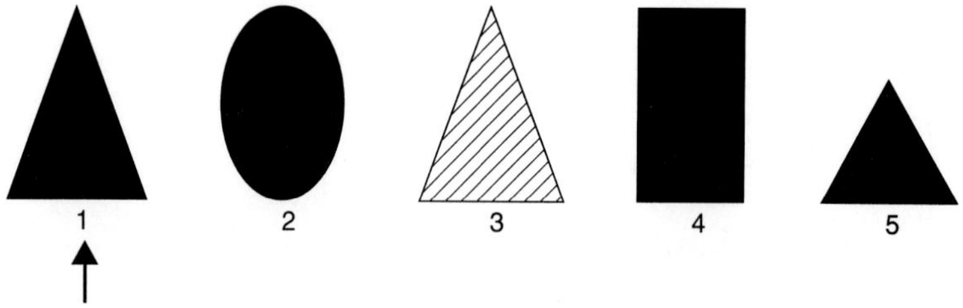

- Write a sentence that rules out only the last object.
- Write a sentence that rules out only the second and fourth objects.
- Write a sentence that rules out only the third object.

Part E Add the words **on the window sill** so the sentence tells about each picture.

The cat looked at the mouse.

Part F Rewrite the sentences. Replace each pronoun with a noun and at least one adjective.

1. He fell from it.
2. She chased them around the barn.
3. It ran into it.
4. They found it under the stairs.

Part G Copy each sentence. Label the nouns and adjectives. Don't label the other parts of speech.

1. The short man fell from the hayloft.
2. My favorite cow chased three mice around the barn.
3. That yellow bulldozer ran into the wall.
4. Those four boys found a ball under the stairs.

Key

1. The short man fell from the hayloft.
   A A N A N
2. My favorite cow chased three mice around the barn.
   A A N A N A N
3. That yellow bulldozer ran into the wall.
   A A N A N
4. Those four boys found a ball under the stairs.
   A A N A N A N

Independent Work

Part H Each item presents two sentences. Copy the sentence that is more specific.

1. Martha works every afternoon.
   Martha will work on Wednesday afternoon.
2. My Uncle Pete makes furniture.
   All my relatives make furniture.
3. Those workers built all the houses on Donner Street.
   The workers built the house at 114 Donner Street.
4. All rivers contain fresh water.
   The Red River contains fresh water.

Part I Write a complete deduction for item 4 in part H. Use the more specific statement as the **conclusion.** Use the more general statement as part of the evidence. Write the missing middle statement.

Part J The map and the statement contradict each other. You don't know whether the map is accurate or the statement is accurate. Tell about the contradication. Follow the outline diagram.

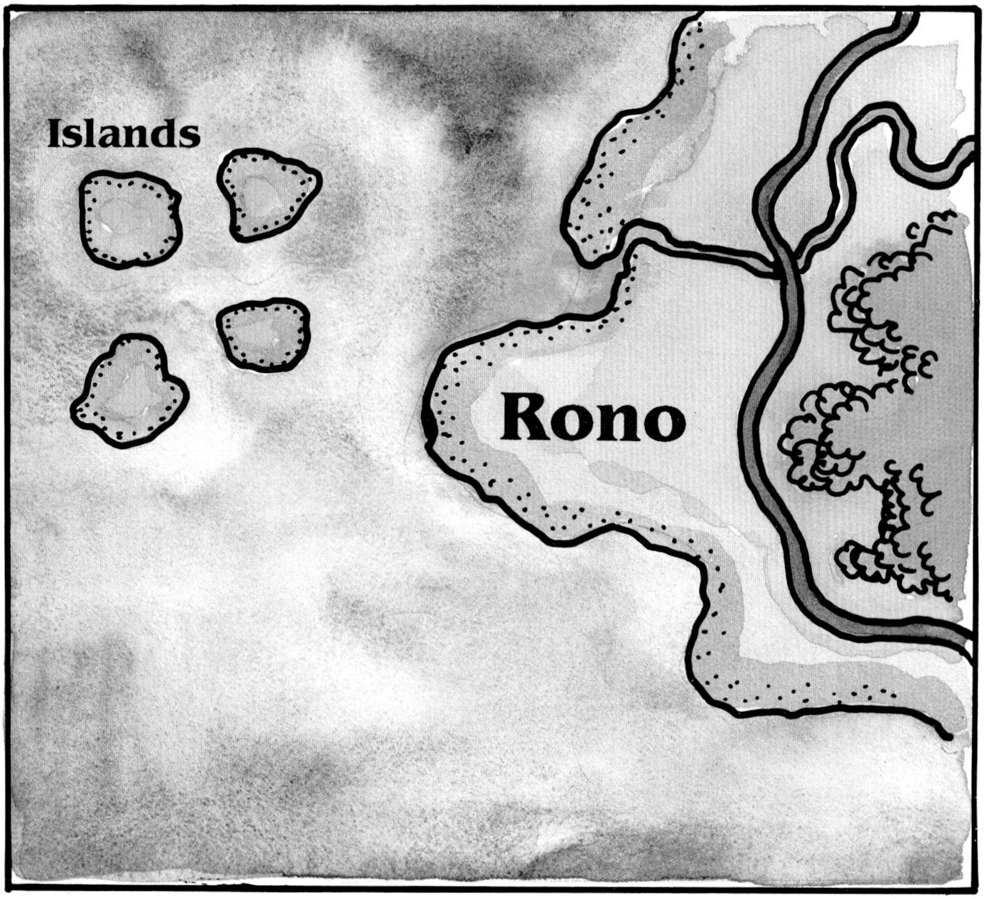

Statement

The islands off the coast of Rono form a triangle.

Outline diagram

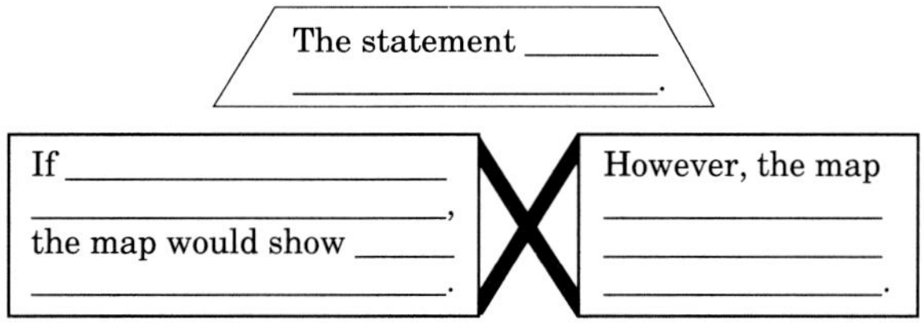

Lesson 40 – Test 4

Part A Follow the outline diagram to write about the inaccuracies in Laura's account. Graph E4 gives accurate information.

Laura's account

My dance school opened in 1981. During the first year, we had 12 students and 3 teachers. By 1984, we had over 30 students and more than 6 teachers. By 1990, our enrollment had grown to 60 students and 10 teachers. Today, we have almost 100 students.

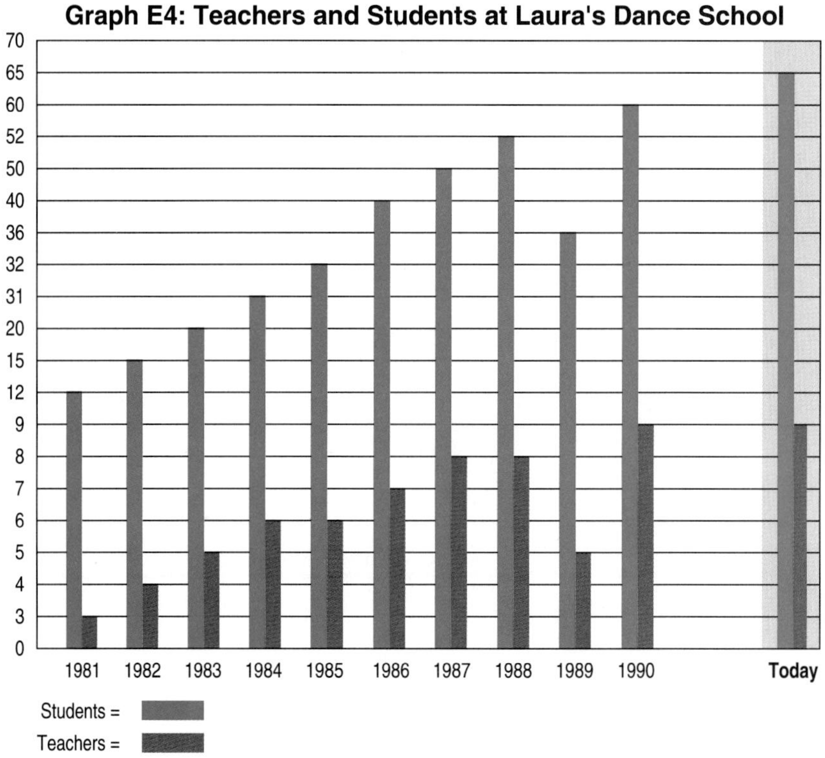

Outline diagram

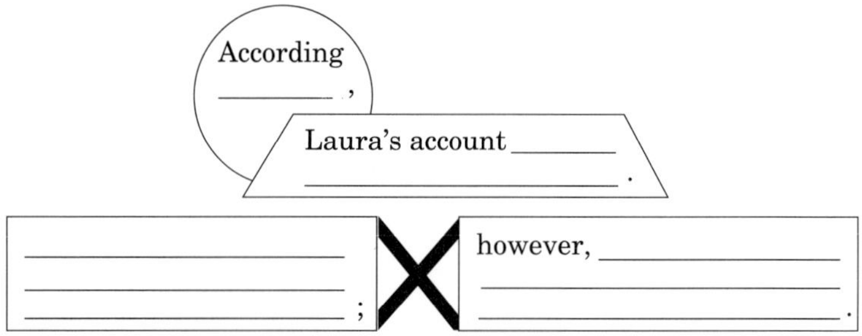

Part B Copy each underlined word. Indicate the part of speech.

1. Tom told them to stop bothering his dog.
2. Their tractor stalled in the middle of a busy intersection.
3. Many bugs near my garden bothered them.
4. She understood that they would be mad at her.

Part C Write three sentences that tell how to make the figure. Tell about the biggest part of the figure first. Start each sentence with the word **Make** or **Draw.**

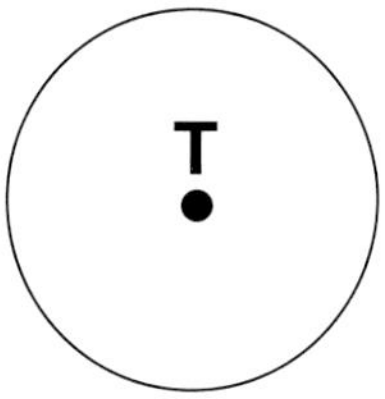

Part D Add the words **in the water** so the sentence tells about each picture.

The man fed the ducks.

Part E For each item, write the complete deduction. Remember the missing middle sentence.

1. Smart shoppers shop at Z-Mart.
   Arnold shops at Z-Mart.
2. Ducks have feathers.
   Birds have feathers.

Part F Write the missing conclusion. Don't copy the rest of the deduction.

All cars that get good mileage cost less to operate.
Bumpos are cars that get good mileage.

Lesson 41

Part A

- Some statements tell about things that you cannot observe on one occasion.
- Here's an example:

  Billy is always losing money.
- On one observation, we cannot see Billy **always** losing money. We might see Billy losing money one time, but not **always.**
- Here's another example:

  Martha takes a nap every afternoon.
- On one observation, we cannot see her taking a nap on **every** afternoon. We can only see her taking a nap on the afternoon we observe.
- Remember, if a statement tells about **always, usually** or **most of the time,** we can't judge whether that statement is true with one observation.

Part B

For each item, write **specific** or **general.**

1. Hilda works in the garden every Tuesday during the summer.
2. My mother lost her purse in Z-Mart.
3. That horse is sweating.
4. Linda's latest picture has a lot of blue in it.
5. Fran is always arguing with Henry.
6. Tim loves to use red crayons when he draws.
7. The children on our block never go to Mr. Smith's house.
8. Tommy was standing on the corner of Elm and Fifth.
9. I have bad dreams whenever I watch a scary movie.

Part C

- Sometimes evidence in an argument is **inadequate.** That means that the evidence does not actually lead to the conclusion the argument draws.
- Here's a conclusion:

  Mary did not fail the exam.
- Evidence that is **adequate** answers the question, **Did she fail the exam?**
- Evidence that is **inadequate** answers some other question.
- Here's evidence that is **inadequate:**

  Mary is a very intelligent person.

  Mary has never failed an exam before.

  Mary's mother works with Mary.

  Everybody in Mary's family is smart.

  Nobody in her family has ever failed an exam.
- None of these statements answers the question, **Did she fail the exam?**
- They answer questions about how smart she is or about how well she has done in the past. All of these statements are **inadequate.**
- Here's evidence that is **adequate:**

  Mary did not miss any items on the test.
- That statement answers the question, **Did she fail the exam?**

Part D

1. Every year Martha plants tomato plants in her garden.
   She was working in her garden the other day.
   Therefore, she was planting tomato plants.

2. There's dirt on the kitchen floor.
   George always tracks dirt into the kitchen.
   Therefore, George must have tracked that dirt into the kitchen.

Outline diagram

The argument concludes ______________________ ______________________;	however, the evidence is inadequate. The specific evidence indicates only that ______________________.

Part E | Rewrite the student's paragraph so it is specific and clear.

Source: **Map E4**

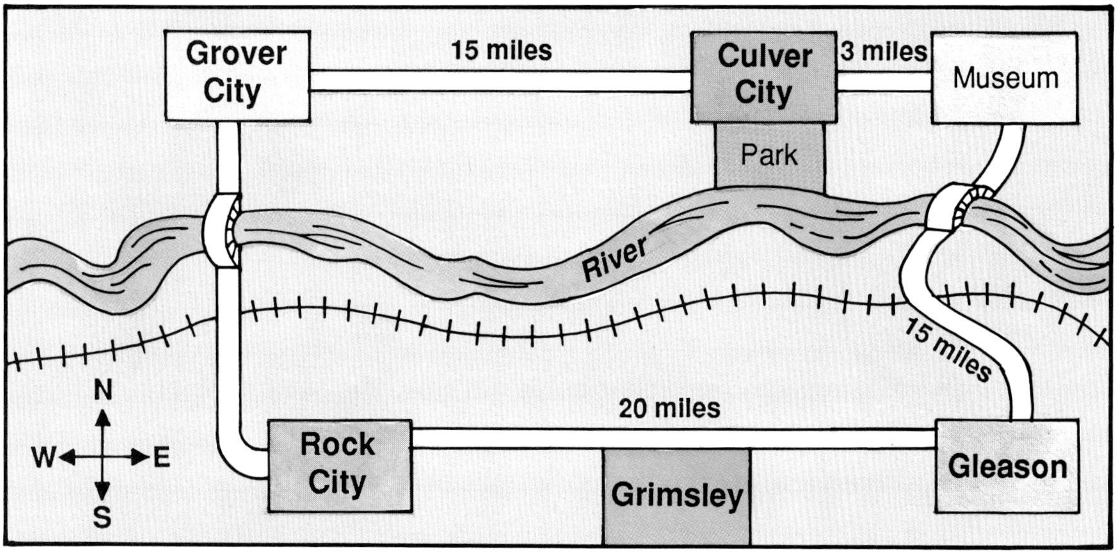

Tim's account

We left Grover City in the morning and drove about 8 miles to Culver City.

We had breakfast in a park just outside Culver City. The park was right on the river.

After breakfast, we drove south 3 miles to the museum. We looked at a lot of old boats.

Then we went south again about 15 miles to the town of Gleason. My cousin lives there, and we visited with her for a while. We had lunch with her.

Then we drove about 20 miles west to the town of Grimsley. We bought some stuff there. Then we drove back to Grover City.

Student's paragraph

[1] According to Map E4, Tim's account contains three inaccuracies. [2] Tim's account indicates that they drove 8 miles; however, they drove 15 miles. [3] Tim's account indicates that they drove south; however, they drove east.

Part F Follow the instructions below each set to write a description of the arrowed object.

Set A

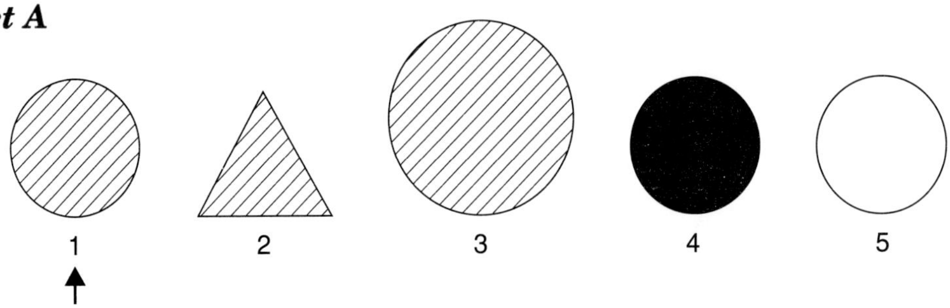

- Write a sentence that rules out only the second object.
- Write a sentence that rules out only the third object.
- Write a sentence that rules out only the fourth and fifth objects.

Set B

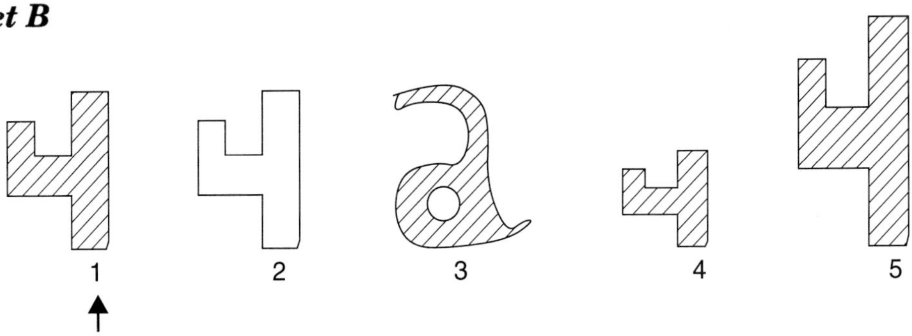

- Write a sentence that rules out only the second object.
- Write a sentence that rules out only the third object.
- Write a sentence that rules out only the fourth and fifth objects.

Part G Follow the outline diagram to write about Lisa's account.

Lisa's account

Sometimes parents are unreasonable. My parents told me that I could have a party on my sixteenth birthday. I told them that I didn't even want a present if I could have a party. They said, "Okay."

But then, just a couple of days before my birthday, they got all upset about the party, and they told me that they would never let me have another one.

A letter that Lisa's sister wrote to a friend:

My sister can be a real pain. She pestered my parents to give her a birthday party. So they finally gave in. Lisa sent out the invitations. Then, a couple of days before the party, my mother was talking to Lisa about the cake. Lisa said that we would need ten cakes.

My mother almost fell over. "Ten cakes?" she screamed. "How many people did you invite to the party?"

Lisa told her. "One hundred."

So now Lisa can't understand why my parents are mad at her.

Outline diagram

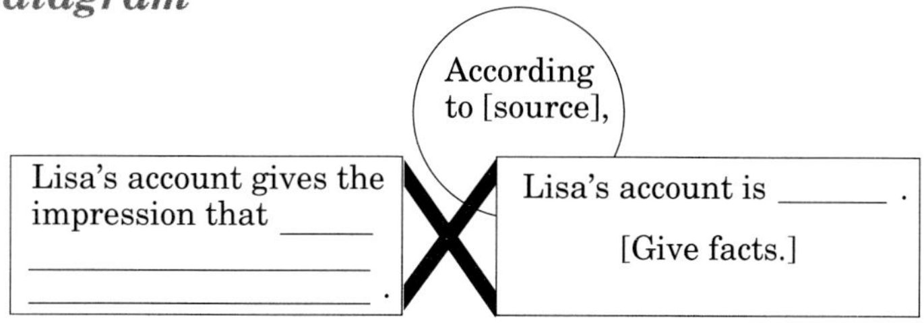

According to [source],
Lisa's account gives the impression that ______ ______ ______.
Lisa's account is ______.
[Give facts.]

Independent Work

Part H

Rewrite each sentence, making it a general sentence by replacing every noun and its adjectives with a pronoun.

1. The boys chased the dogs around the park.
2. Our car drove through the hills.
3. Their team will play three games.

Part I

For each item, use the sentences to write a complete deduction. Figure out the missing middle sentence.

1. The workers painted the office.
   The workers painted every room in the school.
2. All legal papers are legal documents.
   His license is a legal document.

Lesson 42

Part A

Follow the X-box diagram below to write about the problems with these arguments.

1. Debbi is really sunburned.
   Debbi always gets sunburned when she goes fishing.
   Therefore, she must have gone fishing.
2. That picture has a lot of blue in it.
   Linda loves to makes pictures with blue.
   Linda must have made that picture.

Outline diagram

Argument __ concludes ____________________ ____________________;	X	however, the evidence is inadequate. The specific evidence indicates only that ____________________________.

Part B

Rewrite each sentence so it uses one of the new vocabulary words you've learned.

1. I could not remove those terrible images from my mind.
2. The pilgrims began a difficult journey.

Part C

Read the passage. Use context to figure out what the boldface word means. Answer the questions.

Passage

"Stop arguing," Edna said. "You're always **altercating.** And you do it in such a loud voice. Why don't you just sit down and cool off."

"I was not **altercating,**" he said. "You know that I don't like to argue. And I'm not arguing now. You just think that I'm the kind of person who **altercates.** But you're wrong."

Questions

1. What part of speech is *altercate?*
2. What does *altercate* probably mean?

Part D

Rewrite the sentences. Replace each pronoun with a noun and at least one adjective.

1. They met her in front of the school.
2. She put it in her dresser.
3. He loves to eat them.

Part E

Follow the instructions below each set to write a description of the arrowed object.

Set A

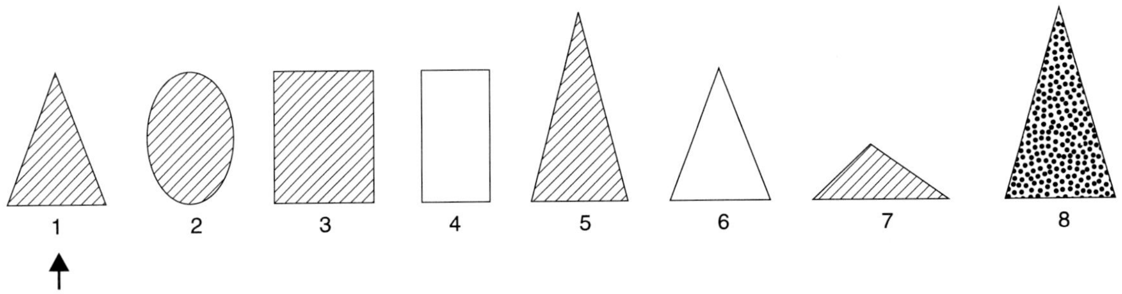

- Write a sentence that rules out only objects 4, 6 and 8.
- Write a sentence that rules out only objects 2, 3 and 4.
- Write a sentence that rules out only objects 5 and 7.

Set B

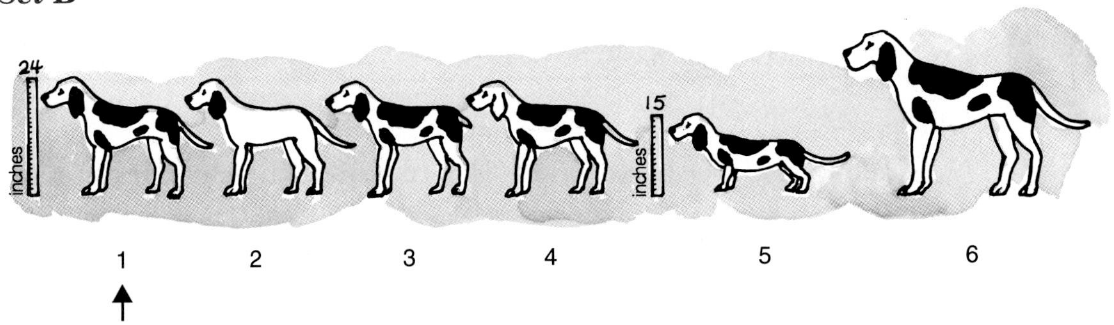

- Write a sentence that rules out dogs 5 and 6.
- Write a sentence that rules out dog 4.
- Write a sentence that rules out dog 3.
- Write a sentence that rules out dog 2.

Part F | Rewrite the sentence so it describes each picture. Add the words **with a long tail.**

The cat chased the kite.

Independent Work

Part G | Write directions for constructing this figure. Write three or more sentences.

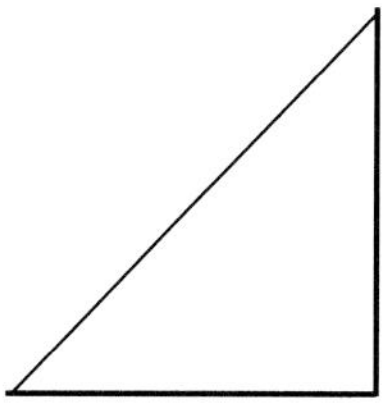

Part H Rewrite the student's work so it is clear and specific. Tell who they were, where they went and the place they came from.

Source: **Map E5**

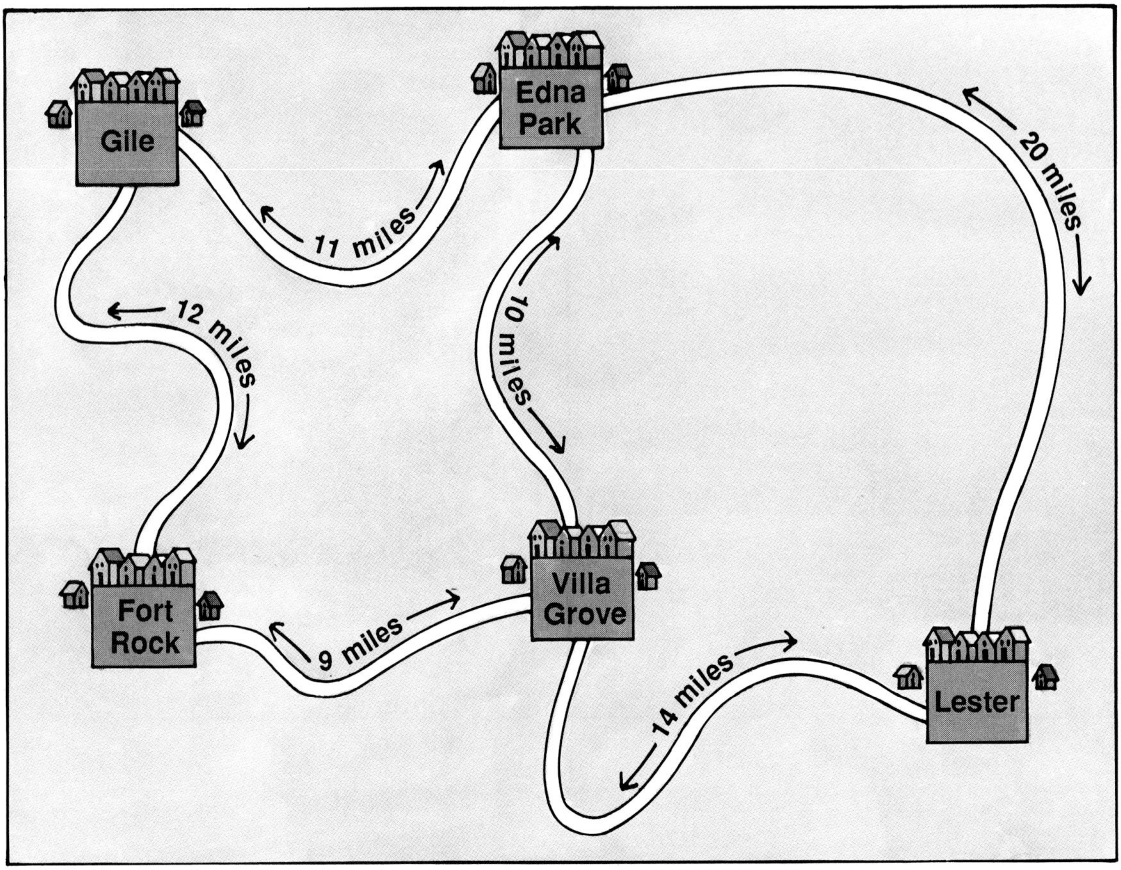

Jan's account

My family left Gile in the morning and drove to Fort Rock. Then we drove all the way to Lester. That's 40 miles from Fort Rock. Then we drove another 20 miles to Edna Park. We had lunch there. Then we drove 4 miles to Villa Grove, where we visited a friend of my mother's. Then we drove 21 miles through Fort Rock and back to Gile.

Student's paragraph

According to Map E5, Jan's account contains two inaccuracies. Jan's account indicates that they drove 40 miles; however, they drove 23 miles. Jan's account indicates that they drove 4 miles; however, they drove 10 miles.

Lesson 43

Part A

Write only the last word in each sentence below. Then write **N** if the word is a noun or **P** if it is a pronoun.

1. They went to her home.
2. They may give peanuts to the girls.
3. Our neighbors don't like it.
4. The dream lasted for several minutes.
5. She gave lots of homework to them.

Part B

- You can use what you know to figure out whether words in the predicate are adjectives.
- Here's a sentence that ends with a noun:

  They talked about that little boy.

- You want to figure out whether the word **about** is an adjective.
- You just replace the end of the sentence with a pronoun. A pronoun **replaces a noun and any adjectives.**
- If the word **about** is an adjective, you'll replace it with the pronoun.
- If the word **about** is **not** an adjective, you **won't** replace it with the pronoun.
- Here's the sentence with the last part replaced by a pronoun:

  They talked about **him.**

- Remember, if a word is not replaced by a pronoun, it is not a noun or an adjective.

Part C

Rewrite each sentence so it ends with a pronoun in place of the noun and adjectives. Then answer the question about the underlined word. Remember, if the underlined word is replaced by a pronoun, it is an adjective.

1. The boys kept shouting at the birds.
   - Is at an adjective?
2. The workers tried to get into a sealed room.
   - Is into an adjective?
3. My mother will buy their fresh vegetables.
   - Is their an adjective?
4. A rusty nail scratched my sister's finger.
   - Is my an adjective?
5. Fran will paint the living room.
   - Is living an adjective?

Part D

- Some reports contradict themselves. When we read those reports, we may not know which statements are true and which statements are false; however, we do know that not **all** of the statements can be true.
- Here are three statements:
  1. **Mark had a lot more money than his little sister.**
  2. **His little sister had the same amount of money that Jane had.**
  3. **Jane had more money than Mark.**
- We can believe any two of those statements, but we can't believe all three. If we believe statement 1 and statement 2, we can't believe statement 3. Jane could not have more money than Mark.
- If we believe statement 1 and statement 3, we can't believe statement 2. The sister and Jane could not have the same amount.
- Remember, if a passage contradicts itself, it's impossible for all the sentences to be true.

Part E Follow the outline diagram to explain the contradiction in Blinky's report.

Here's what Blinky said when he was accused of stealing a watch from a supermarket:

I started out with ten dollars and bought six dollars' worth of groceries. Then I bought the watch for eight dollars.

Outline diagram

Blinky contradicted himself.

If Blinky started out with ten dollars and ______________, his second statement would indicate that ______________.	However, his second statement indicates that ______________ ______________.

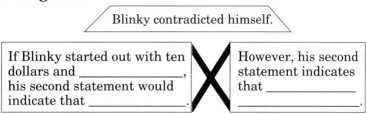

Part F Rewrite each sentence so it uses one of the new vocabulary words you've learned.

1. Four workers got tired of quarreling.
2. The trail was long and difficult.
3. The police broke up a quarrel.

Part G Write **specific** or **general** for each sentence.

1. All puppies are born with their eyes closed.
2. Dogs never sweat.
3. Bill's dog chased a squirrel.
4. Z-Mart stores close at ten o'clock every night.
5. We drove past a mountain with snow on it.
6. Mountains in Montana have snow on them throughout the year.

Part H Follow the X-box diagram to write a paragraph about each argument.

1. Fran is late for dinner whenever she plays with Hilda.
   Fran is late for dinner today.
   Therefore, Fran must be playing with Hilda again.
2. A dollar is in the street.
   Billy is always losing money.
   The dollar must belong to Billy.
3. People sweat after they've been working hard.
   Paul is sweating.
   So, Paul must have been working hard.

Outline diagram

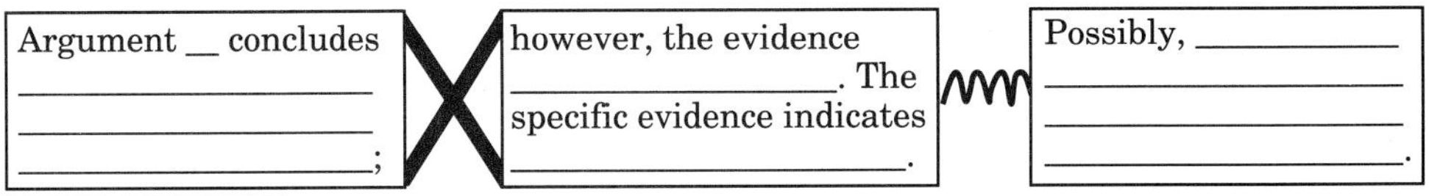
Argument __ concludes
____
____
________________________;
however, the evidence
____________________. The
specific evidence indicates
__________________________.
Possibly, ______________
____
____
________________________.

Independent Work

Part I Here are poor directions for making the figure. Every sentence is unclear. Rewrite each sentence so it is clear and specific. You may write more than one sentence to replace a sentence.

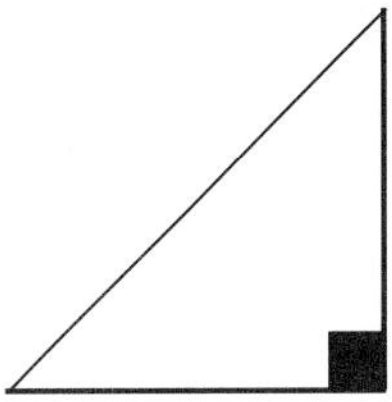

1. Make a triangle that is about an inch high.
2. Make one side of the triangle vertical and the other side horizontal.
3. Draw a small black box in the right corner.

Part J Edit this passage. Write sentences that are not run-ons and that do not have inappropriate words.

The girls in our class went to the White River and we collected rocks and some of them were beautiful. Edna and Lisa had the mostest beautiful rocks and there rocks is red and white. We talked a lot about how to find good rocks on the plane trip home.

Part K Rewrite this sentence so it describes each picture. Add the words **near the bushes.**

The bear watched the bunny.

Lesson 44

Part A Each sentence the student wrote is too general to rule out all of the objects that it is supposed to rule out. Rewrite each sentence so it rules out everything that it is supposed to rule out.

Directions

a. Write a sentence that rules out only objects 4, 5 and 7.

b. Write a sentence that rules out only objects 4, 6 and 8.

c. Write a sentence that rules out only objects 2, 3 and 4.

Student's sentences

a. The object is 1 inch.

b. The object is not solid white.

c. The object is not a rectangle.

Set

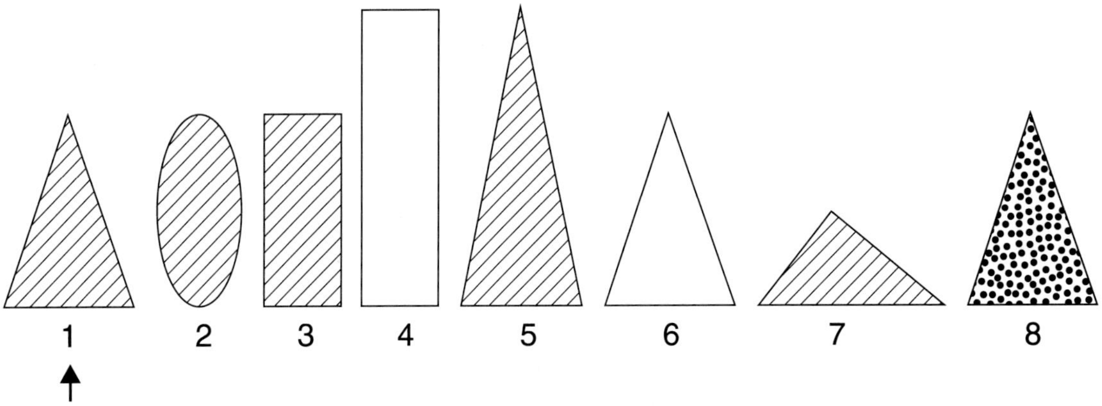

Part B Rewrite the sentences. Replace each pronoun with a noun and at least one adjective.

1. She followed her to the store.
2. It made them wet from head to toe.
3. He gave it to the bus driver.

Part C

Sample Items

a. Mary worked every afternoon last week.
Mary worked every afternoon last month.

b. Fluids flow downhill.
Water flows downhill.

Tell which sentence gives information that is more general.

1. a. She collected birds that were six inches long or shorter.
   b. She collected birds that were one foot long or shorter.
2. a. Food spoils faster when it is not refrigerated.
   b. Mushrooms spoil faster when they are not refrigerated.
3. a. Snow was on the mountaintops during April.
   b. Snow was on the mountaintops during the entire spring.
4. a. The stomach processes food that you eat.
   b. The digestive system processes food that you eat.
5. a. Precipitation returns water to the rivers.
   b. Snow returns water to the rivers.
6. a. Playing tennis helps keep the body in shape.
   b. Exercise helps keep the body in shape.
7. a. The temperature in Illinois was lower 50,000 years ago.
   b. The temperature in North America was lower 50,000 years ago.

Part D

Rewrite each sentence so it ends with a pronoun in place of the noun and adjectives. Then answer the question about the underlined word.

1. That airplane flew <u>after</u> those tiny rockets.
   - Is <u>after</u> an adjective?
2. The old log was filled with <u>lots</u> of little ants.
   - Is <u>lots</u> an adjective?
3. My uncle brought six <u>expensive</u> presents.
   - Is <u>expensive</u> an adjective?
4. My sister did not <u>drop</u> those ripe cherries.
   - Is <u>drop</u> an adjective?

Part E Follow the outline diagram to explain the contradiction in Teeny's report.

Teeny's report about what happened to his brand new coat:

A guy stopped me and made me take my coat off. That guy put the coat on and left. I didn't try to stop him. That guy was at least twice as big as I am.

Outline diagram

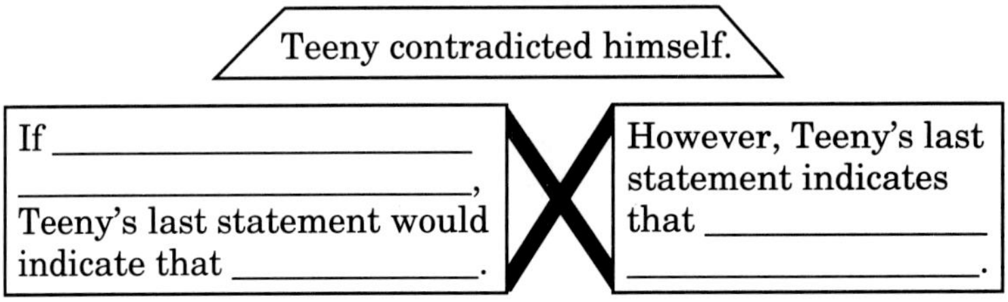

Part F Follow the X-box diagram to tell what is wrong with these arguments.

1. Every time Amy's mother goes to Z-Mart, she spends a lot of money.
   Amy's mother spent a lot of money yesterday.
   So she must have gone to Z-Mart.
2. Smith Pond has water in it.
   Tadpoles always live in water.
   So that pond must have tadpoles in it.

Outline diagram

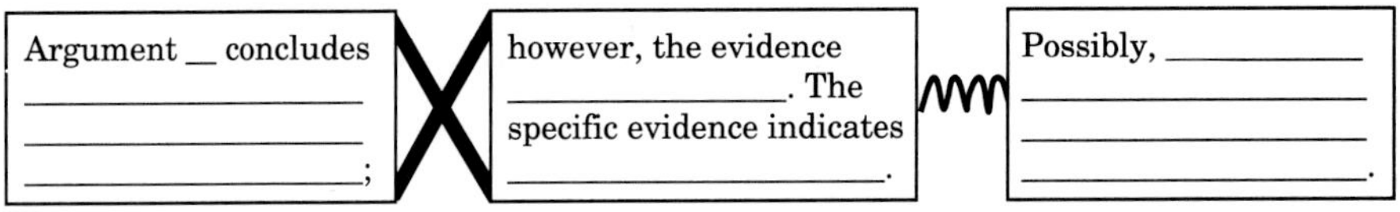

Independent Work

Part G For each item, write the complete deduction. Put the more specific sentence in the conclusion. Figure out the missing middle sentence.

1. My uncle drives a Bumpo.
   All my relatives drive Bumpos.
2. All dangerous chemicals were removed from the factory.
   XXD4 was removed from the factory.

Part H Rewrite each question as a statement. Use all the words. Circle the subject, underline the predicate and indicate the part of speech of each word.

1. Will she buy five more stamps?
2. Are they using a good tool?
3. Were all his sentences long statements?
4. Is he getting good grades?
5. Does his account contradict the map?

Part I Summarize the problems in Willie's account and write a paragraph that follows the outline diagram.

Willie's account

Susan and I went for a drive on Sunday. We ended up a couple of blocks from Big Dad's drive-in. So we drove over to 8th and Wilson and had something to eat at Big Dad's.

I had a hamburger and a milk. That cost $3.00. Susan had a salad and milk. She only had $2.50, so she couldn't pay for her order. She had to borrow 50¢ from me. We laughed.

Outline diagram

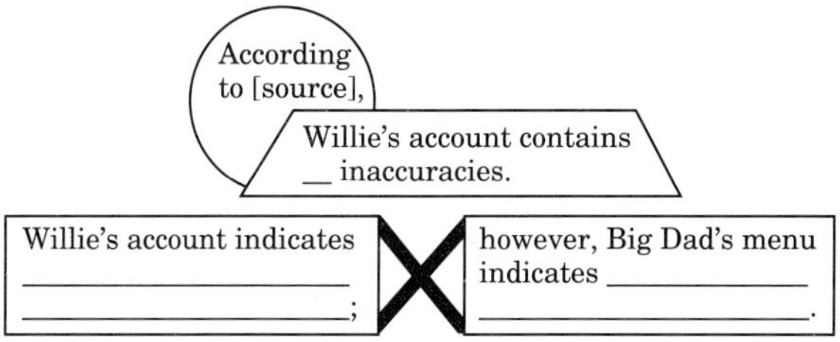

According to [source],
Willie's account contains __ inaccuracies.
Willie's account indicates ________________;
however, Big Dad's menu indicates ________________.

Source

Lesson 45

Part A

- Sentences that tell about one person or one thing are more specific than sentences that tell about a whole class of persons or things.
- Here's a sentence that tells about one house:

  Burglars never go to **Mr. Smith's house.**
- Here's a sentence that tells about more than one house:

  Burglars never go to **any house on Oak Street.**

  This sentence is more general than the sentence about Mr. Smith's house because you'd have to make more observations to figure out whether the sentence is true.

Part B

For each item, write the letter of the **most specific** sentence first, then the letter of the **more general** sentence, followed by the letter of the **most general** sentence.

1. a. Animals were in our tree.
   b. Blackbirds were in our oak tree.
   c. Animals were in our oak tree.

2. a. The boys loved to play baseball.
   b. The girls loved to play games.
   c. The children loved to play games.

3. a. Geese fly.
   b. Water fowl fly.
   c. Ducks sometimes fly over Bay Lake.

4. a. The boys collected beetles.
   b. They collected things.
   c. Jim collected butterflies.

5. a. Most people love to be active.
   b. Those girls love to swim.
   c. Those boys love to be active.

Part C

Follow the outline diagram to write a paragraph about the problem with each argument.

1. Most people who play tennis eat healthy foods.
   Miss Taylor eats healthy foods.
   Therefore, Miss Taylor must play tennis.
2. Birds love high places.
   Andy loves high places.
   Therefore, Andy is a bird.

Outline diagram

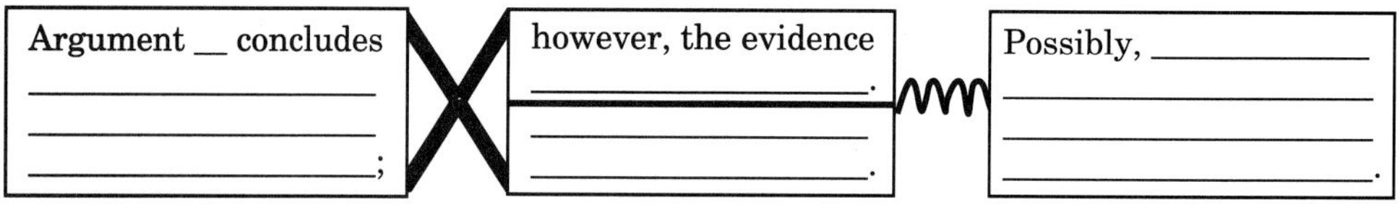

Argument __ concludes
______________________;
however, the evidence
______________________.
______________________.
Possibly, ______________________.

Part D

Rewrite each sentence so it ends with a pronoun in place of the noun and adjectives. Then answer the question about the underlined word.

1. The officers tried to stop those boys.
   - Is stop an adjective?
2. Huge water hoses inundated our neighbor's basement.
   - Is neighbor's an adjective?
3. The police chief said that she would reduce the crime rate.
   - Is crime an adjective?
4. Mrs. Jones watched them go under the bridge.
   - Is under an adjective?
5. A worker stood between Jane's brothers.
   - Is Jane's an adjective?

Part E Follow the outline diagram to explain the contradiction in Laura's report.

Laura's report about why she drove her car off Route 6 into a ditch:

I was heading west on Route 6. The sun was in my eyes and I couldn't see the road. I went off the road at 7 a.m.

Outline diagram

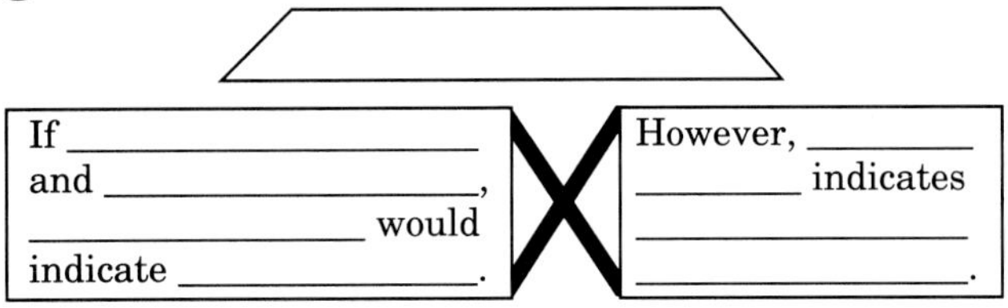
If ____________
and ____________,
____________ would
indicate ____________.
However, ________
________ indicates
____
____________.

Part F For each sentence, indicate the number of each object that is ruled out.

a. The object is striped.
b. The object is about one-half inch high.
c. The object is a rectangle.
d. The object is black.

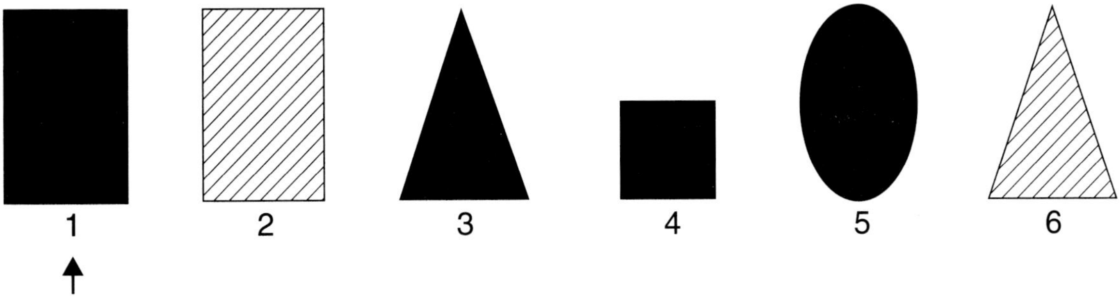
1
2
3
4
5
6

Part G Describe the arrowed object above by following these directions.

- Write the sentence that rules out objects 2 and 6.
- Write the sentence that rules out object 4.
- Write the sentence that rules out objects 3, 5 and 6.

Independent Work

Part H

Copy each sentence. Circle the subject. Underline the predicate. Write the part of speech for each word.

1. Dwayne's account contradicted Ernie's account.
2. Laura's brother was drawing horizontal lines.
3. The document made misleading statements.
4. The army ants expunged a huge wasp nest.

Part I

The directions are supposed to tell about the figure; however, each sentence is too general. Rewrite the directions so the sentences are clear and specific.

- Make a **T** that is one inch wide.
- Make an **S** that is one-half inch high.
- Put the **S** so its top touches the left half of the horizontal line.

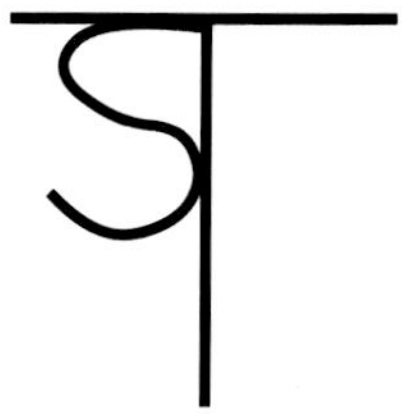

Part J

Write the complete deduction. Write the more general sentence, the missing middle sentence, then the conclusion.

1. All the documents that Herbert made were inaccurate.
   The map of Rono was inaccurate.
2. Timmy has a picture of a square.
   Timmy has a picture of every kind of rectangle.

Lesson 46

Part A Follow the outline diagram to explain the problem with each argument.

Argument 1

An animal is sitting in that tree.
Birds sit in trees.
Therefore, the animal must be a bird.

Argument 2

Watchdogs keep burglars away from houses.
Burglars never go to Mr. Smith's house.
So, Mr. Smith must have a watchdog.

Outline diagram

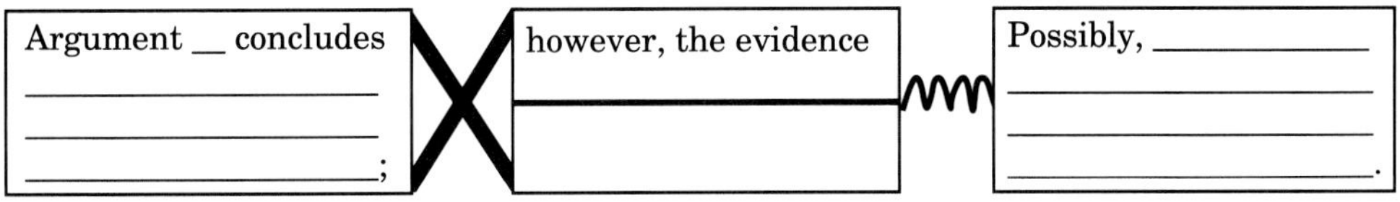

Part B Follow the outline diagram to write about the contradiction in Blinky's account.

Blinky's account

I left work at 5 p.m. It takes me 30 minutes to get home. When I got home, I saw two men sneaking around the house. So I called the police at 5:15 p.m.

Outline diagram

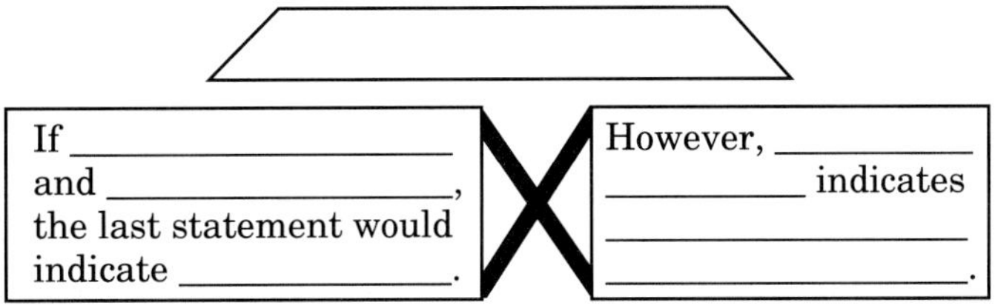

If ____________________
and ____________________,
the last statement would indicate ____________________.
However, ____________ indicates ____________________.

Part C

- Most words can be more than one part of speech. You can figure out what part of speech they are by analyzing the sentence.
- Here are two sentences using the word **ball:**

  The **ball** game lasted two hours.

  The **ball** sailed over their house.
- The word **ball** is an adjective in one sentence and a noun in the other.
- Here are two sentences using the word **sail:**

  A **sail** caught the wind.

  A **sail** boat left the harbor.
- The word **sail** is a noun in one sentence and an adjective in the other.

Part D

For each sentence, write a different sentence that uses one of the adjectives in the subject as a noun.

1. A street sign fell down.
2. Her story book has lots of pictures.
3. The bus station was on Tenth Avenue.
4. Her rose garden was beautiful.

Part E For each sentence, write the number of each object that is ruled out.

a. The object is a rectangle.
b. The object is striped.
c. The object is black.
d. The object is a four.
e. The object is white.

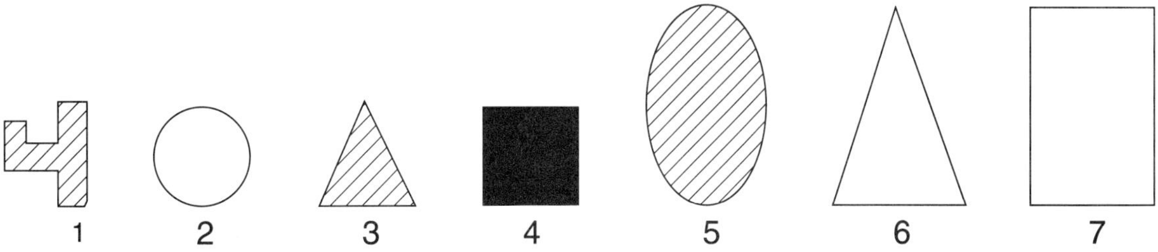

Part F

- You've learned that you can often rewrite sentences that begin with the word **there.**
- Here's an example:

  There were three cats in the tree.
- Here's the rewritten sentence:

  Three cats were in the tree.
- Some sentences use the word **they** in a way that is not clear.
- Here's a sentence:

  They opened a dance school in Glenwood.

  We don't know who **they** refers to.
- We can rewrite the sentence so it does not have the word **they:**

  A dance school opened in Glenwood.

Part G Rewrite all of the sentences so they do not have the word **they** or the word **there.**

1. They had more than 300 parents at the meeting.
2. They have a lot of new cars coming out this year.
3. There was a big spot in the middle of the rug.
4. They have people waiting in line at Z-Mart stores.
5. There are fifteen new models of Bumpos coming out next year.

Independent Work

Part H Rewrite the sentence so it describes each picture. Add the words **in the truck.**

The mail carrier delivered a package to the woman.

Part I

Rewrite each sentence so it contains a new vocabulary word. Then circle the subject, underline the predicate and write a letter above each word to show the part of speech.

1. Did the bulldozer destroy all the gopher holes?
2. The assignment required hard work.
3. Will all that rain flood our patio?

Part J

Rewrite each sentence so it is clear.

1. We asked if her tree was still growing fast yesterday.
2. They told us about their trip around the world in less than twenty minutes.
3. We watched a shooting star streak across the sky from the kitchen window.

Key

1. More than 300 parents were at the meeting.
2. A lot of new cars are coming out this year.
3. A big spot was in the middle of the rug.
4. People are waiting in line at Z-Mart stores.
5. Fifteen new models of Bumpos are coming out next year.

Lesson 47

Part A Follow the outline diagram to explain the problem with each argument.

Argument 1

Elephants have stayed away from our city for years.
Elephants avoid very dry areas.
Therefore, our city must be a very dry area.

Argument 2

The best arguments end with a short conclusion.
Terry's argument has a very short conclusion.
Therefore, Terry's argument must be a good one.

Outline diagram

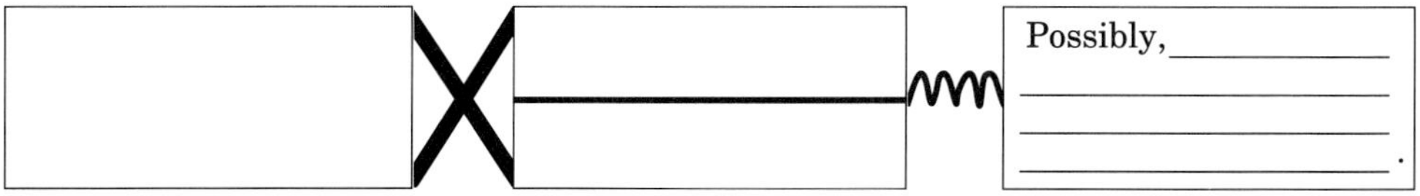

Part B

- One way to test whether a word is a noun is to put an **s** ending on the word. If the word **names more than one thing,** the word is a noun.
- Here's a word: **sentence.**

  Here's the word with an **s** ending: **sentences.**

  That word names more than one thing. So **sentence** and **sentences** are nouns.
- Here's a word: **sad.**

  Here's the word with an **s** ending: **sads.**

  The word makes no sense. **Sad** is not a noun.
- Here's a word: **think.**

  Here's the word with an **s** ending: **thinks.**

  The word makes sense, but it does not name more than one thing. It's not a noun.

Part C Write each word with an **s** ending. If the word names more than one thing, the word is a noun. Write **N** above it.

1. contradiction	4. writing	7. cloud
2. rug	5. situation	8. cheap
3. write	6. loud	9. listen

Part D Read each passage. Use **context** to figure out what each bold-faced word means and answer the questions below.

Passage 1

Jenny said, "Your problem is that you do not **adapt** to new situations."

George said, "I do too **adapt.** The first time I gave a speech in class, I had a lot of trouble, but now I can do it with no problem at all."

"No," Jenny said, "I don't mean **adapt** to schoolwork. You don't **adapt** well in getting along with other people."

"I do too **adapt** well. When I forgot my lunch, I **adapted** and ate Tina's lunch."

"That's not **adapting** well," Jenny said. "You want everyone to adjust to your needs. You don't adjust to what other people need or feel. You are very weak at **adapting** when people criticize you."

George started to jump up and down. He shouted, "That's a lie, and you're a liar. Everybody knows that I can adjust to any situation, especially to taking criticism."

a. What part of speech is **adapt?**
b. What does **adapt** probably mean?

Passage 2

They watched the brightly colored birds disappear before their eyes. As soon as the birds landed in the field, they became invisible. Mrs. Brown pointed out, "Their coloring **conceals** the birds when they are on the ground."

Donna said, "Those birds are so well **concealed** that I can't even see them any more."

Anthony said, "It's impossible for birds with such bright coloring to be **concealed** in a field that is brown and green."

Just then the birds took off. Mrs. Brown said, "The birds are not **concealed** now. They are easily seen."

a. What part of speech is **conceal?**
b. What does **conceal** probably mean?

Part E

- You've learned about adjectives in the predicate. Sometimes, an adjective in the predicate is the last word in the sentence.
- Here's a sentence that ends with an **adjective,** not a noun:

  The boys were **handsome.**
- You can show that the word **handsome** is an adjective by adding a word to the predicate:

  The boys were **handsome boys.**
- That sentence says the same thing as the sentence:

  The boys were **handsome.**

Part F

Say each sentence so the last noun is missing.

a. The girls were happy girls.
b. Our dog is an energetic dog.
c. The game was a very difficult game.

Part G

Rewrite each sentence so it ends with an adjective. Then write a letter above each word: **N** for noun, **A** for adjective, **V** for verb, **P** for pronoun.

1. The boy was a busy boy.
2. The mother bear was a grumpy bear.
3. His car was a rusty car.

Part H

Write answers to the questions after each sentence.

1. A farmer from Texas ordered soap for cleaning sheep.
   a. Does statement 1 tell where the farmer came from?
   b. Does statement 1 tell where the soap came from?
   c. Does statement 1 tell where the sheep came from?

2. A farmer ordered soap for cleaning sheep from Texas.
   d. Does statement 2 tell where the farmer came from?
   e. Does statement 2 tell where the soap came from?
   f. Does statement 2 tell where the sheep came from?

3. A farmer ordered soap from Texas for cleaning sheep.
   g. Does statement 3 tell where the farmer came from?
   h. Does statement 3 tell where the soap came from?
   i. Does statement 3 tell where the sheep came from?

Part I Write the number of each tree that is ruled out by each sentence. Write the letter of the most specific sentence. Write the letter of the most general sentence.

a. This tree has a thick trunk.
b. This tree is the shape of a tall lollipop.
c. This tree is tall.
d. This tree is shaped like a Christmas tree.

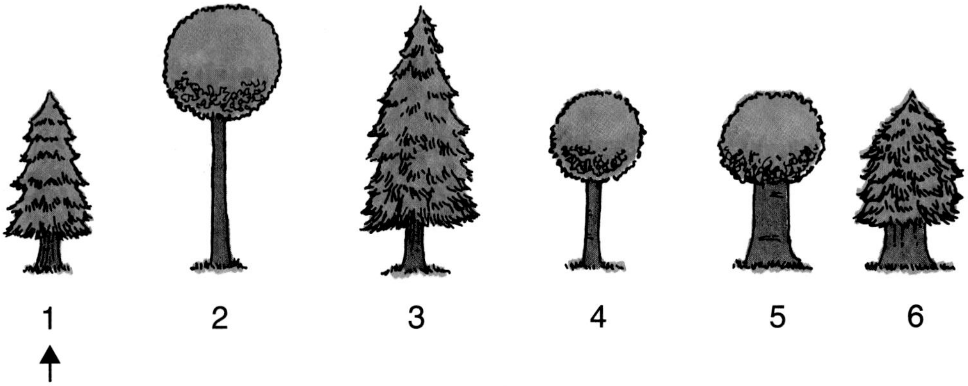

Part J Write a description of the arrowed tree.

- Write a sentence that rules out trees 2, 4 and 5.
- Write a sentence that rules out tree 3.
- Write a sentence that rules out tree 6.

Independent Work

Part K

The directions are supposed to tell about the figure; however, each sentence is too general. Rewrite the directions so the sentences are clear and specific.

- Make a letter that is one inch high.
- Make a $\frac{1}{2}$ inch square.
- Make another $\frac{1}{2}$ inch square.
- In each square, make a diagonal line.

Part L

Fix this passage.

They opened a new mall and we went to it with Jerry and his mother. There were lots of clowns who gave away balloons and we had so many balloons we were getting dizzy from blowing them up. One balloon kept losing it's air.

Part M

Tell whether each sentence tells about something **specific** or something **general.** A sentence that tells about a specific thing tells about something you could observe on one occasion.

1. Horses get longer hair at the end of each summer.
2. Our stream dries up every August.
3. Jimmy lost his left shoe.
4. My mother always gets up before 6:30 in the morning.
5. We saw a bald eagle on top of that cliff.

Lesson 48

Part A For each sentence, write a different sentence that uses an adjective in the subject as a noun.

1. The street corner was dark.
2. That book store is always crowded.
3. Their house pets were mice.

Part B Rewrite the description so it uses only two sentences to describe the arrowed object.

Description

a. The object has three sides.
b. The object is striped.
c. The object is one inch high.

Outline diagram

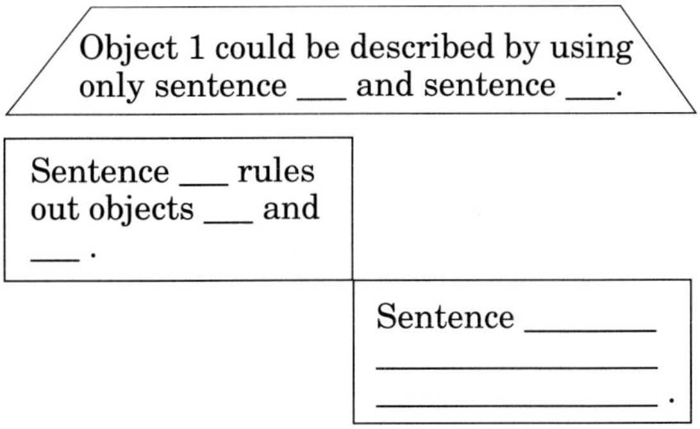

Object 1 could be described by using only sentence ___ and sentence ___.
Sentence ___ rules out objects ___ and ___ .
Sentence ________ ________________ ________________ .

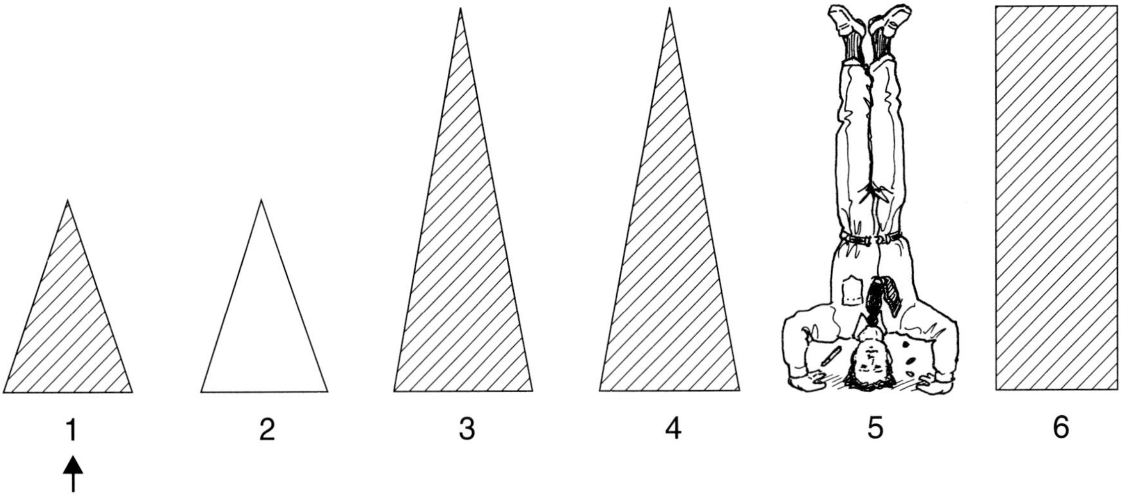

Part C

Sample Sentences

a. His car looked like a dirty car.

b. Her voice sounded like a strange voice.

c. His argument seemed to be a silly argument.

Write each sentence so it ends with an adjective. Then write a letter above each word to show its part of speech.

1. My little brother looked like a tired brother.
2. The animals sounded like loud animals.
3. Her favorite bracelet was a colorful bracelet.

Part D

- Sometimes people decide to do things. They may decide to buy a car, go on a trip or learn how to ride a horse.
- After deciding on a goal, a person must figure out the steps needed to reach the goal. If the person doesn't identify the steps and take them, the person may not reach the goal.
- Here's a goal:

  Donna decides that she would like to learn how to ride a horse.

- Here are the facts:

  She lives in a city.

  She has never ridden a horse.

  To reach her goal, Donna must **learn some things** and **do some things.**

- Here are some of the most important questions she must answer:
  1. How can she get **information** about learning to ride a horse?
  2. How will she **learn** to ride a horse?
  3. How will she **pay** for the lessons?
  4. How will she **get to and from** the location where horses are?

  When she answers these questions, she'll have a good plan.

- Here's the outline diagram for writing about the plan:

Paragraph 1

Donna wants to ______________.
Donna needs to do four things to reach this goal.

First, ______________________________
______________________________.

Paragraphs 2 and 3

The next thing Donna should do is ________
______________________________.

Paragraph 4

The last thing ______________________
______________________________.

Independent Work

Part E Rewrite each sentence so it ends with an adjective. Write a letter above every word to indicate the part of speech.

1. Jim Taylor is a friendly man.
2. Their argument was a complicated argument.
3. That house is an expensive house.
4. Her accident was a careless accident.

Part F Follow the outline diagram to tell what's wrong with the argument.

Argument

Tim is going to Milltown tomorrow.
Tim likes to run.
So, Tim will run to Milltown.

Outline diagram

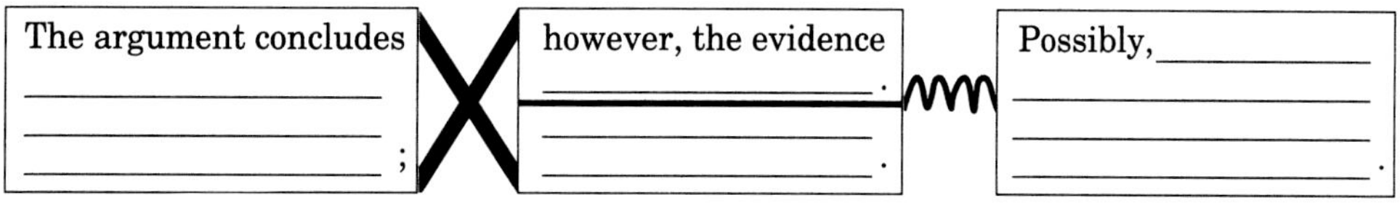
The argument concludes ______ ;
however, the evidence ______ . ______ .
Possibly, ______ .

Lesson 49

Part A

For each sentence, write the two nouns and circle the more general noun. Then rewrite each sentence so it ends with an adjective.

1. The church bell was an enormous object.
2. Jim's car is a reliable vehicle.
3. Earthquakes can be terrible disasters.
4. His earlier letters are interesting documents.

Part B

Rewrite the description so it uses only two sentences to describe the arrowed object.

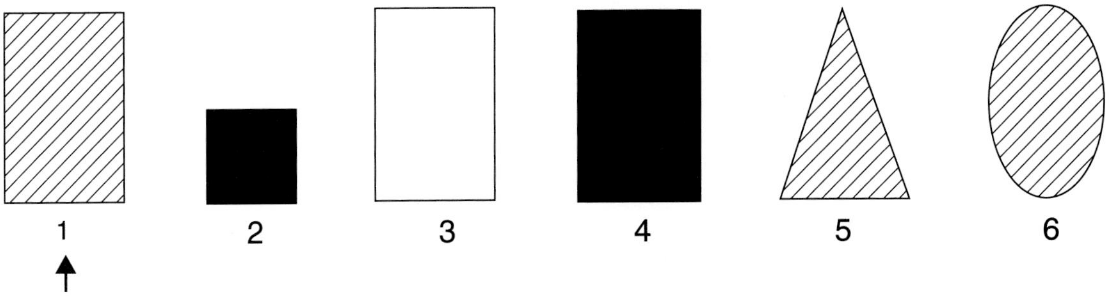

Description

a. The object is striped.
b. The object is about one inch high.
c. The object is a rectangle.

Outline diagram

Object 1 could be described by using only sentence ____________________.

Sentence ___ rules
____
____________________.

____
____
____________________.

Part C

Rewrite the second sentence in each item so the sentence is clear.

1. Billy moved to a farm, and he finally adapted to getting up at 5 a.m. That took over three months.
2. Billy had the chore of milking the cows every morning. Billy's mother had to remind him to do that chore on three occasions.
3. Billy lost his calculator in the barn. It was full of mice.
4. Billy and Jimmy altercated near the bus stop. That didn't last long.

Independent Work

Part D

Write each word with an **s** ending. If the word names more than one thing, the word is a noun. Write **N** above it.

1. pillow
2. sensation
3. beside
4. decide
5. decision
6. clear
7. stripe
8. wide

Part E

Write each question as a statement. Mark the subject and the predicate, and indicate the part of speech for every word.

1. Can she go?
2. Will those weeds conceal the gophers?
3. Do old dogs learn new adaptations?
4. Was the water inundating all the houses?

Part F For each sentence, indicate the number of each object that is ruled out.

a. The object is striped.
b. The object is about one-half inch high.
c. The object is a rectangle.
d. The object is black.

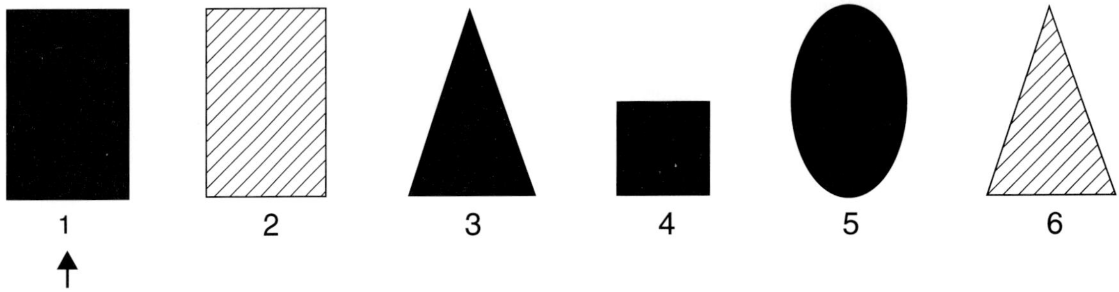

Part G Describe the arrowed object above by following these directions.

1. Write a sentence that rules out objects 2 and 6.
2. Write a sentence that rules out object 4.
3. Write a sentence that rules out objects 3, 5 and 6.

Key

1. The church bell was enormous.
2. Jim's car is reliable.
3. Earthquakes can be terrible.
4. His earlier letters are interesting.

Lesson 50 – Test 5

Part A In each subject, find the adjective that can also be a noun. Write a sentence with that word as the noun in the subject.

1. That toy shop is always crowded.
2. Her last tire repair cost $6.00.
3. Our only pear tree is dying.

Part B Follow the outline diagram to write about the contradiction in Blinky's account.

Blinky's account

I had to mow my lawn so I borrowed a lawn mower from Eddie. I pulled and pulled on the starting cord, but the lawn mower never started.

The next day I returned the lawn mower to Eddie, and he got mad at me. He said that the lawn mower wasn't broken when I borrowed it. I told him that it was. Besides, it was such an old machine that it took me over an hour to mow my lawn.

Outline diagram

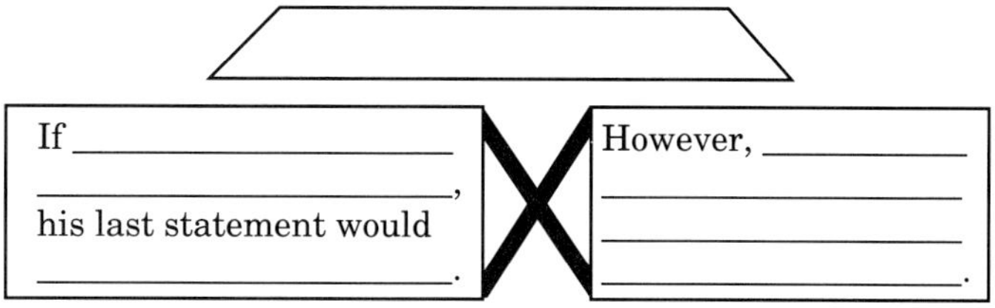

Part C

Follow the directions to write a description of the arrowed tree.

Directions

1. Write a sentence that rules out trees 5 and 6.
2. Write a sentence the rules out trees 2 and 3.
3. Write a sentence that rules out tree 4.

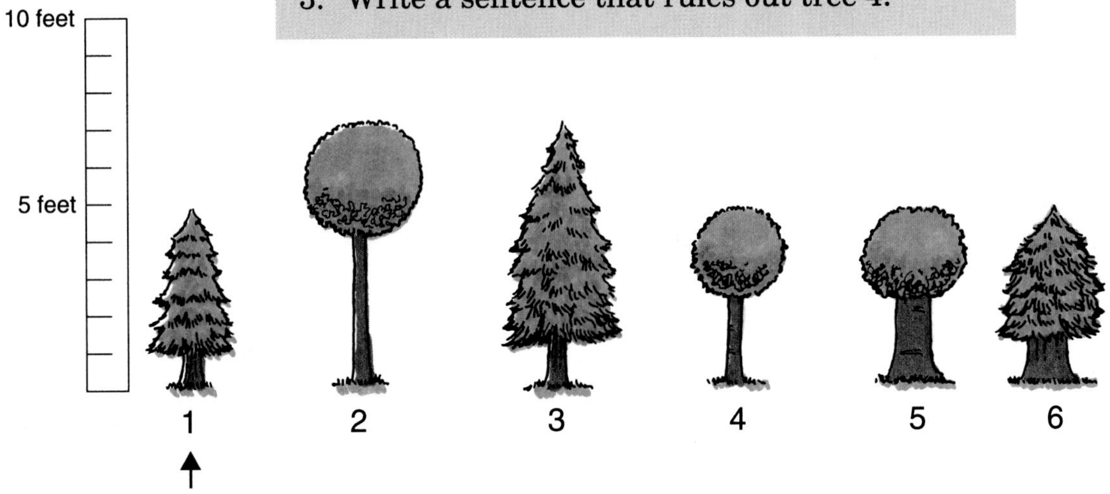

Part D

Follow the outline diagram to explain the problem with this argument.

Argument

Mr. Jackson always drives carefully.
There's a dent in the side of Mr. Jackson's car.
Therefore, Mr. Jackson's son must have had an accident.

Outline diagram

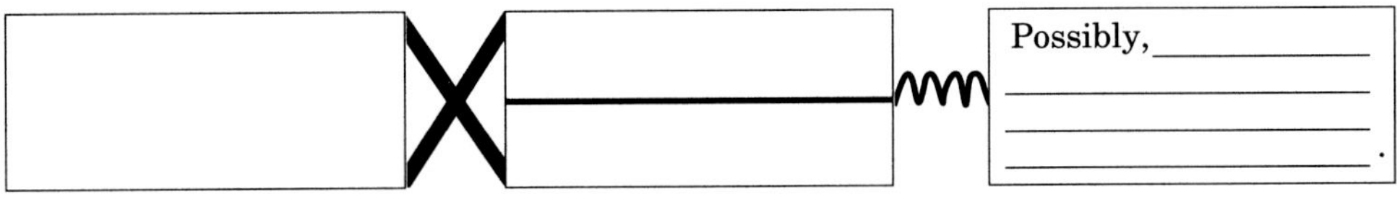

Lesson 51

Part A

Use the vocabulary box to help you with difficult words.

Vocabulary Box

pattern	invisible	arctic
region	plentiful	scarce

Part B

- You've worked with arguments that have inadequate evidence. The conclusion these arguments draw is not the **only** conclusion that is possible.
- You can show how far from correct these arguments are by **changing the evidence** so that the conclusion shown is the only conclusion a person could draw.
- When you change the evidence, you create a whole new argument, but the new argument has the evidence a person would need to draw the conclusion of the original argument.
- Here's an argument that has inadequate evidence:

  The big clock always chimes at 10 p.m.
  I hear the big clock chiming.
  Therefore, it must be 10 p.m.

- That conclusion is not the only one that's possible.
- If the argument presented **different** evidence, we could safely draw the conclusion that it is 10 p.m.

Part C

Change the more general evidence so it uses the word **only.**

1. Every time Amy's mother goes to Z-Mart, she spends a lot of money.
   Amy's mother spent a lot of money yesterday.
   Therefore, she must have gone to Z-Mart.
2. George always tracks dirt into the kitchen.
   There are dirt tracks on the kitchen floor.
   George tracked that dirt into the kitchen.
3. Linda always gets sick after she travels to Texas.
   Linda is really sick.
   She must have traveled to Texas recently.

Part D

For each sentence, write the two nouns. Circle the noun that is more general. Then rewrite each sentence so it ends with an adjective.

1. Their wedding was a delightful event.
2. Our family reunion was a memorable occasion.
3. Fear is a powerful emotion.
4. Their first house was an old building.
5. Her horse was a magnificent animal.

Part E

- Soon you'll be working with arguments that tell about cause and effect.
- The **cause** is something that happens first.
- The **effect** is what **always happens next.**
- You hold a pencil up in the air, and then you let go of it. **Letting go of it is the cause.**
- The effect is what happens to the pencil.

Part F

For each item, identify the cause and the effect.

1. Jimmy hit Angela. Therefore, she hit him back.
2. Ginger was laughing because Billy made a funny face.
3. When Sam walked out into the bright light, he had to squint.

Part G

Follow the outline diagram to explain how you identified the mystery object.

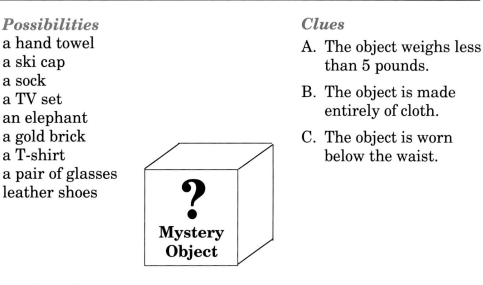

Possibilities

a hand towel
a ski cap
a sock
a TV set
an elephant
a gold brick
a T-shirt
a pair of glasses
leather shoes

Clues

A. The object weighs less than 5 pounds.

B. The object is made entirely of cloth.

C. The object is worn below the waist.

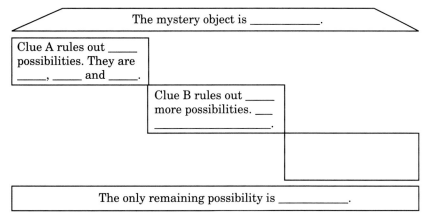

Outline diagram

The mystery object is ___________.

Clue A rules out _____ possibilities. They are _____, _____ and _____.

Clue B rules out _____ more possibilities. ___ ____________________.

The only remaining possibility is ___________.

Independent Work

Part H Follow the instructions to write three sentences that describe the arrowed object. Start each sentence with **The line is.**

- Write a sentence that rules out objects 2, 3, 5 and 7.
- Write a sentence that rules out objects 4 and 6.
- Write a sentence that rules out object 8.

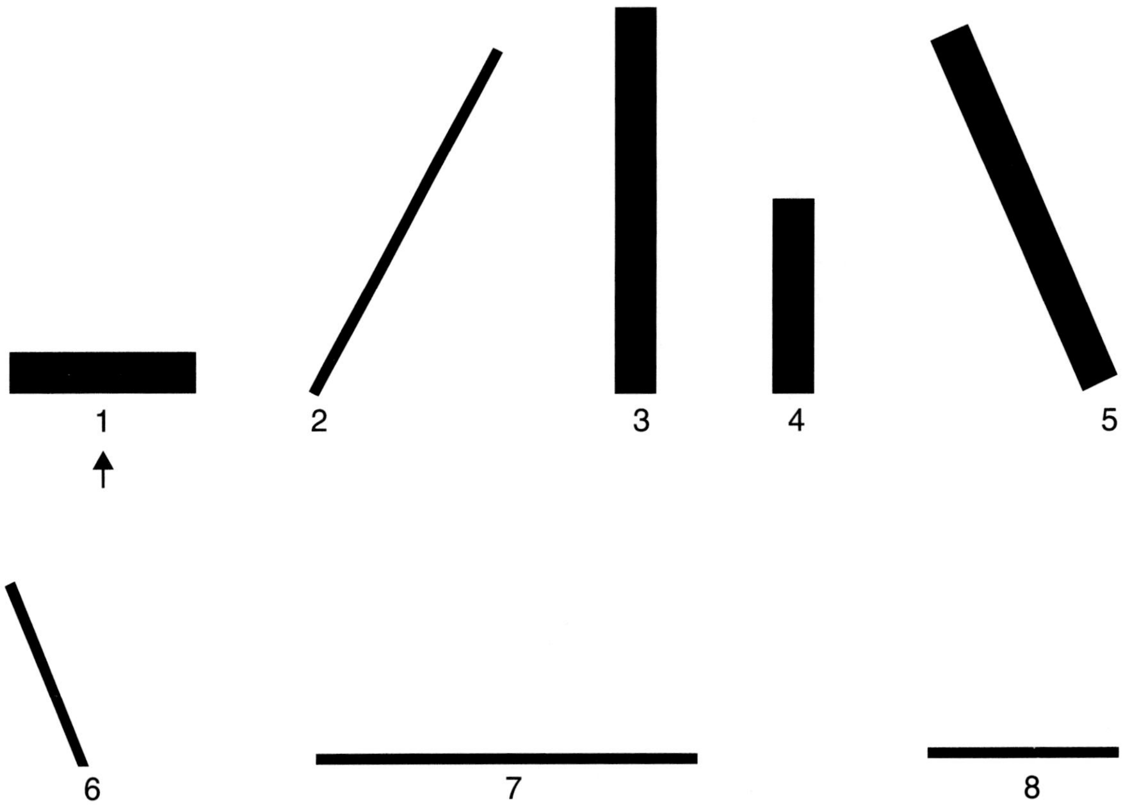

Part I Follow the appropriate outline diagram and write about the problem with Hilda's account.

Hilda's account

I have three sisters. All are older than I am. Ellen is the oldest. Diana is the youngest. She was very small when she was a baby. I remember seeing her just after she was born. She looked like a tiny doll. You would not believe how big she is now.

Key

1. A N V A
   Their wedding was delightful.
2. A A N V A
   Our family reunion was memorable.
3. N V A
   Fear is powerful.
4. A A N V A
   Their first house was old.
5. A N V A
   Her horse was magnificent.

Lesson 52

Part A Change the more general evidence so it uses the word **only.**

1. That picture has a lot of blue in it.
   Linda makes pictures that have a lot of blue in them.
   Linda must have made that picture.
2. Watchdogs keep burglars away from houses.
   Burglars never go to Mr. Smith's house.
   So he must have a watchdog.
3. Jim always wears striped shirts.
   That person in the distance is wearing a striped shirt.
   That person must be Jim.

Part B Follow the outline diagram to explain how you identified the mystery object.

Mrs. Johnson goes to the grocery store and purchases one food item. That item fits into a small bag.

Possibilities

an apple
a can of dog food
yogurt
a banana
a can of soup
a jar of olives
a dog bone
a jar of mustard

Mystery bag

Clues

A. The food is in a container.
B. The container is not a jar.
C. The food is served in a dish or bowl that is placed on the floor.

Outline diagram

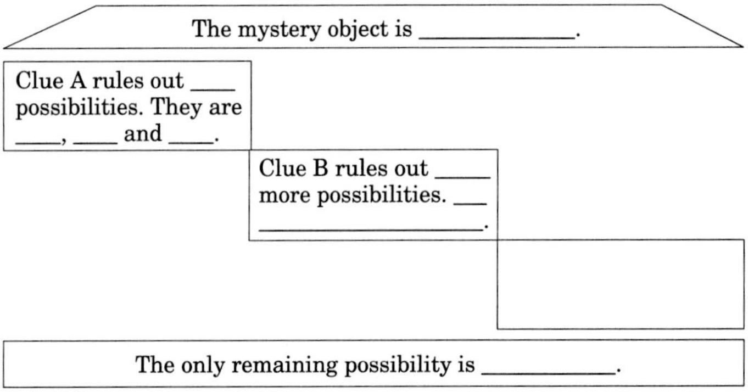

The mystery object is ____________.
Clue A rules out ____ possibilities. They are ____, ____ and ____.
Clue B rules out ____ more possibilities. ____ ________________.
The only remaining possibility is ___________.

Part C **Sample Items**

a. She was a girl.
   She was smart.

b. That bird is active.
   That bird is a rooster.

Combine these pairs of sentences so they end with a noun. Skip a line between each item.

1. The dinner was delicious.
   The dinner was a meal.
2. Our trip was an experience.
   Our trip was terrific.
3. Their room was a place.
   Their room was enormous.

Part D For each item, identify the cause and the effect.

1. People put on their coats because the temperature dropped 18 degrees.
2. Joe skinned his knee when he fell off the bike.
3. Jan put the burner on high. The water boiled harder.

Part E For each question, write the statement that uses all the words. Then circle the subject, underline the predicate and label the part of speech for every word.

1. Did they find all the concealed eggs?
2. Was Martha concealing her feelings?
3. Can those plants adapt?
4. Was their altercation a serious one?

Part F You're going to write a plan for Amy to reach her goal.

Amy's goal is to make an oak rocking chair.

Facts

- Amy has never built things out of wood.
- She does not have the tools or materials she needs to build the chair or to varnish it.
- She does not have any money, but she has a job, and she would be able to save as much as $30 each week if she was careful.

Here are the questions Amy's plan should answer:

1. Where is Amy going to get information about making furniture?
2. How will she learn to make furniture?
3. Where is she going to get the tools and materials she needs to make her chair?
4. How is she going to get the money necessary to pay for materials and training?

Independent Work

Part G Find out the answer to question 1 in part F. Find out who Amy could talk to or what she could read to give her the information she needs.

Part H For each sentence, write the two nouns and circle the more general noun. Then rewrite each sentence so it ends with an adjective. Indicate the part of speech for each word.

1. His birthday party is a delightful celebration.
2. The other boy was a colorful character.
3. Their houses were tiny buildings.
4. Her frequent altercations are disturbing events.

Part I Rewrite the description so it uses only two sentences to describe the arrowed object. Then write about your description.

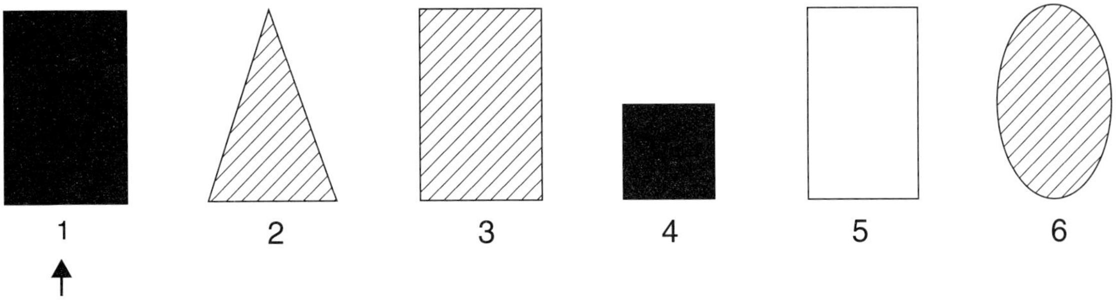

Description

A. The object is 1 inch high.
B. The object is a solid color.
C. The object is black.

Outline diagram

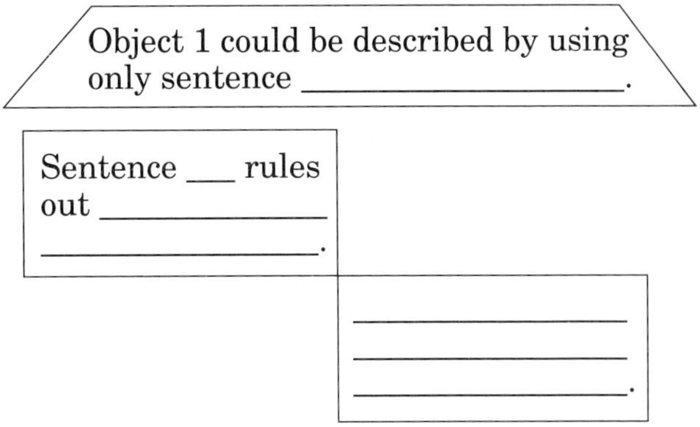

Object 1 could be described by using only sentence ____________.
Sentence ___ rules out ____________ ____________.
____________ ____________ ____________.

Lesson 53

Part A Follow the outline diagram to write about the most practical route from Milltown to Billtown.

Map

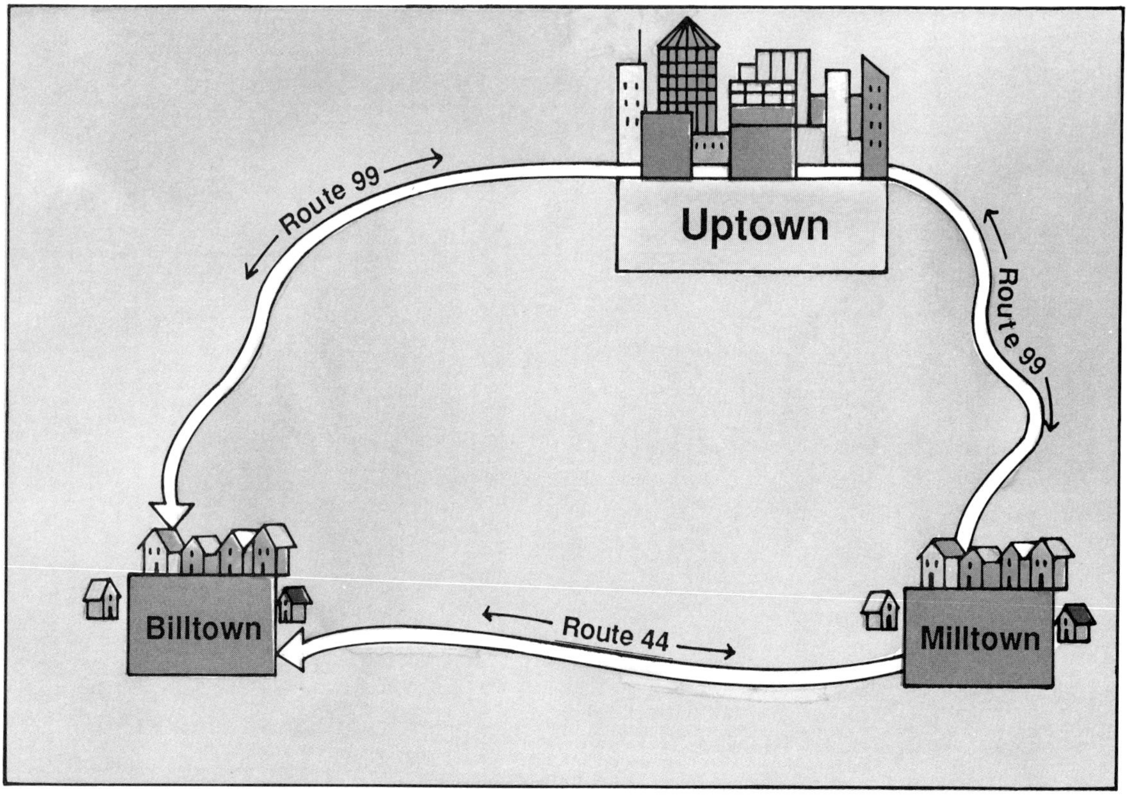

Outline diagram

The most practical route is ______________________ ______________________ .	=	That route has these advantages: it ____ ____ ; it __________ .

Part B For each sentence, describe the cause and the effect.

1. Ted got mad when his bike tire went flat.
2. Mr. Brown turned red from working in the sun all day.
3. Jenny got soaked when it started to rain.

Part C **Follow the outline diagram to explain how you identified the mystery object.**

Possibilities

a TV set
a brick
a wallet
a pencil
a shoelace

Clues

A. The object is smaller than a notebook.

B. The object weighs less than a pound.

C. The object is not flexible.

Outline diagram

The mystery object is ______________.

Clue A rules out _____.
That object is _______
____________________.

The only remaining possibility is ____________.

Part D **Write the combined sentence for each pair of sentences.**

1. The document was an article.
   The document was long.
2. The boy was obnoxious.
   The boy was a child.
3. That device is expensive.
   That device is a printer.
4. The program was a comedy.
   The program was outrageous.

Part E Follow the outline diagram to write a plan for Amy.

Amy's goal is to make an oak rocking chair.

Facts

- Amy has never built things out of wood.
- She does not have the tools or materials she needs to build the chair or to varnish it.
- She does not have any money, but she has a job, and she would be able to save as much as $30 each week if she were careful.

Here are the questions Amy's plan should answer:

1. Where is Amy going to get information about making furniture?
2. How will she learn to make furniture?
3. Where is she going to get the tools and materials she needs to make her chair?
4. How is she going to get the money necessary to pay for materials and training?

Outline diagram

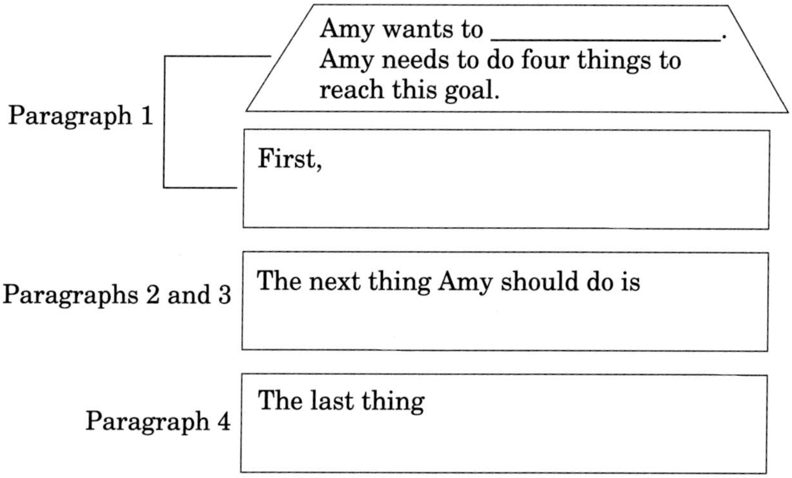

Amy wants to ________________.
Amy needs to do four things to reach this goal.
Paragraph 1
First,
Paragraphs 2 and 3
The next thing Amy should do is
Paragraph 4
The last thing

Independent Work

Part F Complete your plan for Amy (if you haven't completed it).

Part G Write specific directions for making this figure.

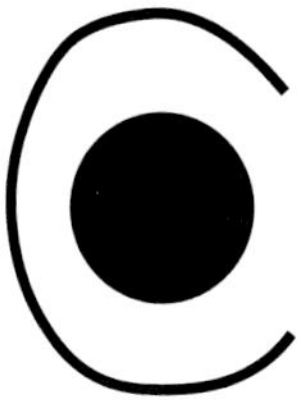

Lesson 54

Part A Follow the outline diagram and write two paragraphs about the most practical plan for Donna.

Donna's goal is to learn to ride a horse.

Facts

- She lives in a city.
- She has never ridden a horse.
- She has to figure out some way to pay for learning how to ride.

Possible ways that Donna could learn to ride a horse:

Plan 1 (Buying a horse): Donna could buy a horse, saddle and gear.

Plan 2 (Moving): Donna could move 40 miles away to the country and live on a farm that has horses.

Plan 3 (Taking lessons): Donna could take riding lessons at a nearby community college.

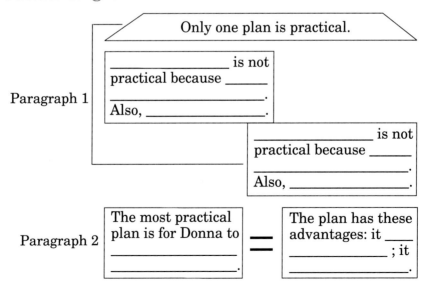

Outline diagram

Only one plan is practical.

Paragraph 1

______________ is not practical because ______ ______________.
Also, ______________.

______________ is not practical because ______ ______________.
Also, ______________.

Paragraph 2

The most practical plan is for Donna to ______________ ______________. = The plan has these advantages: it ____ ______________; it ______________.

Part B

- You've worked with compound sentences. Compound sentences are really two sentences that are linked together with one of these words: **and, but, or.**
- You punctuate compound sentences by writing a comma just before the linking word.
- Here are two sentences:

  His grandmother is old. She is very fast.

- Here are the sentences written as a compound sentence:

  His grandmother is old, but she is very fast.

- If the part of the sentence that follows the linking word is **not** a complete sentence, you do not write a comma before the linking word:

  His grandmother is old but very fast.

- The part after the linking word is not a sentence. So you do not write a comma before **but.**

Part C

Sample Sentences

a. The day was rainy and cold.

b. The day was rainy and the night was cold.

Write **compound** or **no** to tell about each of these sentences.

1. The baby drank a bottle of milk and he went to sleep.
2. His mother was pretty and quite young.
3. The servings were small but they were tasty.
4. In the morning, the wind was cold but it died down in the afternoon.
5. She writes fast but not carefully.

Independent Work

Part D Write the compound sentences from part C. Mark both subjects and predicates. Then place the comma correctly.

Part E Follow the appropriate outline diagram to write about the problems with the newspaper account. Table E6 is accurate.

Newspaper account

Iowa has the fourth largest number of trails and the fourth highest number of miles. Washington has over 430 miles of trails. Washington is sixth in both total miles and number of trails. Missouri has only four trails, but they are long ones. Missouri has a total of about 210 miles of trails. Wisconsin tops all the states in the total miles of trails with 751.8 miles, but Wisconsin is only fifth in the number of trails, with 39.

Table E6: Rail-Trail Mileage in Top 10 States

The United States has 514 trails where railroad tracks used to be. The rail trails total 6,384 miles. Average trail length is 12.4 miles.

	Total Mileage of Trails	Number of Trails
Wisconsin	751.8	39
Michigan	710.4	48
Pennsylvania	545.7	45
Iowa	544.4	37
Minnesota	486.5	22
Washington	433.1	30
Illinois	323.9	29
New York	298.7	24
Missouri	209.7	4
West Virginia	191.5	10

Source: Rails to Trails Conservancy

Part F Write a complete deduction for each pair of sentences. Show the more specific sentence as the conclusion of the deduction.

1. She collects shirts.
   She collects objects made of cloth.
2. Iron floats in mercury.
   Iron floats in liquids that are more dense than iron.

Lesson 55

Part A Follow the outline diagram to explain how you identified the mystery object.

Possibilities

banana
cherry
strawberry
apple
raspberry

Clues

A. The object is red.

B. The object in not taller than a silver dollar.

C. The object has a "stone" inside.

Outline diagram

The mystery object is ______________.

Clue A rules out ______.
That object is ________
____________________.

The only remaining possibility is ____________.

Part B

- You've worked with faulty arguments. Some arguments don't have evidence that would permit you to draw the conclusion that the argument draws.
- If you change the evidence by using the word **only,** you create a new argument. But the new argument has evidence that makes it possible to draw the conclusion that the original argument draws.
- Some faulty arguments are different. You make it possible to draw the conclusion that the argument draws by adding the words **all** or **every** to the evidence.
- Here's an argument of that type:

  Tadpoles live in ponds.
  I see a pond.
  Therefore, it must have tadpoles in it.
- The evidence is not strong enough to permit somebody to draw the conclusion.
- You could fix up the evidence with the word **all.**

  Tadpoles live in all ponds.
  I see a pond.
  Therefore, it must have tadpoles in it.
- The statement, **Tadpoles live in all ponds,** is not true; however, that statement would have to be in the evidence for you to draw the conclusion that there are tadpoles in the pond.

Part C

Change one of the sentences in the evidence so it draws the conclusion that is given. Use the word **all** or **every.**

Argument 1: Many people who wear Craddy running shoes run faster.
J.J. Terry wears Craddy running shoes.
Therefore, J.J. must be running faster than he did.

Argument 2: Liver is a food that contains iron.
You should eat foods that contain iron.
Therefore, you should eat liver.

Argument 3: George has lots of tools.
A level is a type of tool.
Therefore, George has a level.

Part D

The girls were happy. Their mother said, "Why are you girls so chipper today?"

Molly said, "Because our teacher gave prizes to Hilda and I."

Their mother said, "You should say, 'Our teacher gave prizes to Hilda and **me.**' "

Molly said, "But Mom, you didn't get any prizes. Hilda and me got the prizes."

"No, no," their mother said. "you should say, 'Hilda and **I** got the prizes.' "

"But Mom," Hilda said, "you weren't even there. The prizes went to Molly and me."

"That's the way to say it," their mother said. "The prizes went to Molly and **me.**"

"But Mom . . . "

- The words **I** and **me** are pronouns. People often misuse pronouns when a sentence tells about more than one person.
- Here's how to test whether you're using the right pronoun: **Say the sentence so it tells about only one person.**
- Sample sentence:

  Hilda and me received a prize.

- The underlined part names two persons.
- Here's the sentence with only the pronoun:

  Me received a prize.

- If you were the only person, you'd say,

  I received a prize.

- So, when there's more than one person, you'd say,

  Hilda and I received a prize.

Part E

Sample Item

That dog followed Hilda and I.

For each sentence, write a correct sentence that tells about one person and uses the pronoun **I** or **me.**

1. The party was for Fran and me.
2. Sally and me worked very hard.
3. Alex and I had fun at the park.
4. A dog followed the boys and I.
5. The boys and I looked forward to vacation.

Part F

- This is Herbie's faulty argument:

  Every time I wear my blue socks, the Tigers win.
  I'm going to wear my blue socks tonight.
  The Tigers are going to win again.

- This argument doesn't really show that one thing causes another.
- Here's how you'll write about arguments like this one:

  The argument concludes that the Tigers are going to win again; however, the evidence is inadequate. The evidence indicates only that when Herbie wore blue socks, the Tigers won. The evidence doesn't indicate that Herbie wearing blue socks **causes** the Tigers to win.

Outline diagram

The argument concludes that ________________ ________________ ________________;	however, the evidence is inadequate. The evidence indicates only that when [one thing happened], [another thing happened].	The evidence doesn't indicate that ______ ____________ causes ________________.

Part G Follow the X-box diagram in part F to write about the problem with this argument.

Every time George went to Detroit, it rained in Texas.
George is going to Detroit tomorrow.
Therefore, it's going to rain in Texas.

Part H Write **compound** or **no** to tell about each of these sentences. Then copy the compound sentences and place the comma. Circle the subjects and underline the predicates.

1. They found it in the front yard or in the driveway.
2. The rain was heavy but the wind was calm.
3. Mary will go to the park or she will read a book.
4. He was sweating and breathing fast.
5. Their eyes were alert and their muscles were tense.

Independent Work

Part I Write directions for drawing this figure.

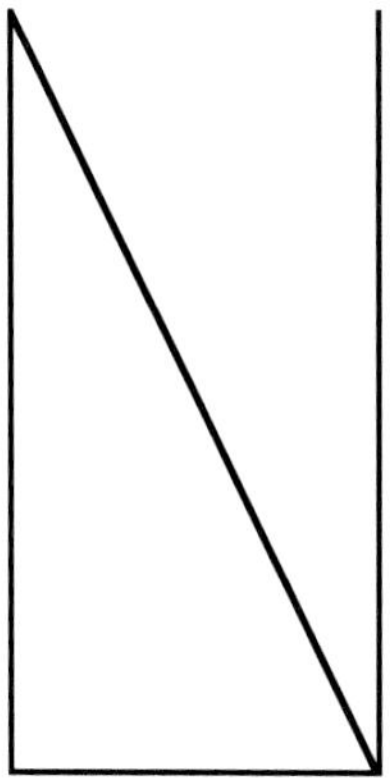

Part J Follow these instructions to describe the arrowed object.

A. Write a sentence that rules out objects 2, 5 and 6.

B. Write a sentence that rules out object 3.

C. Write a sentence that rules out object 4.

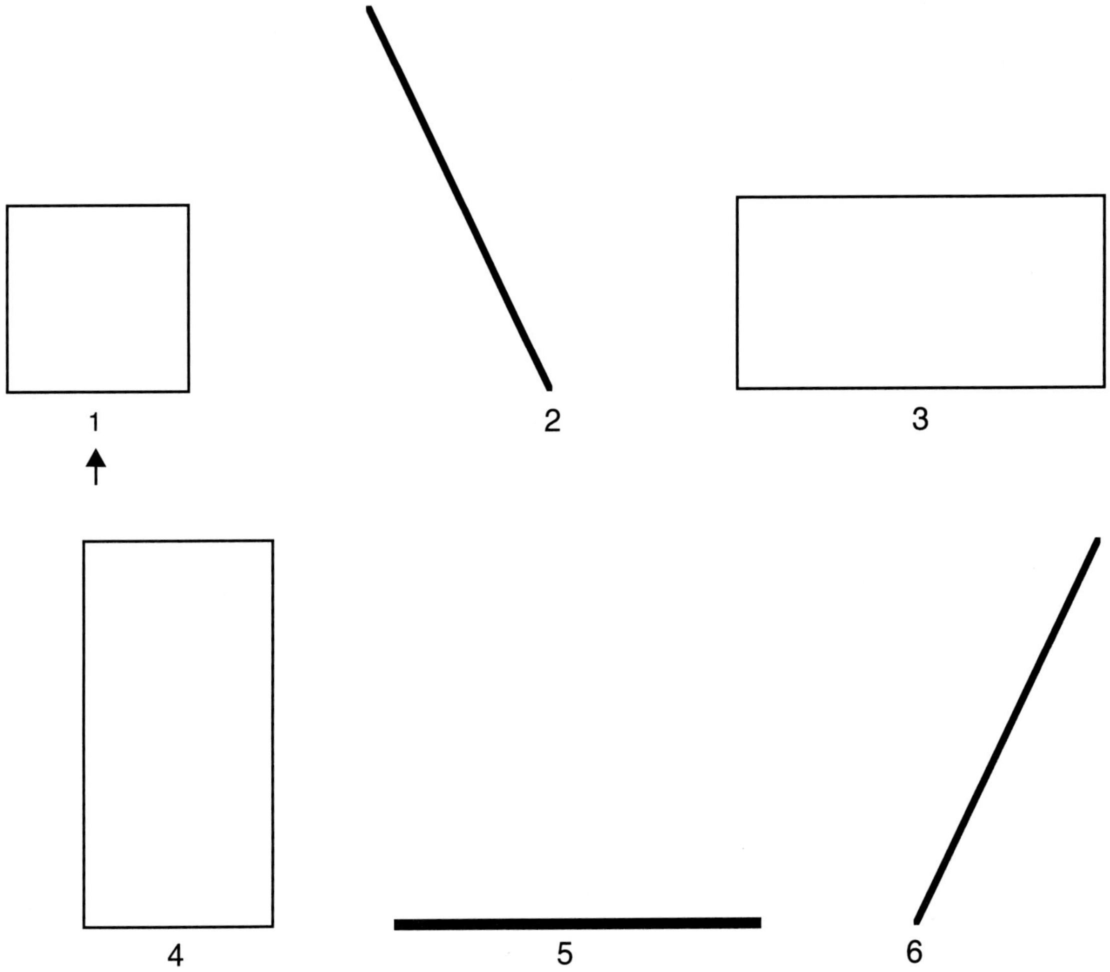

Part K You could probably describe object 1 in part J by using only two of your sentences. Follow the outline diagram to tell about those sentences.

Object 1 could be described using only sentence ________.

Sentence ___ rules
____
________.

____
____
________.

The only remaining possibility is ______.

Key

2. The rain was heavy, but the wind was calm.
3. Mary will go to the park, or she will read a book.
5. Their eyes were alert, and their muscles were tense.

Lesson 56

Part A Follow the outline diagram to write how you selected the best jacket for Henry.

Henry's requirements

1. The jacket must cost less than $200.00.
2. The jacket must be washable.
3. The jacket must offer superior protection against the cold.
4. The jacket must weigh no more than 4 pounds.

Facts

Jacket	Stormbuster	Windblaster	Leader	King Kold	Wilderness
Price	$179.00	$187.99	$156.00	$206.00	$187.00
Weight	4 lb.	3 lb. 2 oz.	2 lb. 8 oz.	3 lb. 7 oz.	4 lb. 3 oz.
Protection against cold	superior	superior	good	superior	superior
Cleaning	washable	dry clean only	washable	washable	washable

Outline diagram

The only jacket that meets all Henry's requirements is ______________.

Requirement __ rules out ___________. That jacket ____________.

The only remaining jacket is__________.

Part B

Write each compound sentence, place the comma, and mark both subjects and predicates.

1. Ducks can fly and ducks can swim.
2. She slipped and she fell.
3. My brother can fly planes and skydive.
4. Mary gathered nuts and washed them in the backyard.
5. The police officer stopped her but he did not arrest her.

Part C

Follow the outline diagram to write about the problem with the argument.

Here's what Herbie said:

If I wear my red shirt when we take a test, Jan does well. I'm not going to wear that shirt tomorrow. Jan won't do well on tomorrow's math test.

Outline diagram

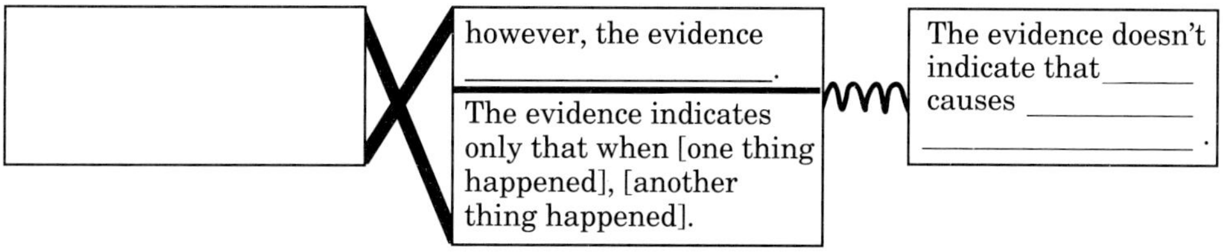
however, the evidence ____________________.
The evidence indicates only that when [one thing happened], [another thing happened].
The evidence doesn't indicate that ______ causes ____________ ____________________.

Part D **Sample Items**

a. George and her liked the movie.

b. Henry and him argued in the yard.

Rewrite each sentence so it tells about only one person and uses the correct pronoun.

1. Jerry and him painted the bike.
2. He and Mary laughed a lot.
3. The cat looked at Luisa and I.
4. Her and Fran went swimming.
5. The car almost ran into Sara and her.

Part E Fix the evidence in these arguments by rewriting one sentence. Use the word **all** or **every.**

Argument 1: Mrs. Jones has lots of jewelry.
An emerald necklace is a type of jewelry.
Therefore, Mrs. Jones must have an emerald necklace.

Argument 2: Radiator hoses are parts of cars.
Many parts of Bumpo cars are excellent.
Therefore, Bumpos must have excellent radiator hoses.

Argument 3: You should do exercises to improve your endurance.
Running 300 miles every week improves your endurance.
Therefore, you should run 300 miles every week.

Independent Work

Part F Write the combined sentence for each pair of sentences.

1. They were noisy.
   They were robins.
2. She is an inventor.
   She is brilliant.
3. The vehicle was damaged.
   The vehicle was a bus.
4. Their pet is an elephant.
   Their pet is enormous.

Part G Write about the problem with each argument. Follow the appropriate outline diagram.

Argument 1: Wolves love to eat chickens.
The entire Jones family loves to eat chickens.
Therefore, the Jones family must be a pack of wolves.

Argument 2: The best swimmers have great big feet.
Denny has huge feet.
Therefore, Denny must be a super swimmer.

Key

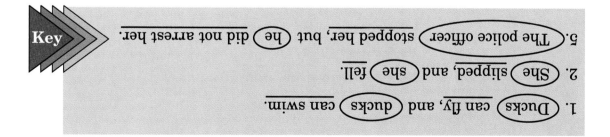

1. Ducks can fly, and ducks can swim.
2. She slipped, and she fell.
5. The police officer stopped her, but he did not arrest her.

Lesson 57

Part A Add the word **all, every** or **only** to one sentence in the evidence to make the evidence lead to the conclusion.

Argument 1: Millionaires have lots of possessions.
Mrs. Anderson has lots of possessions.
Therefore, Mrs. Anderson must be a millionaire.

Argument 2: Becky is a good basketball player.
Good players are on our school's basketball team.
Therefore, Becky must be on our school's basketball team.

Argument 3: Redwood trees grow in California.
Sandy saw a redwood tree growing.
Therefore, she was in California.

Part B

- You can combine some sentences by using the word **who** or **that.**
- You usually use the word **who** to refer to humans. You use the word **that** to refer to things that are not human.
- Here are sample sentences that can be combined:

  They had **gloves.**
  The **gloves** were dirty.
- Here's the combined sentence:

  They had **gloves that** were dirty.
- Here's another sample of sentences that can be combined:

  The **girls** made a poster. All those **girls** were in Ms. Ander's class.
- Here's the combined sentence:

  The **girls who** were in Ms. Ander's class made a poster.
- Here are the steps:
  - ✔ Find the part of the first sentence that is repeated.
  - ✔ Change the second sentence so it starts with **who** or **that.**
  - ✔ Write all the words from the first sentence.
  - ✔ Put the part from the second sentence that begins with **who** or **that** just after the word that part refers to.

Part C Combine these sentences. Use the word **who** or **that.**

1. The boys took a shortcut. Those boys lived on Oak Street.
2. The trucks stopped at a rest station. The station was teeming with people.
3. They helped a little girl. The little girl was lost.
4. The mountain was foggy. The mountain was next to the lake.
5. Pens were on sale. All those pens had a five-year guarantee.

Part D **Sample Argument**

Trucks have tires.
The vehicle in our garage has tires.
Therefore, the vehicle in our garage must be a truck.

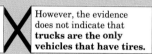

The sample argument concludes that **the vehicle in our garage is a truck.**	X	However, the evidence does not indicate that **trucks are the only vehicles that have tires.**	=	Therefore, **the vehicle in our garage** might be **a motorcycle** or **tricycle.**

Follow the outline diagram to tell about the problem with each argument.

Argument 1: There's a dollar in the street.
Billy is always losing money.
Therefore, that dollar must belong to Billy.

Argument 2: There's an animal sitting in that tree.
Birds sit in trees.
Therefore, that animal must be a bird.

Outline diagram

Argument ___ concludes that ______________ ______________ ______________.	X	However, the evidence does no indicate that ________ [all/only] ______________ ______________.	=	Therefore, ______________ ______________ might ____________ or ______________.

Part E

Sample Sentences

a. Donna and me met Andy.

b. Alex saved some dessert for my friends and me.

c. Marilyn and her stayed up too late.

If a sentence has the wrong pronoun, rewrite the sentence so it is correct.

1. Joel and me watched the ball game.
2. Maggie drove Fred and I to the game.
3. Sally, Amy and I get good grades.
4. Why do you question Donna and I?
5. She and Alex wore running shoes.
6. Him and his brother talk too much.

Part F

- Some rules are **if** rules. These rules have two parts:
  - ☞ The **if** part tells about the things that must take place.
  - ☞ The last part tells what else will happen.
- Here's an **if** rule:

  If an animal runs faster, the animal burns more calories.

- That rule covers many parallel rules that are more specific:

  If a **horse** runs faster, the horse burns more calories.

  If a **goat** runs faster, the goat burns more calories.

- The rule doesn't tell you anything about a **robot** running faster or a **car** running faster, because those things are not animals.

Part G For each rule, write a specific sentence that is covered by the rule.

Rule 1: If you put plants where there is no sunlight, the plants will die.

Rule 2: If an animal gets hungry, the animal will try to find food.

Independent Work

Part H Write about the problem with each argument. Follow the outline diagram.

Here's what Dan said:

Every time my elbow is sore, it rains. I just hurt my elbow. So, it's going to rain pretty soon.

Here's what Julie said:

Every time I walk under a ladder, I have bad luck. I didn't walk under any ladders today. So, I will have good luck tomorrow.

Outline diagram

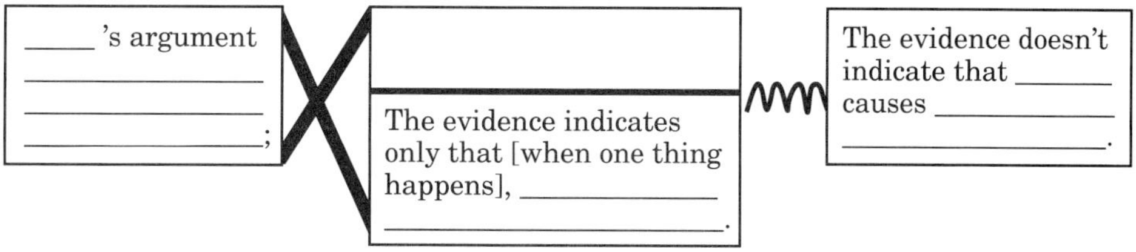

_____ 's argument _____ _____ _____;
The evidence indicates only that [when one thing happens], _____ _____.
The evidence doesn't indicate that _____ causes _____ _____.

Part I Copy each sentence that is a compound sentence. Punctuate it properly. Then circle both subjects and underline both predicates.

1. Her sister is only 8 years old but she looks older.
2. Our neighbors make noise in the morning and very late at night.
3. Candy may taste good but you should avoid eating too much candy.
4. We will go to the mountains or to a wonderful place on the coast.

Lesson 58

Part A

Combine these sentences. Use the word who or that.

1. They went swimming in a river. The river was polluted.
2. The girls found twenty dollars. The girls live next door to me.
3. The scouts slept in a tent. The scouts were studying survival techniques.
4. They bought sweaters. The sweaters had short sleeves.
5. The travelers listened to an old man. That man was very wise.

Part B

Follow the outline diagram to tell about the problem in each of these arguments.

Argument 1: Hammers are tools that have no moving parts.
Uncle Bill has a tool that has no moving parts.
Therefore, Uncle Bill has a hammer.

Argument 2: Days that are warm and sunny occur in spring.
April 3 is a day in spring.
Therefore, April 3 will be warm and sunny.

Argument 3: Plants need sunlight to live.
That plant is dying.
Therefore, that plant must not be getting enough sunlight.

Outline diagram

Argument ___ concludes that ________________ ________________ ________________.	X	However, the evidence does not indicate that ________ [all/only] ________________ ________________.	=	Therefore, ________________ ________________ might ____________ or ________________.

Part C For each rule, write a more specific sentence that is covered by the general rule.

Rule 1: If an object floats in water, the object is less dense than water.

Rule 2: If a solid object cools, the object gets smaller.

Part D Follow the outline diagram to write how you selected the best bike for Carla.

Carla's requirements

1. The bike must have more than 10 speeds.
2. The bike must have a front fender and a rear fender.
3. The bike must weigh no more than 22 pounds.
4. The bike must cost less than $250.

Facts

Bike	Mountain Buddy	Climber	Dirt Scrambler	Speed More	Pedal Pal
Price	$300	$267	$229	$195	$236
Weight	18 lb.	20 lb.	21 lb.	20 lb.	24 lb.
Fenders	none	front and rear	front and rear	front and rear	front and rear
Number of speeds	12	15	18	10	18

Outline diagram

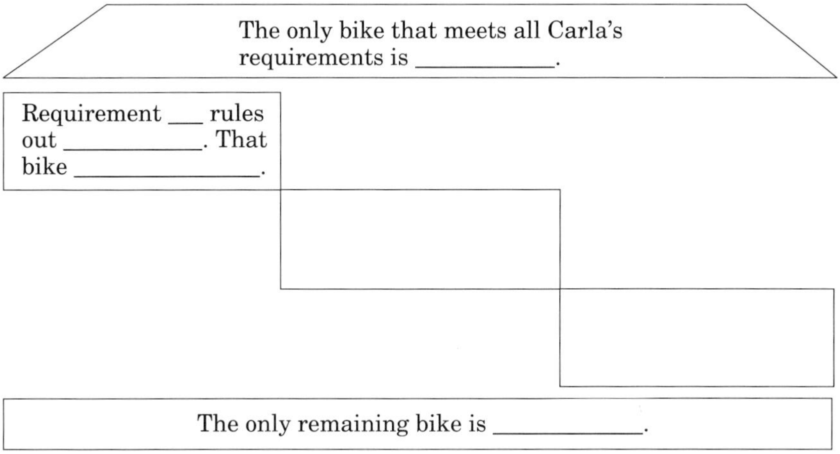

The only bike that meets all Carla's requirements is ___________.
Requirement ___ rules out ___________. That bike ______________.
The only remaining bike is ___________.

Independent Work

Part E Write about the problem with this argument. Follow the appropriate outline diagram.

Here's what Roy said:

Every time our gas gauge reaches empty, our car stops. I'm going to fix that gas gauge so it can't reach the empty mark. Our car will never stop running again.

Part F If a sentence has a wrong pronoun, rewrite the sentence so it is correct.

1. I went to the game with Sam and the rest of them.
2. Will Shirley and me be able to go on the trip?
3. Why did they laugh at him and his dog?
4. Her and her mother are always doing things together.

Part G Copy each sentence that is a compound sentence. Punctuate it properly. Then circle both subjects and underline both predicates.

1. She went to the mall and to the train station near the mall.
2. They indicated that they would have pizza or Chinese food.
3. Their car is old and it has a large dent on one side.
4. Mr. Edison does a lot of complaining but he is nice.

Part H Rewrite each sentence so it is clear.

1. Tammy's father told us about all the fun Tammy had at camp and about the songs she learned after Tammy came home.
2. We learned about the longest war that ever took place in yesterday's reading period.
3. Ms. Anderson told us the story of a puppet who got a longer nose every time he told a lie in the lunchroom.

Lesson 59

Part A Follow the outline diagram to explain the problem with each argument.

Argument 1: Jamal always tracks dirt into the kitchen.
Dirt tracks are in the kitchen.
Therefore, Jamal must have made those dirt tracks.

Argument 2: That picture has a lot of blue in it.
Linda makes pictures with a lot of blue.
Linda must have made that picture.

Outline diagram

Argument ___ concludes that ________________ ________________ ________________.	X	However, the evidence does not indicate that ________ [all/only] ________________ ________________.	=	Therefore, ________________ or ________________ might ________________ ________________.

Part B Use **who** or **that** to combine the sentences in each item.

1. The basketball game was exciting. We saw the basketball game on Saturday.
2. The presents were costly. Uncle Henry bought those presents.
3. We went to a new grocery store. My mother recommended that grocery store.
4. They stopped near a waterfall. The waterfall was over 100 feet high.

Part C

- You've written specific sentences that are based on more general rules. You can also use more general rules to draw conclusions.
- To draw a conclusion you must have a fact that tells about the **if** part of the rule.
- Here's a rule:

  If an object is more dense than water, the object will sink in water.
- Here's a fact that lets you draw a conclusion:

  A rock is more dense than water.
- Here's the conclusion:

  The rock will sink in water.
- Here's another fact that lets you draw a conclusion:

  A steel bar is more dense than water.

Part D

For each **if** rule, write the conclusions that can be made by using the facts.

Rule 1: If an object is left out in the rain, that object will get wet.

Fact A: A shirt is left out in the rain.

Fact B: A dog is left out in the rain.

Fact C: A towel gets wet.

Fact D: A cat gets wet.

Rule 2: If a person runs faster, the person burns more calories.

Fact A: Alice started burning more and more calories.

Fact B: Five girls started running much faster.

Fact C: Tom exercised very hard.

Fact D: Jim started running faster.

Fact E: Andy began to burn lots of calories.

Part E

Rewrite the incorrect sentences so they use the correct pronoun.

1. Tommy didn't say a word to Rita and I.
2. I get angry every time I think about Donald and her.
3. Bob and him played catch in the yard.
4. Tony's brother and me raced to school.

Part F

Follow the outline diagram to write how you selected the best jacket for Terry.

Terry's requirements

1. The jacket must weigh less than 4 pounds.
2. The jacket must be washable.
3. The jacket must provide superior protection against the cold.

Facts

Jacket	Stormbuster	Windblaster	Leader	King Kold	Wilderness
Price	$179.00	$187.99	$156.00	$206.00	$187.00
Weight	4 lb.	3 lb. 2 oz.	2 lb. 8 oz.	3 lb. 7 oz.	4 lb. 3 oz.
Protection against cold	superior	superior	good	superior	superior
Cleaning	washable	dry clean only	washable	washable	washable

Outline diagram

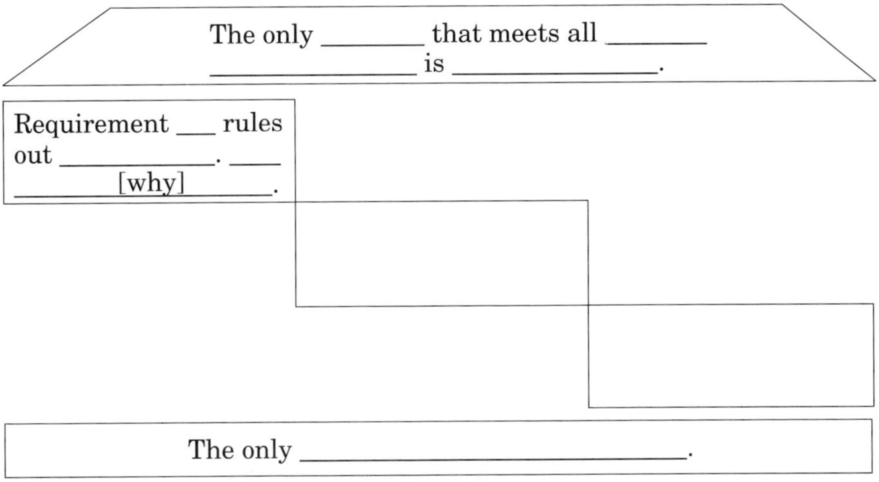

The only ______ that meets all ______
______________ is ______________.
Requirement ___ rules out ____________. ____
________ [why] ________.
The only ____________________.

Independent Work

Part G Copy each sentence. Indicate the subject, the predicate and the part of speech for every word.

1. They discovered a large cave.
2. Will all those clowns chase the baby elephant?
3. Is that fog bank concealing a steep cliff?

Part H Write the two nouns in each sentence. Circle the noun that is more general. Then rewrite the sentence so it ends with an adjective. Indicate the subject, the predicate and the part of speech for every word.

1. His summary was a confusing passage.
2. My mother is a thoughtful person.
3. Their altercation was a disturbing event.

Part I List the objects that each sentence in the description rules out. Then follow the outline diagram to tell about the shorter description.

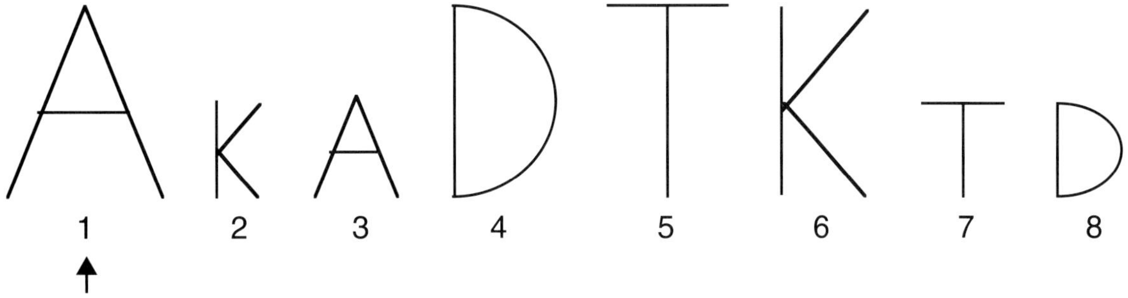

Description

A. The object is one inch high.

B. The object is one of the first six letters of the alphabet.

C. Part of the object is a triangle.

Outline diagram

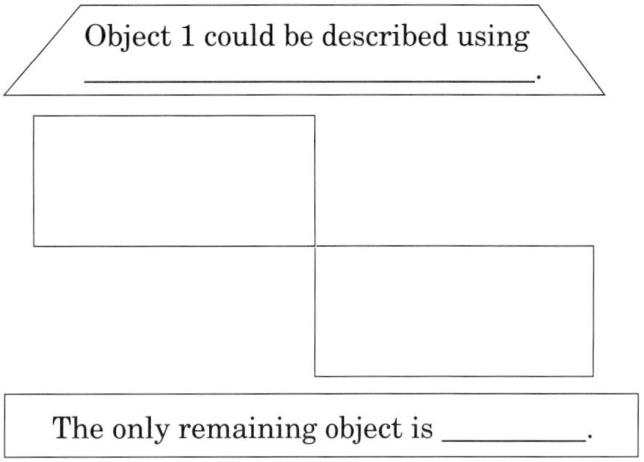

Object 1 could be described using ________________.
The only remaining object is ________.

Lesson 60 – Test 6

Part A For each item, write the combined sentence. Indicate the part of speech for each word.

1. She was ambitious.
   She was a student.
2. My uncle is a plumber.
   My uncle is thorough.

Part B If a sentence has a wrong pronoun, rewrite the sentence so it is correct.

1. She wanted to go to the party with Shay and I.
2. Sally and me are pretty good friends.
3. Rita, Pearl and I are going to meet in front of school.
4. Did they buy gifts for David, Alex or me?

Part C Follow the outline diagram and write two paragraphs about the most practical plan for Don to get to River City and back home.

Don's goal is to visit a friend who lives in River City.

Facts

- River City is 450 miles away.
- Don plans to go there next month.
- Don has 4 days to get to River City, visit with his friend and return.
- Don has $200 for his trip.

Possible ways that Don could visit his friend

Plan 1 (Building a car): Don could build a car and then drive it to River City.

Plan 2 (Taking the bus): Don could take the bus to River City and back.

Plan 3 (Walking): Don could walk to River City and back.

Plan 4 (Hitchhiking): Don could hitchhike to River City and back.

Outline diagram

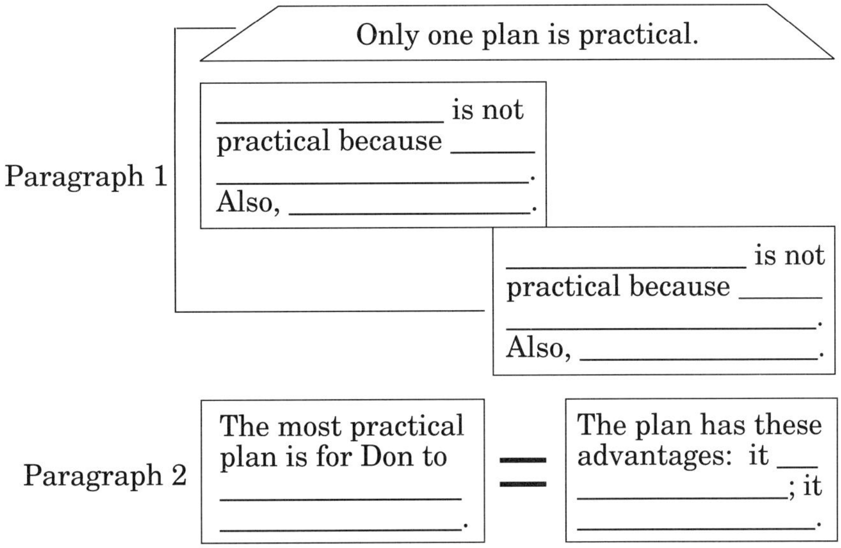

Lesson 61

Part A

- Sometimes a person says things that let you know the general rule the person is using.
- Here's something that Bill said:

  "I know my teacher hates me because my teacher gave me a bad grade."
- Bill believes that the teacher follows a rule about giving students bad grades.
- Here's how to figure out the **rule:**

  You start with the part of the sentence that begins with **because** and make a general **if** rule that's based on that part:

  I know my teacher hates me **because my teacher gave me a bad grade.**
- Here's the **if** rule:

  If my teacher gives any student a bad grade, she hates that student.
- Here's the whole argument:

  If my teacher gives a student a bad grade, she hates that student. My teacher gave me a bad grade. Therefore, my teacher hates me.

Part B

Sample Item

Rita said, "I'll vote for Kenya because I know that she'll win the election."

If I know that a person will win an election, . . .

Write the **if** rule for these statements.

1. Andy said, "Ted got warts because Ted touched a toad."
2. Mr. Rowe said, "I know it will rain soon because my knee hurts."

Part C

- Some sentences have more than one noun in the subject. Those subjects may have the word **of**.
- The word that comes before **of** is usually a noun.
- The last word in the subject is usually a noun.
- Here are subjects:

  a. Five rings of fire ________.

  b. A handful of salty peanuts ________.

Part D

For each sentence, write the subject and write **N** above each noun in the subject.

1. The group of girls looked at photographs.
2. Ten tall trees cast long shadows.
3. That bunch of grapes looks delicious.
4. Those large bundles of brown paper were recycled.

Part E Follow the outline diagram to write how you selected the best house for the Hunters.

Requirements for the Hunter family's new house

1. The house must be within 6 blocks of an elementary school.
2. The house must be within 1 mile of a shopping center.
3. The house must have 4 bedrooms and 2 baths.
4. The house must cost no more than $100,000.
5. The house must be in good repair.

Facts

Location	33 Elm	18 Maple	26 W. 5th	200 Laurel	56 E. Main
Distance from elementary school	4 blocks	5 blocks	7 blocks	4 blocks	5 blocks
Distance from shopping center	$\frac{7}{10}$ mile	$1\frac{1}{2}$ miles	4 blocks	3 blocks	3 blocks
Number of bedrooms	4	4	4	4	3
Number of baths	2	2	2	2	2
Cost	$99,000	$98,000	$97,000	$86,000	$103,000
Condition	good	needs repairs	good	superior	good

Outline diagram

Paragraph 1

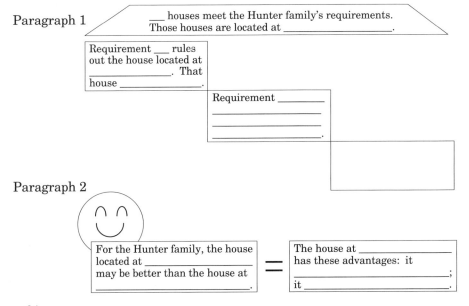

___ houses meet the Hunter family's requirements. Those houses are located at ________________.

Requirement ___ rules out the house located at ________________. That house ________________.

Requirement ________ ________________ ________________ ________________.

Paragraph 2

For the Hunter family, the house located at ________________ may be better than the house at ________________.

=

The house at ________________ has these advantages: it ________________; it ________________.

Part F

- You've learned that you can make a deduction using two sentences that have some of the same parts.
- Here are two sentences that can be used to form a deduction:

  Sally has all types of jewelry.
  Sally has a necklace.

- One of those sentences goes in the evidence, and one goes in the conclusion.
- The more general sentence goes in the evidence, and the more specific sentence goes in the conclusion.
- Here's the whole deduction:

  Sally has all types of jewelry.
  A necklace is a type of jewelry.
  Therefore, Sally has a necklace.

- Sometimes, people make up arguments that are upside-down. They are upside-down because they have the more specific sentence in the evidence and the more general sentence as the conclusion.
- Here's an upside-down argument:

  Sally has a necklace.
  A necklace is a type of jewelry.
  Therefore, Sally has all types of jewelry.

Part G For each argument, write **more specific** or **more general** to tell about the conclusion. Then rewrite those arguments that have a conclusion that is more general than the evidence.

Argument 1: This pizza came from Tony's.
This pizza is terrible.
Therefore, all the food from Tony's is terrible.

Argument 2: Dan is good at all sports.
Football is a sport.
Therefore, Dan is good at football.

Argument 3: Tom is from Calhoun County.
Tom is tall.
Therefore, all men from Calhoun County are tall.

Argument 4: All the Rothbergs have airplanes.
Mary is a Rothberg.
Therefore, Mary has an airplane.

Argument 5: Mrs. Smith loves flowers.
Petunias are flowers.
Therefore, Mrs. Smith loves petunias.

Independent Work

Part H Rewrite each sentence that has an incorrect pronoun.

1. She was jealous of Marvin and I.
2. They had presents for James, Wendy and me.
3. David and me like swimming in the new pool.
4. Martin kept arguing with his brother and I.
5. I played ball with Julio and him.

Part I

Copy each compound sentence and place the comma. Mark both subjects and predicates. Don't copy sentences that are not compound sentences.

1. Edna wanted to go with us but she had no money.
2. His new car had lots of room and was fun to drive.
3. They decided that they would go to the park or stay at home and watch the game on TV.
4. She went skating but she did not have much fun.

Part J

Read the if rule and the facts. Write all the conclusions that are possible.

If Rule: If you add pepper to food, the food will taste hotter.

Fact A: Don added pepper to his salad.

Fact B: Penny made her hamburger much hotter.

Fact C: Jose's tacos are hotter than Hilda's tacos.

Part K

Write about the problem with this argument.

Jill said, "When the rooster crows the sun comes up. I'm going to try to make the rooster crow. Then the sun will come up."

Lesson 62

Part A

For each item, write the subject and write **N** above each noun.

1. The shingles on the roof started sliding.
2. The batch of cookies tasted good.
3. Three pairs of green pants were in the dryer.
4. Twenty members of the club worked with orphans.
5. The worms in the sand pile were pink.

Part B

Figure out the **if** rule for these statements.

1. Rita said, "I know Jimmy will get rich because he has rich relatives."
2. Mrs. Finch said, "The weather will change because there's a halo around the moon."
3. Dennis said, "I know that boy is a basketball player because he is very tall."

Part C

Sample Item

Peter said, "I know Alice is mad because she is frowning."

For each sentence, write a three-sentence deduction.

1. Heather said, "I know Mr. Green is rich because he drives an expensive car."
2. Denny said, "Today will be a bad day because it is Friday the 13th."

Part D

- For some of the work you'll do, you'll draw inferences.
- Inferences are like conclusions. When you don't know exactly what happened but you use clues to figure out what you think happened, you're **drawing an inference,** or **inferring.**
- If you see a dent in a car and if that dent has red paint on it, you could draw the inference that a red vehicle banged into the car. You could be wrong because the paint may have been on the car before the dent was created. But if you use the clues that are present to figure out what **probably** happened, you're drawing a **reasonable** inference.
- Look at the picture of Peter.
- You know how to infer Peter's rule from what he is saying.

- Look at the picture of the footprints. Those footprints match Jimmy's shoes.

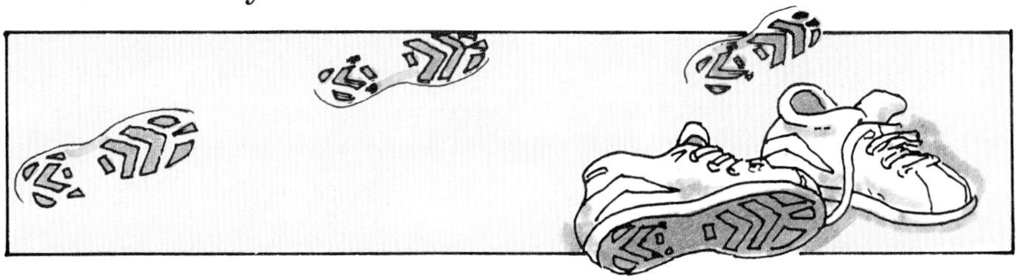

- We can infer that Jimmy made those prints, but we can't be positive. Maybe somebody else wore Jimmy's shoes. However, it's more likely that Jimmy wore the shoes.

Part E Follow the outline diagram to write about the problem with Blinky's account.

Blinky's account

Two giants rode their horses into Lisa's campsite. One of them pulled down the clothesline and sent Lisa's clothes flying onto the ground. The other giant grabbed the rope and rode up under the tree. He reached up and tied one end of the rope to the tree. Then both giants rode away. One of them called back to Lisa, "Have a good day."

Outline diagram

________ inferred that ____________________ ____________________;	however, that inference is not probable. A more probable inference is that _____ ____________________________________.

Part F For each argument, write **more specific** or **more general** to tell about the conclusion. Then rewrite those arguments that have a conclusion that is more general than the evidence.

Argument 1: Mrs. Smith make clothes for all of her children.
Meg is one of Mrs. Smith's children.
Therefore, Mrs. Smith makes clothes for Meg.

Argument 2: Jane is rich.
Jane is from Billtown.
Therefore, everyone in Billtown must be rich.

Argument 3: It rained on Tuesday.
Tuesday was the fourth day in March.
Therefore, it rained on all the days in March.

Argument 4: Every tide pool is full of living things.
There are tidepools in Bay City.
Therefore, all the tide pools in Bay City are full of living things.

Independent Work

Part G Use **who** or **that** to combine the sentences in each item.

1. The men were cold. The men were working on top of the tower.
2. We went to the park. The park was near our house.
3. They looked at the mountains. The mountains were 50 miles away.
4. The girls were proud. Those girls won the contest.

Part H Write about the problem with this argument.

Argument: Crickets make noise at night.
There was a lot of noise last night.
Therefore, there must have been a lot of crickets out last night.

Part I Follow the outline diagram and write two paragraphs about the most practical plan for Hilda.

Goal

Hilda's goal is to have a new car.

Here are facts about Hilda:

- Hilda is 18 years old.
- She has saved $17.50.
- She does not have a job.
- She is very talented and could easily work as an artist.
- The car she wants costs $24,600.

Possible ways that Hilda could buy a car:

Plan 1 (Marrying):	Marry a millionaire and have him buy the car.
Plan 2 (Getting a job):	Get a job as an artist and save enough money to make payments on the car.
Plan 3 (Waiting for a gift):	Wait for somebody to give her the money.

Outline diagram

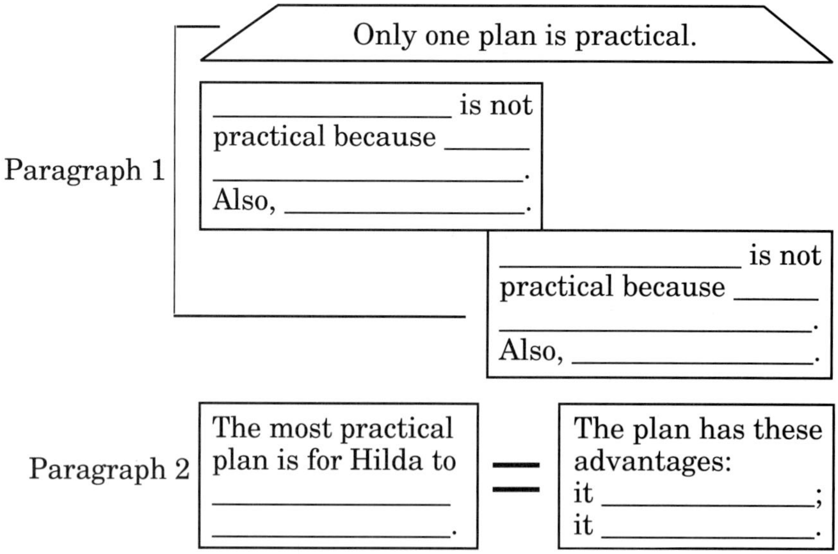

Lesson 63

Part A Follow the outline diagram to write about the problem with Blinky's account.

Blinky's account

Tom and Shola went inside. Then twelve neighbors with shovels quickly shoveled the walk. When Tom and Shola finished putting on their snow outfits, the walk was cleaned, and the neighbors had left two shovels on the porch.

Tom said, "We don't have to shovel the walk, so let's build a snowman."

Outline diagram

________ inferred that ____________________ ____________________;	however, that inference is not probable. A more probable inference is that _____ ____________________.

Part B Write the subject of each sentence. Write **N** above each noun.

1. Many children prefer milk.
2. A gathering in Oklahoma took place last week.
3. A collection of paintings burned last year.
4. Four teams of players went to Chicago.
5. A very large pile started to form.

Part C **Sample Argument**

I know three men who have long hair.
All of them are lazy.
Therefore, all men with long hair are lazy.

Argument 1 concludes that all men with long hair are lazy;	however, the conclusion is more general than the evidence. Evidence about **three men with long hair** cannot lead to a proper conclusion about **all men with long hair.**

Follow the outline diagram to tell about the problem with the arguments.

Argument 1: This pizza came from Tony's.
The pizza is terrible.
Therefore, all food from Tony's must be terrible.

Argument 2: Tom is from Calhoun County.
Tom is tall.
Therefore, all men from Calhoun County are tall.

Outline diagram

Argument __ concludes ____________________ ____________________;	however, the conclusion is more general than the evidence. Evidence about [a specific category] cannot lead to a proper conclusion about [a general category].

Part D Follow the outline diagram to write about the possibility that Tom's test does not rule out.

Here's Tom's problem:

Tom has three large bags. One of them is not the same weight as the other two. Tom doesn't know which bag that is. He doesn't know whether that bag is lighter or heavier than the other two. So Tom puts bags A and B on a balance scale. The side with bag A goes down.

Tom's conclusion

Bag A is the bag that doesn't weigh the same amount as the other bags. Bag A is heavier than the others.

Outline diagram

Paragraph 1

Tom's test is inadequate. It does not rule out the possiblity that ______________.

To rule out that possibilty, Tom could ___________ _________________________.

Paragraph 2

If the scale ___________, _______ is not the same weight as the other bags. _______ is ____________.

If the scale ___________, _______ is not the same weight as the other bags. _______ is ____________.

Independent Work

Part E Write about the problem in Roger's account. Use the appropriate outline diagram.

Roger's account

We went on a trip from our house. First we went 5 miles north to Tiny Town. Then we went 5 miles east to the river. Then we went 5 miles south to the park. After leaving the park, we went back home. That trip was 12 miles.

Part F Write about the problem with this argument.

Argument: Many animals that fly have feathers.
I see a flying animal.
It must have feathers.

Lesson 64

Part A Follow the outline diagram to tell about the problem with the argument.

Argument: Jane is rich.
Jane is from Billtown.
Therefore, everybody from Billtown must be rich.

Outline diagram

The argument concludes ______________________ ______________________;	however, the conclusion is more general than the evidence. Evidence about [a specific category] cannot lead to a proper conclusion about [a general category].

Part B

- Sometimes adjectives have two words.
- Here's a sentence:

  Jimmy had a dog.
- Here's a sentence with a two-word adjective:

  Jimmy had a short-tailed dog.
- The words **short-tailed** have a hyphen between them to show that the dog wasn't **short.** And the dog wasn't just a dog **with a tail.** The dog was **short-tailed.**
- Here's another sentence:

  Jimmy has a short-tailed, long-eared dog.
- The adjective **long-eared** is also made up of two words. The hyphen tells you that the dog wasn't **long;** the dog was **long-eared.**

Part C

Sample Item

Mary sat on it.

Make each description more specific by writing a two-word adjective.

a. A dog followed Henry home.

b. Fran found a toad.

Part D

Sample Items

a. A sack of peanuts ______ on the table.

b. A group of soldiers ______ near the river.

c. A batch of cookies ______ in the oven.

d. Three cups of sand ______ on the floor.

Write each sentence with the correct verb.

1. Three bowls of brown rice ______ expensive.
2. A group of bunnies ______ on the lawn.
3. The citizens of Canada ______ angry.
4. A stack of pancakes ______ on her plate.
5. A ton of bricks ______ in the truck.

Part E Follow the outline diagram to write about the problem with Fran's test.

Fran's test

Fran said, "My brother is amazing. He cannot tell the color of cards or blocks or any solid object. He's colorblind. But he can tell whether traffic lights are red or green. I guess there is something about lights that is different from solid objects. He can see the color of lights."

Blake disagreed. So Fran did a test with her brother. They went to a corner and looked at the traffic light. When it was red, her brother said, "It's red." When it was green, he said, "It's green."

Fran concluded, "I told you that he can see the color of lights."

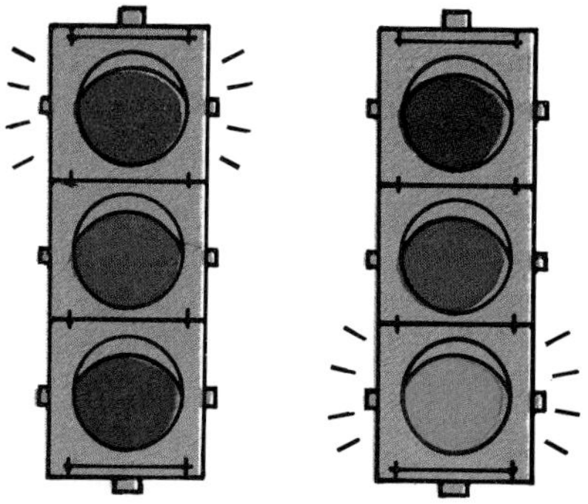

Outline diagram

Paragraph 1

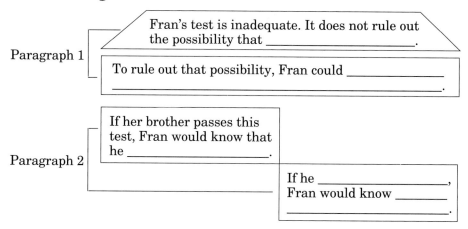

Fran's test is inadequate. It does not rule out the possibility that ______________________.

To rule out that possibility, Fran could ______________ ______________________________.

Paragraph 2

If her brother passes this test, Fran would know that he ____________________.

If he ____________________, Fran would know ________ ____________________.

Independent Work

Part F For each item, write a three-sentence deduction. Write the **if** rule, the fact and the conclusion.

1. I know that Bob won't be ready on time because he's telling jokes.
2. Frita can't be trusted because she has a brother who went to prison.

Part G Write about the problem with this argument.

Argument: Mrs. Johnson makes delicious chicken dinners.
The chicken dinner I had the other day was super.
It must have been prepared by Mrs. Johnson.

Part H Rewrite each sentence that has an incorrect pronoun.

1. We wanted to buy presents for Charley and him.
2. Her and her parents went fishing.
3. My brother and me had a jumping contest.
4. She laughed at Mark and me.

Lesson 65

Part A Follow the outline diagram to write about the problem with Blinky's account.

Blinky's account

Ted said to Sally, "I know a person who sells hats. She lives a few blocks from here. We can buy hats from her. Then we won't get wet."

So Ted and Sally went to Mrs. Rodriguez's house. They looked at different hats and decided to buy a couple of big ones. Then they put on the hats and went back to the bus stop. By now the rain was coming down pretty hard.

Outline diagram

________ inferred that ____________________ ____________________;	however, that inference is not probable. A more probable inference is that _____ ______________________________.

Part B **Sample Items**

a. She was on a diet that was free of fat.

b. He had a body that was shaped like a bell.

Rewrite each sentence so it has a two-word adjective.

1. We watched a spider with long legs.
2. They looked at a shirt that had short sleeves.
3. I like rooms with light colors.

Part C Write these sentences with the correct verb, **is** or **are.**

1. The players on the team ______ angry.
2. The box of toys ______ open.
3. The cartons of milk ______ leaking.
4. Six chairs in the room ______ dusty.
5. The bunch of bananas ______ still green.
6. Groups of children ______ singing.

Part D Follow the outline diagram to write about the problem with Sam's test.

Sam's test

Sam and Sid saw an old man in the park. The man seemed to be lost.

Sid said, "I wonder if that old man knows how to speak English."

"I'll find out," Sam said. He went over to the old man and said, "Do you know how to speak English?"

The old man said, "Yes, indeed."

Sam said, "Do you live nearby?"

"Yes, indeed."

Sam said, "Are you waiting for somebody?"

The old man said, "Yes, indeed."

Sam reported back to Sid. "He can speak English, and he's not lost. He's just waiting for somebody."

Outline diagram

Paragraph 1

Sam's test ________________. It does not ______________________________.

To rule out ______________________________ ______________________________.

Paragraph 2

If ________________ ________________ ________________.

If ________________ ________________ ________________.

Independent Work

Part E Follow the outline diagram to explain how you identified the mystery word.

Possibilities

dog	Dan
dig	sled
girl	bad

?
Mystery Word

Clues

A. One letter in the word is the fourth letter of the alphabet.

B. The letter is a small d, not a capital D.

C. The word is usually an adjective.

Outline diagram

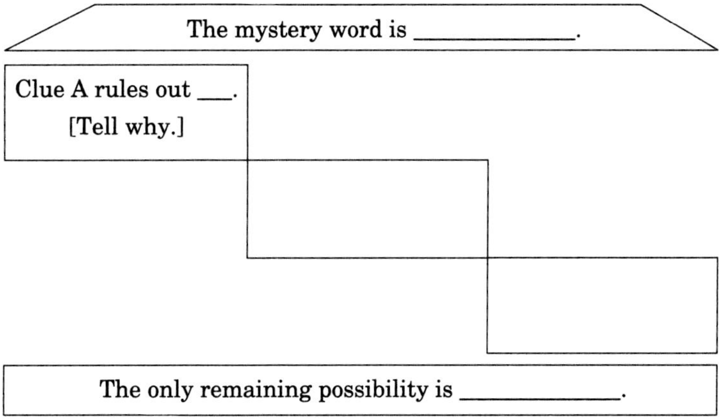

The mystery word is ______________.
Clue A rules out ___.
[Tell why.]
The only remaining possibility is ______________.

Part F Write directions for making this figure.

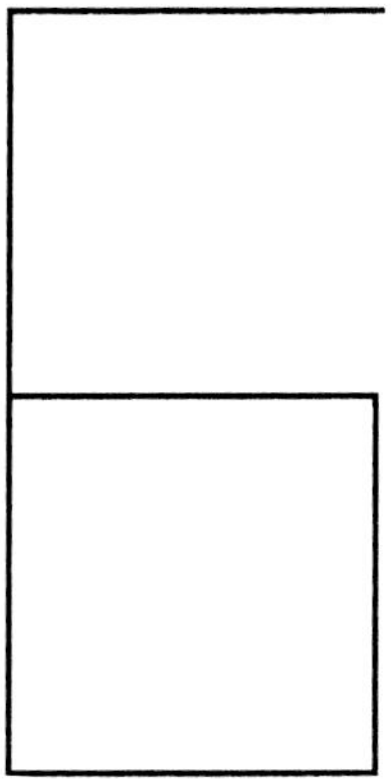

Lesson 66

Part A | Rewrite each sentence that has the wrong verb.

Passage

1 James picked flowers. 2 He put them inside his house. 3 A large bunch of bright red flowers was on the kitchen table. 4 Five vases of flowers were in the dining room. 5 A rose with many yellow petals were in the living room. 6 The windows of the garage were decorated with blue flowers. 7 A large bunch of red-and-yellow daisies were in the hall.

Part B | Rewrite each sentence so it has a two-word adjective in front of the noun.

1. They listened to a sound that had a high pitch.
2. Mrs. Brown was a person who dressed well.
3. Jimmy was a boy with a happy face.
4. They sat in a room that was half painted.

Part C | Follow the outline diagram to write about the problem with the argument.

Argument

I know that everybody in our class voted for Kim to be the new school president. Therefore, everybody in the whole school must have voted for Kim.

Outline diagram

Part D Follow the outline diagram to write how you selected the best bike for Sid.

Sid's requirements

1. The bike must cost less than $300.
2. The bike must weigh less than 24 pounds.
3. The bike must have more than 12 speeds.

Facts

Bike	Mountain Buddy	Hill Boy	Dirt Climber	Speed More	Pedal Pal
Price	$300	$267	$229	$195	$236
Weight	18 lb.	20 lb.	21 lb.	20 lb.	24 lb.
Fenders	none	front and rear	front and rear	front and read	front and rear
Number of speeds	12	15	18	10	18

Outline diagram

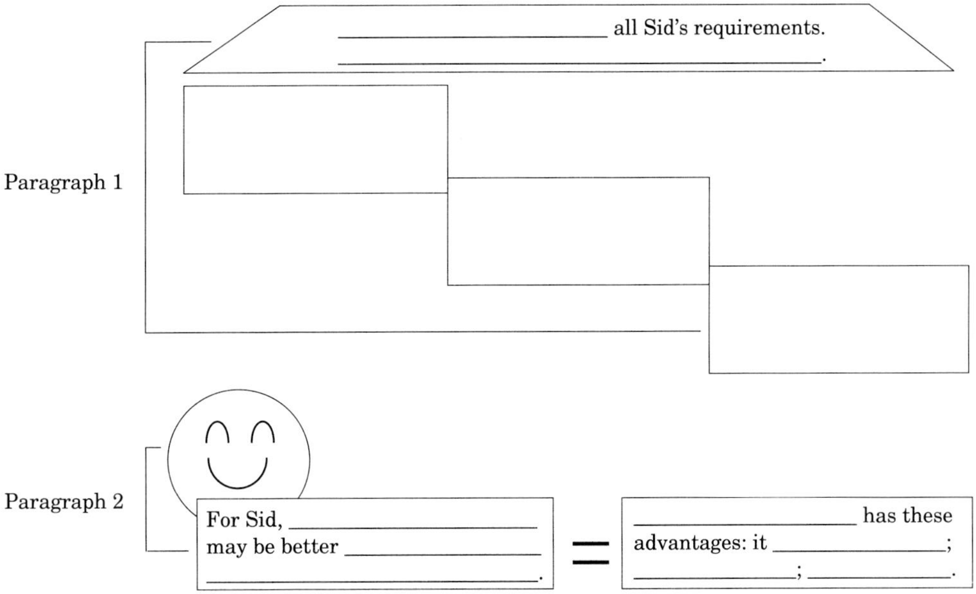

__________ all Sid's requirements.
__________.
Paragraph 1
Paragraph 2
For Sid, __________ may be better __________ __________.
=
__________ has these advantages: it __________; __________; __________.

Independent Work

Part E Explain the problem with each argument.

Argument 1: Mr. Briggs loves to buy things that are on sale.
Speedfreak running shoes are on sale.
Therefore, Mr. Briggs is going to buy a pair of Speedfreaks.

Argument 2: Joe plays on the Blaster football team.
That team is very bad.
Therefore, Joe must be a very bad player.

Outline diagram

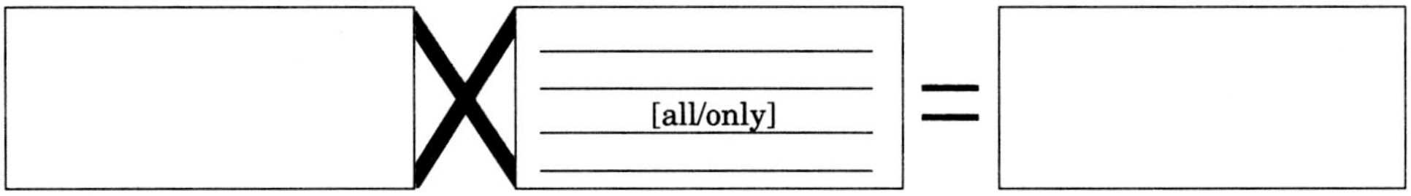

Lesson 67

Part A Follow the outline diagram to write about the problem with Sam's test.

Sam's test

Sam did an experiment with maple seeds. He planted 600 seeds at a depth of one-half inch below the surface of the dirt. He controlled the temperature of the soil so it was above 60 degrees Fahrenheit. Nearly all the seeds sprouted.

He planted another batch of seeds two inches deep. He put them in a place that had a temperature that was less than 60 degrees. Almost none of those seeds sprouted.

Sam's conclusion

A temperature above 60 degrees causes the seeds to sprout.

Outline diagram

Paragraph 1

Sam's test is inadequate. It does not rule out ______________________________.

To rule out that possibility, Sam could ______________ ______________________________.

Paragraph 2

If ____________________, Sam would know ________ ____________________.

If ____________________, Sam would know ________ ____________________.

Part B The passage and graph do not agree. Write about the problems.

Passage

The United States uses a higher percentage of its grain to feed livestock than any other nation uses. The country with the second-highest percentage is Germany. Japan, China and India use less than 40% of their grain to feed livestock. Brazil uses a higher percentage of grain to feed livestock than Japan does.

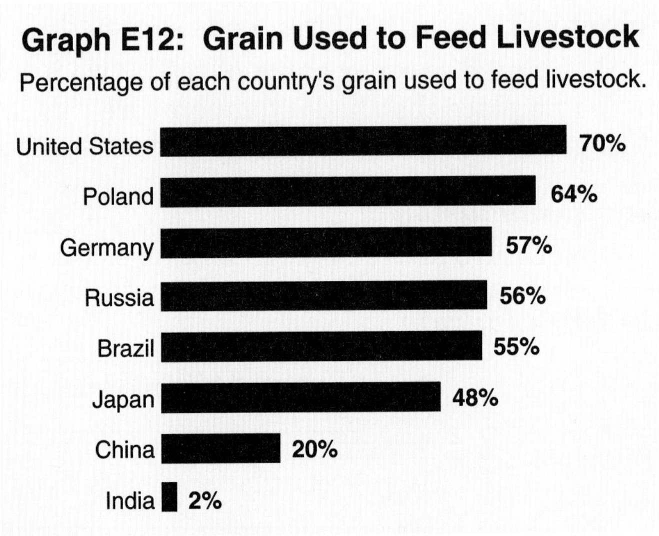

Part C **Sample Sentence** They sat near a stream that was flowing fast.

Rewrite each sentence so it has a two-word adjective. Then mark the part of speech for nouns, verbs, pronouns and adjectives.

1. They laughed at a dog that looked funny.
2. They picked flowers that had a sweet smell.
3. They listened to music that sounded strange.

Independent Work

Part D Explain the problem with each of these arguments.

Here's what Joey said:

Watchdogs keep burglars away from houses. Burglars never go to Mr. Smith's house. Therefore, Mr. Smith must have a watchdog.

Outline diagram

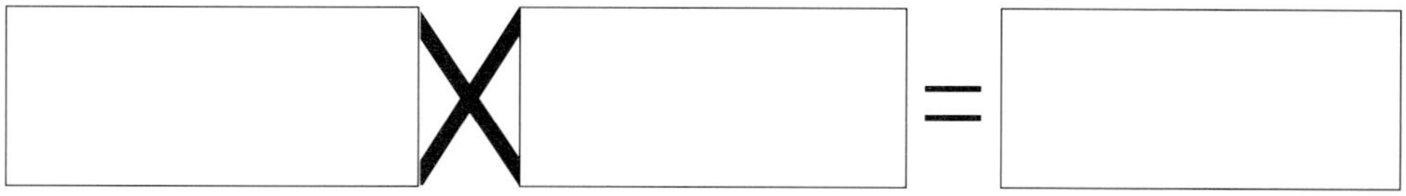

Here's what April said:

Mr. Harrison became richer every time he got another dog. He has 11 dogs. I'm going to get 12 dogs. Then I'll be richer than Mr. Harrison.

Outline diagram

Part E Write a three-sentence deduction. Construct the **if** rule that Edna uses. Then write the fact and the conclusion.

Here's what Edna said:

You can tell that James will never succeed in business because he doesn't look at you when he talks to you.

Lesson 68

Part A

- Some two-word adjectives do not end in **i-n-g** or **e-d.** Those are adjectives that have a number.
- Sample sentence:

  They wrote an adjective with two words.
- The noun for the sentence is **adjective.**
- Here's the sentence:

  They wrote a two-word adjective.
- Remember, if the adjective has a number, you usually don't have to end the other word in **e-d** or **i-n-g.**

Part B

Rewrite these sentences. Use two-word adjectives.

1. The man bought a suit that had three pieces.
2. Mary went on a vacation that lasted five days.
3. They watched a show that was in two parts.
4. We are going on a run that is five miles.

Part C Follow the outline diagram to write about the problems with Dr. Jason's account.

Dr. Jason's response to the question, "How many bones are in the human body?"

Dr. Jason said, "There are 206 bones in the human body."

He added, "It's easy to remember the number of bones in the human body and where they are. There are 75 on the left side of the body. There are 75 on the right side of the body, and there are 50 in the middle of the body. The bones in the middle include the spine. There are 33 separate bones in the spine."

Dr. Jason added, "One of the easiest bones to remember is the humerus. Think of where your funny bone is. Very close to the funny bone is the humerus, which is in your lower arm."

Outline diagram

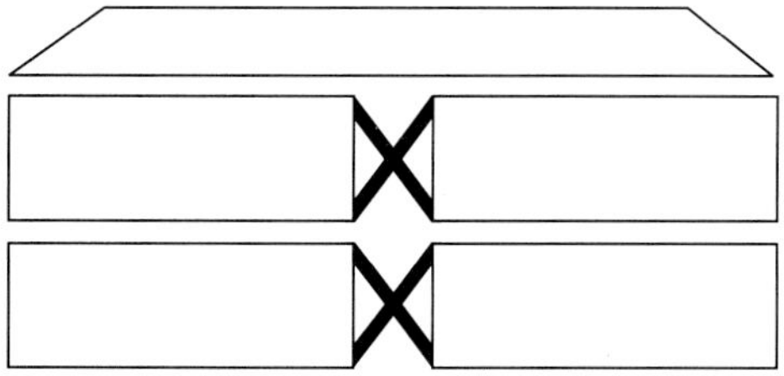

Part D Write about the problem with Blinky's account.

Blinky's account

A fire maniac saw the cat jump onto the shelf and knock the candle off. That gave the maniac an idea. He snuck into Mrs. Smith's house, and while she wasn't looking, he found the candle on the floor. He lit it and set fire to the papers. Then he ran out of the house so that Mrs. Smith wouldn't know what he'd done.

Outline diagram

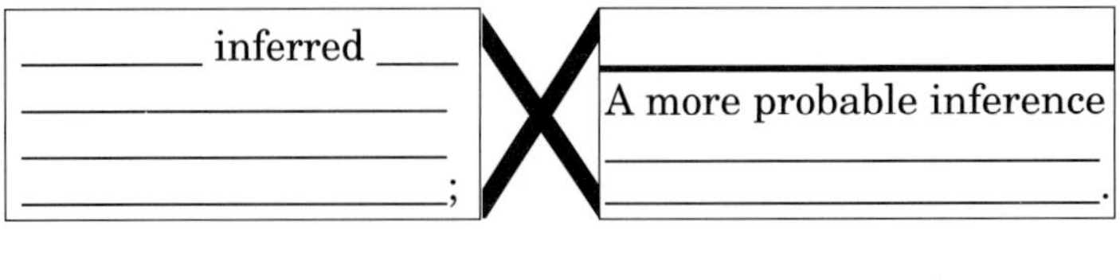

Independent Work

Part E Write about the problem with Pam's account.

Pam's account

Jerry thinks that I gave him the three-day measles, but that's not possible. I looked up the facts on the three-day measles, and here's what I found out. You can spread the disease to other people on the first day you come down with the measles and for four days after that. I came down with the measles on April 1st. I didn't see Jerry until April 5th, so I couldn't have given him the measles.

Part F Edit this passage. Every sentence has a problem. Rewrite the entire passage.

Passage

A large flock of birds were flying south. The birds flew directly over my mother and I. My mother took some excellent pictures of those birds using a camera and a tripod. One of her best pictures are in our living room.

Part G Follow the directions to write a four-sentence description of the arrowed object.

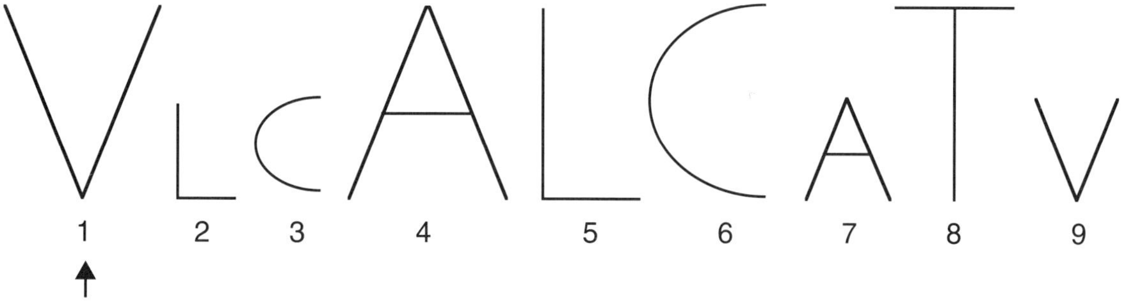

1. Write the sentence that rules out only objects 3 and 6.
2. Write the sentence that rules out only objects 4 and 7.
3. Write the sentence that rules out only objects 2, 5 and 8.
4. Write the sentence that rules out only object 9.

Lesson 69

Part A Write about the problem with Hilda's argument.

Here's what Hilda said:

I was in the gym at Dunn School. The gym was very noisy. Therefore, Dunn School must be a terribly noisy place.

Part B

- These words are **conjunctions:**

  and **but** **or**

- **Conjunctions** join, and that's what these words do when they combine parts or combine sentences.
- To indicate what part of speech a conjunction is, you'll write the letter **C** above the word.

Part C For each sentence pair, write a combined sentence with the appropriate conjunction. Punctuate the sentence correctly. Label the parts of speech, including conjunctions.

1. The field had short grass. The grass concealed 50 quail.
2. Their hands were filthy. Their clothes were black.
3. She had group-leader skills. She worked long hours.

Part D Write about the problem with Fran's statements.

Here's what Fran said:

Mrs. Johnson fixes wonderful chicken and makes great pizzas. She's going to fix a stew for us. I know it will be wonderful.

Part E Explain the problem with the situation described below. Start with a summary. Tell what Henry could do to rule out the possibility that he did not consider. Then tell what he would know from either outcome of the experiment you design.

Situation

Jill and Henry each made a batch of fudge. Jill used two cups of sugar in her fudge. She also allowed the fudge to reach a temperature of 235 degrees before she poured it into a pan. Henry used three cups of sugar and allowed his fudge to reach 275 degrees before he poured it into a pan. Jill's fudge was perfect, but Henry's was as hard as a rock.

Henry concluded, "I know what I did wrong. I used too much sugar. If I had used less sugar, my fudge would have been perfect."

Independent Work

Part F Follow the instructions to write a description about the arrowed object.

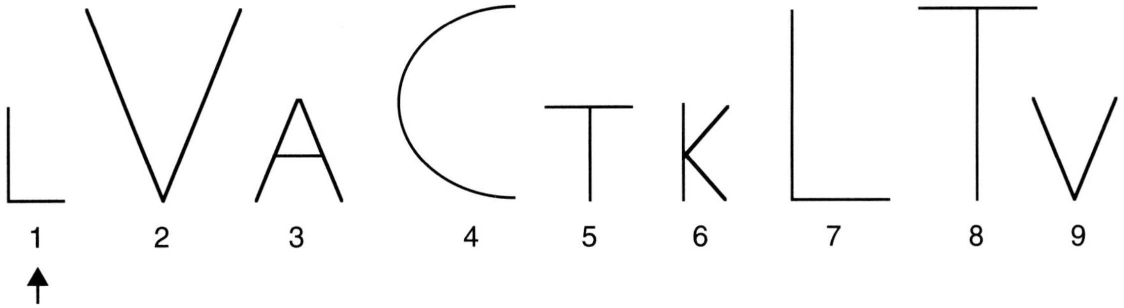

1. Write the sentence that rules out only objects 3, 4 and 6.
2. Write the sentence that rules out only objects 2, 7 and 8.
3. Write the sentence that rules out only object 9.
4. Write the sentence that rules out only object 5.

Part G

1. Write one sentence that tells how to make object 1 in part F.
2. Write one sentence that tells how to make object 2 in part F.

Part H

Write a three-statement deduction. Start with the **if** rule. Write the fact and the conclusion.

I haven't done very well in math before, but I know that I will do well this year because I'm working hard in math, and I'm thinking about math more.

Key

1. The field had short grass, but the grass concealed 50 quail.
   A N V A N C A N V A N
2. Their hands were filthy, and their clothes were black.
   A N V A C A N V A
3. She had group-leader skills, and she worked long hours.
   P V A N C P V A N

Lesson 70 — Test 7

Part A Explain the problem with Amy's experiment.

Here's what Ted said:

Amy has a very interesting theory about liquids. She told me about it the other day. She said, "If you take two liquids that are really different from each other and pour them into a container, the liquid that you pour in first will stay on the bottom, and the liquid that you pour in second will stay on top."

I told her that her theory didn't make any sense. So she said that she'd prove her theory. She got a large glass. Then she got a bottle of oil and a bottle of cola.

She said, "Oil and cola are liquids that are greatly different from each other."

She poured the cola into her glass. She said, "The cola is on the bottom, and it will stay on the bottom when I add the oil."

Then she poured in oil. And what do you know? The oil stayed on top, just like she said it would. You could see the cola on the bottom and oil on top. Wow. That convinced me that she was right about the first liquid staying on the bottom.

Part B Explain the problem with Blinky's explanation.

Blinky's account

The good witch of the south waved her wand above Sandra and her dog. The dog suddenly had little ice skates on his little feet. Sandra suddenly had big ice skates on her big feet. And the horse was suddenly tied to the tree. The good witch walked around near the horse, leaving footprints in the snow. Then she said, "Have a good day," and she disappeared.

Part C Explain the problem with Blinky's argument.

Blinky's argument

Blinky said, "Sandra loves lemons. Lemons are a type of citrus fruit. Therefore, Sandra loves all types of citrus fruit."

Part D Write a three-statement deduction for this statement. Write the inferred **if** rule, the fact and the conclusion.

I know that the new boy in our class is an animal lover because he has two cats.

Lesson 71 – Team Activity

- You've worked with outline diagrams that tell about problems with different kinds of arguments, but you've never made up arguments for these outline diagrams.
- Your team is going to construct an argument for the diagram below. Your argument won't be exactly like any of the arguments you've worked with, but it will be faulty, just like the other arguments.
- After your team makes up the argument, you'll explain the problems with the argument by following the outline diagram and writing a passage.

Outline diagram

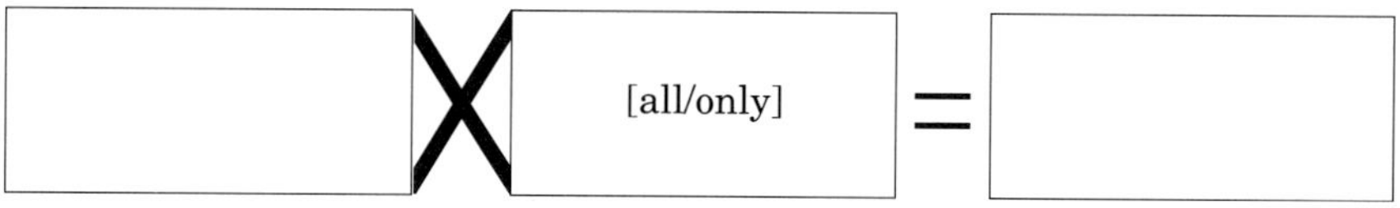
[all/only]

Lesson 72 – Team Activity

- Here's another outline diagram that you've used:

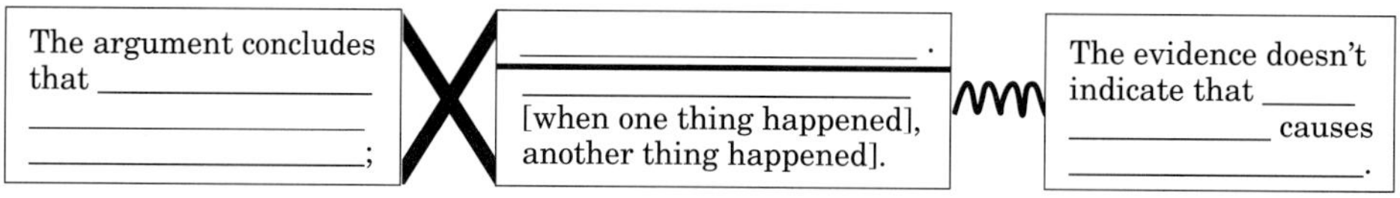
The argument concludes that ______ ______ ______;
______.
______ [when one thing happened], another thing happened].
The evidence doesn't indicate that ______ ______ causes ______.

- Your team is going to make up an argument for the outline diagram. Then your team will write a passage to explain the problem with your argument.
- Your argument will be original. It will not be exactly like any of the arguments in your book.
- For this diagram, think of people you know who have strange superstitious behaviors. You may be able to use one of those behaviors for your argument.

Lesson 73 – Team Activity

Rewrite the landlord's instructions. Use only simple words. Then write a report explaining the problems with his restrictions.

Here's what Mr. Thompson's landlord said:

You are permitted to have pets in your apartment; however, not all pets are permitted. No aquatic creatures are allowed. A pet must be an arboreal creature, but the pet cannot be in the class of Mammalia. The pet must be aerial. However, the pet may be a feline.

Lesson 74 – Team Activity

- The people at the Gregory Company made up rules about how to hire successful product designers.
- Here are the questions they asked to determine whether a person applying for the job would be a good designer:
    1. Does the person dress well?
    2. Does the person speak well?
    3. Does the person seem to be polite and cooperative?
    4. Has the person worked for another company that designs new products?
- If the answer is **yes** to all the questions, the folks at the Gregory Company give the person the highest possible rating.
- If the answer is **no** to all the questions, the person receives the lowest possible rating.
- Here are the scores the Gregory Company gave different people who applied for designer jobs:

Fran	Dan	Andy	Candy	Hilda	Ted
4	4	3	2	0	0

- Here's how good those people actually are at designing new products:

Fran	Dan	Andy	Candy	Hilda	Ted
good	fair	good	excellent	poor	excellent

- Work in teams and make up an outline diagram that explains the general problem with the standards the Gregory Company uses. Then explain what they should do instead.

Lesson 75 – Team Activity

- Here's an outline diagram for writing about one of Blinky's accounts:

Outline diagram

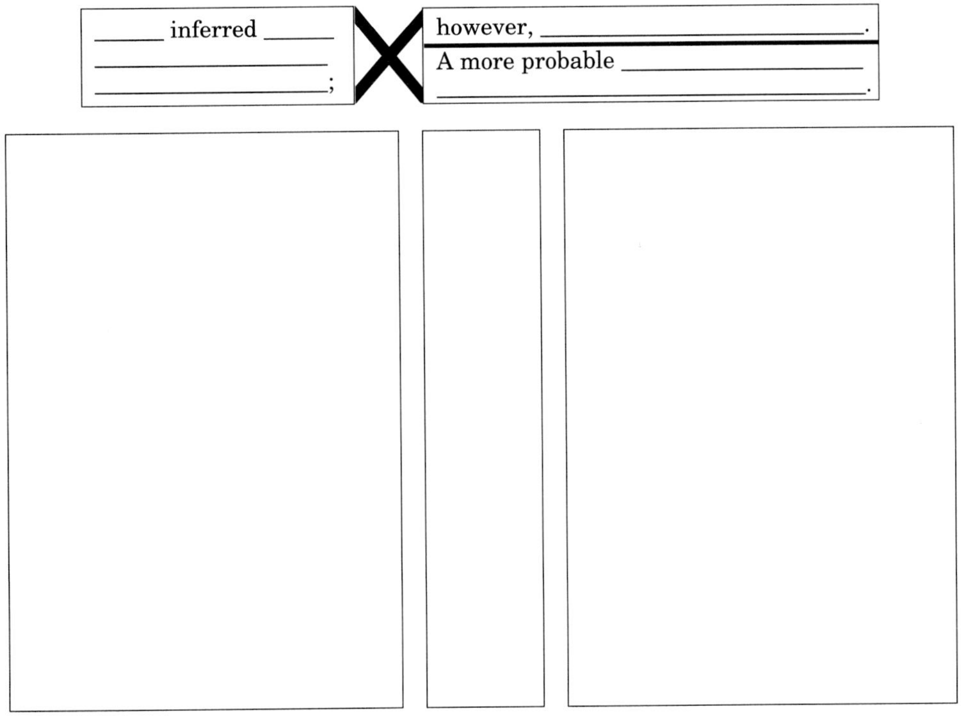

- Your team is going to make up an item:
  1. First, your team will write instructions for making the pictures. You will describe what's in the first picture and what's in the last picture. Remember, these are the kind of pictures that Blinky has problems with.
  2. Next, your team will write Blinky's account. Remember, he makes up those very improbable inferences. Write what Blinky said just the way he would write it.
  3. Then we'll see if we can get some good artists to make the illustrations.
  4. Finally, another team will read the account your team wrote and tell what's wrong with the account.

Lesson 76 – Team Activity

- Mr. Thompson's landlord wrote a new policy for having pets. But he didn't write his policy in simple language. He used the same kind of fancy words that he used before.
- If he had used simple language, he would have written these sentences:

  The pet must be an animal with a backbone.

  The pet must be in the class of warm-blooded animals that nurse their young.

  The pet must live in trees.

  The pet must be a flying animal.

  The pet must be a plant eater.

  And it must be a member of the squirrel family.

- Your team is going to make up the sentences that the landlord could have written.
- You'll look up different words and ask people if they know the fancy name or scientific name for the things that the landlord describes.
- You'll need fancy words for:
  - animals with backbones
  - warm-blooded animals that nurse their young
  - animals that live in trees
  - flying animals
  - plant-eating animals
  - members of the squirrel family
- After you find out all these names, you'll write sentences that are parallel to the sentences in the simple account; however, your sentences will have the fancy names.

Lesson 77 – Team Activity

- Mr. Thompson's landlord went on a vacation. He told Mr. Thompson that, if Mr. Thompson could figure out where the vacation spot was, Mr. Thompson would not have to pay rent for two months.
- Here are the clues the landlord gave Mr. Thompson:
    1. The vacation spot is not in the southern hemisphere and not in the eastern hemisphere.
    2. This place is between the latitudes of 22° and 16°. This place is between the longitudes of 85° and 90°.
    3. The neighboring state to the west of the vacation spot has a name with these letters: **CTAYUNA**, but the letters are in a different order.
    4. This place is an island. Its name begin with **C** and ends with **L.**
- Your team is going to locate the mystery place:
    1. Use an atlas or a globe.
    2. Find the area that is in both the northern hemisphere and western hemisphere.
    3. Find the area described by the latitude and longtitude numbers. **Latitudes** are shown with horizontal lines on the map or globe. **Longitudes** are shown with vertical lines.
    4. Find the neighboring state that has a name with these seven letters: **CTAYUNA**
    5. Go east and look for an island that has a name beginning with **C** and ending with **L.**

Lesson 78 – Team Activity

- Your team is going to make up another set of pictures and another account that Blinky wrote.
- Remember the steps:

  1. First, your team will write instructions for making the pictures. You will describe what's in the first picture and what's in the last picture.
  2. Next, your team will write Blinky's account. Remember, he makes up those very improbable inferences. Write what Blinky said just the way he would write it.
  3. Then we'll see if we can get some good artists to make the illustrations.
  4. Finally, another team will read the account your team wrote and tell what's wrong with the account.

Lesson 79 – Team Activity

- Each team is going to write a paper about homework.
- Some of the teams will write papers that are in favor of lots of homework.
- Other teams will write papers that argue for less homework.
- Papers that argue for homework will give their reasons. They will argue that
  - homework is good for students
  - homework is good for parents
  - homework is good for teachers
- Papers that are in favor of less homework will argue that
  - less homework is good for students
  - less homework is good for parents
  - less homework is good for teachers
- The arguments will present evidence based on the team's experiences.
- When writing your arguments, state what you believe and tell **why.** Make your reasons and evidence as clear and convincing as you can.
- Then state what you think your opponents would say and tell why you think they are wrong.
- After you write your arguments, you'll have a debate.

Outline diagram

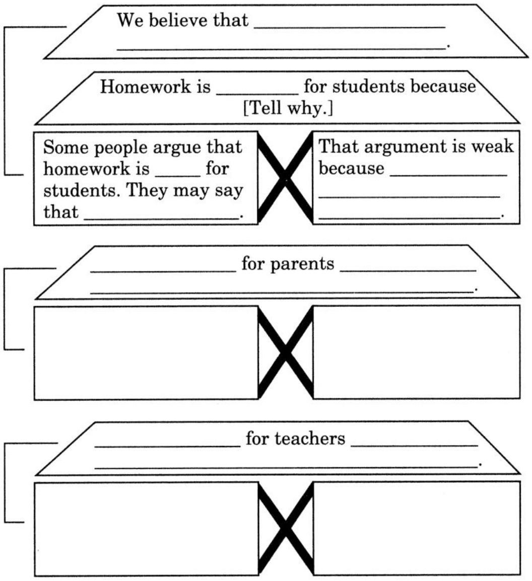

Lesson 80 – Team Activity

- Your team is going to write a proposal for improving schools.
- Your proposal could deal with
  - the length of the school day
  - whether more of the school day should be outside the classroom or outside the school
  - how the schedule could change to provide more work for some subjects and less work for others
  - what kind of new subjects could be put in school
  - how the way teachers grade students could be improved
  - whether more time or less time should be spent in school
  - whether school should operate all year long or during only part of the year
- When your write your proposal, you won't write about every change you think would be nice; you'll write about the most important changes that would benefit students, teachers and parents.
- Here's a very general outline diagram for writing a proposal for improving schools.

Our Proposal for Changing Schools

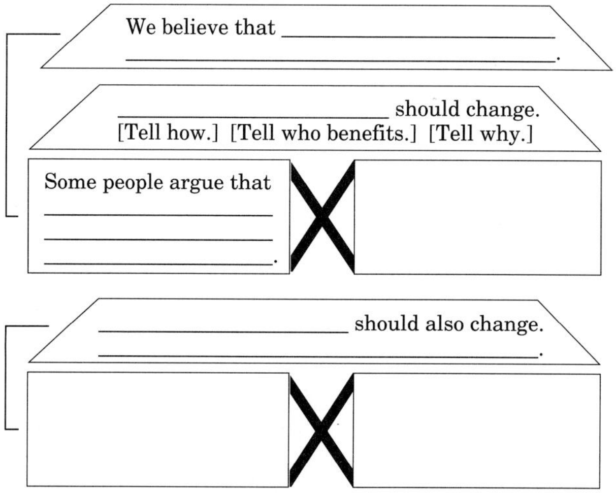

- It looks something like the diagram for the debate.
- You'll tell the reasons for your changes. Then you'll indicate what the opposition might say and tell why that position is weak.

Reference Section

Facts

birds – Birds, class Aves, are warm-blooded, egg-laying animals with a backbone. Birds are covered with FEATHERS and have wings. A few families of birds (such as OSTRICHES, EMUS and RHEAS) and some species of otherwise flying families (for example, some GREBES, RAILS and CORMORANTS) cannot fly. Others (such as PENGUINS) have become adapted to flying in water, but not in air.

bones – (See *skeleton.*)

Columbus – Columbus was a European who landed in America in 1492.

corn – Corn is an important farm crop. Corn is a plant of the grass family. The plant possesses both male and female flowers. The male flowers are borne in the tassel at the top of the stalk, and the female is a cluster, called a cob, at a joint of the stalk. Among the world's four most important crops (the others are wheat, rice and potatoes), corn is native to America. The United States produces over 40 percent of the world output. Countries with large areas devoted to corn include the United States, China, Brazil, Mexico, Argentina, Romania, France, India and South Africa.

fowl – The term is usually used with an adjective, for example, wild fowl or water fowl. If the term is used without an adjective, it means birds that are raised for food, or it means bird meat.

mammals – The largest mammal is the blue whale. Seals, dolphins, otters, walruses and whales are mammals that live in the ocean.

mountains – The tallest mountain in the world is Mt. Everest, which is 29,028 feet high (almost 5-1/2 miles).

Mountains	Feet	Meters	Location
Everest	29,028	8,848	Nepal-Tibet
K 2	28,250	8,611	Kashmir
Kanchenjunga	28,168	8,586	Nepal-Sikkim
Lhotse 1	27,923	8,516	Nepal-Tibet
Makalu 1	27,790	8,470	Nepal-Tibet

skeleton – The adult human skeleton is comprised of 206 individual bones. The three main functions of the skeletal system are protection, motion and support. The following diagram shows some of the important bones in the skeleton.

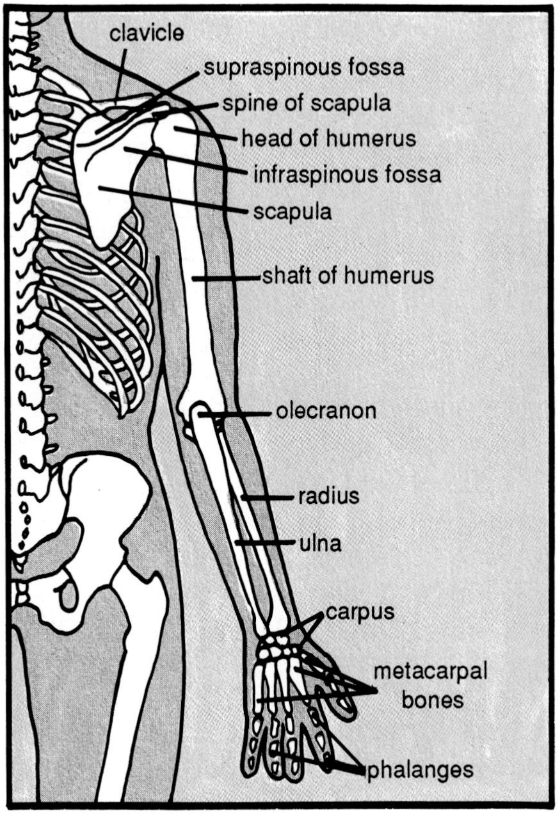

water – Water freezes at 32° Fahrenheit (0° Celsius) and boils at 212° Fahrenheit (100° Celsius).

wheat – Wheat is second only to rice in importance as a world food source. Wheat is grown on more of the world's acreage than any other food.

year – 365 days make a year, except leap year (every fourth year). Leap year equals 366 days.

Contractions

I am --------------I'm
I have ------------I've
I will --------------I'll
I would-----------I'd

you are ----------you're
you have --------you've
you will ----------you'll
you would ------you'd

he is --------------he's
he will ------------he'll
he would --------he'd

she is ------------she's
she will ----------she'll
she had ---------she'd

it is----------------it's

we are -----------we're
we will -----------we'll
we have ---------we've
we would -------we'd

they are ---------they're
they have -------they've
they would ------they'd
they had---------they'd
they will ---------they'll

here is -----------here's
that is ------------that's
there is ----------there's
what is -----------what's
where is ---------where's
who is------------who's
who will ---------who'll
let us -------------let's

are not-----------aren't
does not---------doesn't
do not ------------don't
has not ----------hasn't
have not---------haven't
is not -------------isn't
should not ------shouldn't
was not ----------wasn't
were not---------weren't
would not -------wouldn't

cannot -----------can't
will not -----------won't

Figures

Figure 1

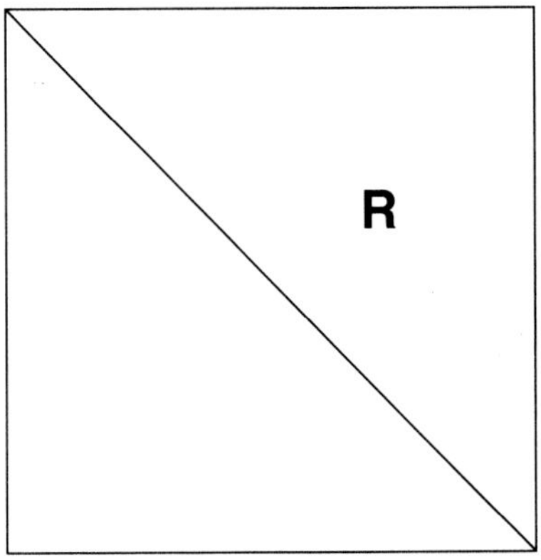

Figure 2

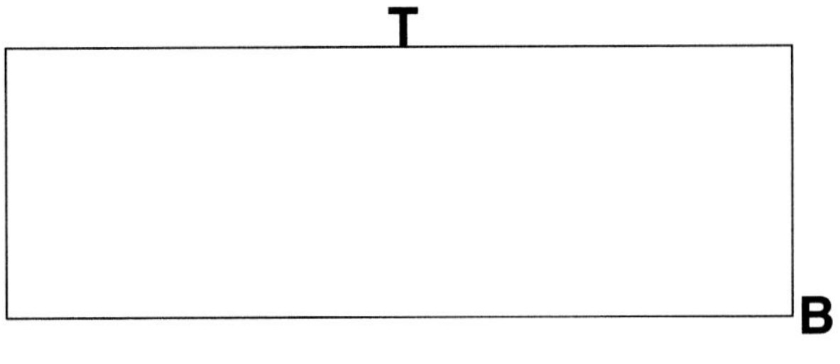

Verb–Noun List

VERB	NOUN
adapt	adaptation
adjust	adjustment
agree	agreement
altercate	altercation
apply	application
appoint	appointment
argue	argument
arrange	arrangement
assert	assertion
assign	assignment
assist	assistance
associate	association
assume	assumption
attach	attachment
attend	attendance
behave	behavior
believe	belief
bite	bite
choose	choice
collect	collection
collide	collision
communicate	communication
compare	comparison
compete	competition
complain	complaint
compose	composition
conclude	conclusion
confess	confession
confuse	confusion
connect	connection
conserve	conservation
construct	construction
contradict	contradiction
contribute	contribution
converse	conversation
cooperate	cooperation
criticize	criticism
declare	declaration
decorate	decoration
dedicate	dedication
deduct	deduction
demonstrate	demonstration
describe	description
destroy	destruction
develop	development
differ	difference
direct	direction
disagree	disagreement
discover	discovery
distract	distraction
disturb	disturbance
divide	division
educate	education
elevate	elevation
entertain	entertainment
erase	erasure
erode	erosion
erupt	eruption
establish	establishment
estimate	estimation
evacuate	evacuation
evaporate	evaporation
evolve	evolution
exaggerate	exaggeration
examine	examination
except	exception
excite	excitement
exclaim	exclamation
exclude	exclusion
exhibit	exhibition
exist	existence
expand	expansion
expect	expectation
explain	explanation
explode	explosion
explore	exploration

VERB	NOUN
extend	extension
fail	failure
fascinate	fascination
fertilize	fertilization
flatter	flattery
fulfill	fulfillment
fuse	fusion
gather	gathering
glorify	glorification
graduate	graduation
gravitate	gravitation
grow	growth
happen	happening
harass	harassment
harmonize	harmony
hate	hatred
hesitate	hesitation
horrify	horror
hypnotize	hypnotism
identify	identification
ignore	ignorance
illuminate	illumination
illustrate	illustration
imagine	imagination
impede	impediment
impress	impression
improve	improvement
improvise	improvision
include	inclusion
indent	indentation
indicate	indication
induct	induction
infect	infection
infer	inference
inherit	inheritance
injure	injury
inquire	inquiry
insist	insistence
inspect	inspection
inspire	inspiration

VERB	NOUN
install	installment/installation
instruct	instruction
interfere	interference
interpret	interpretation
interrogate	interrogation
interrupt	interruption
introduce	introduction
invade	invasion
invest	investment
invite	invitation
involve	involvement
jeopardize	jeopardy
join	joint
judge	judgment
kill	killing
kindle	kindling
locate	location
marry	marriage
object	objection
observe	observation
perform	performance
practice	practice
prepare	preparation
propose	proposal
punctuate	punctuation
relate	relation
remind	reminder
request	request
require	requirement
rotate	rotation
sing	song
state	statement
study	study/studying
summarize	summary
theorize	theory
transform	transformation
vacate	vacation
vaccinate	vaccination
warn	warning

Lesson 23

We watched rockets take off from our couch.

Figures

Lesson 28

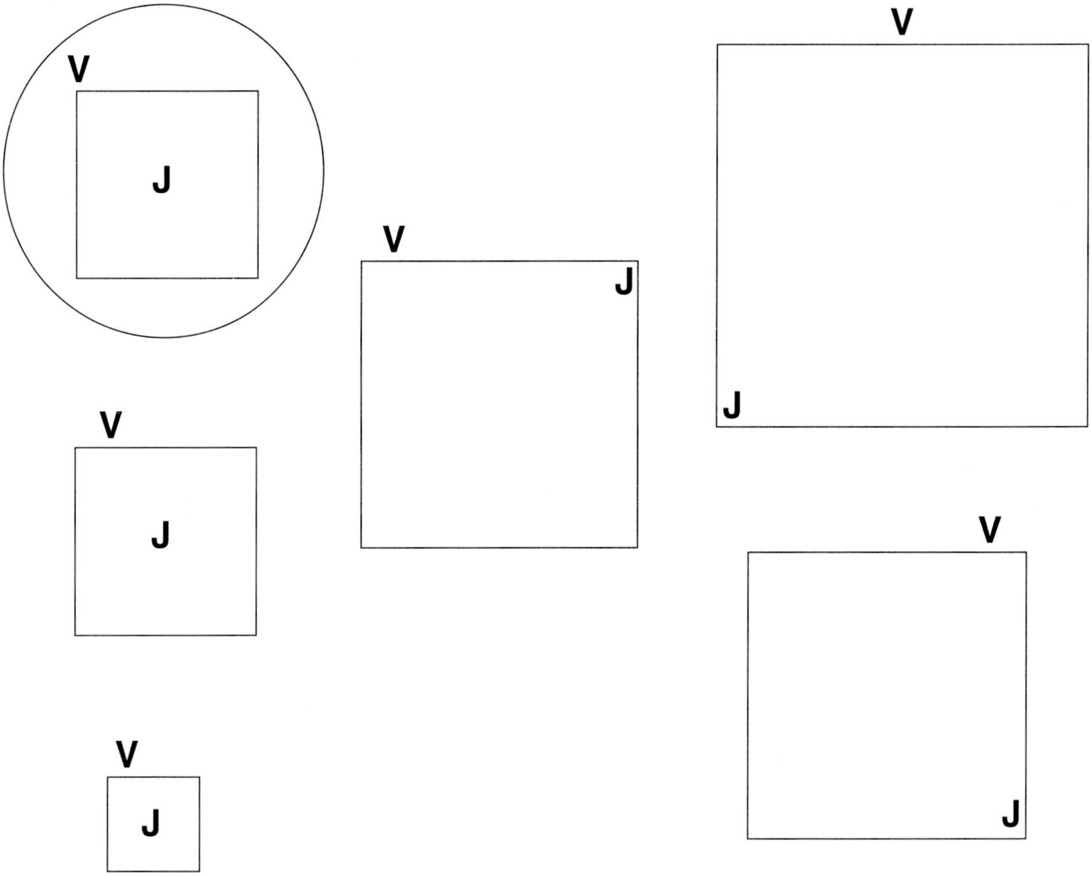

Parts of Outline Diagrams

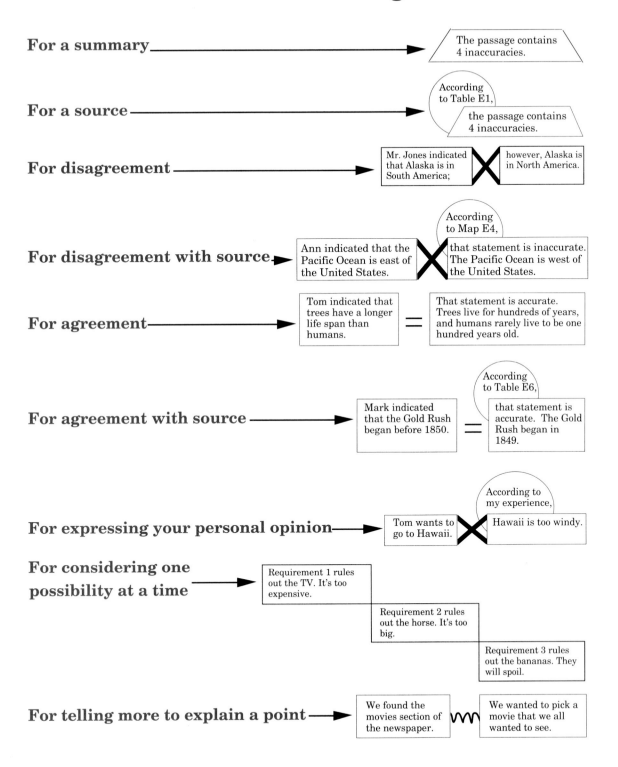

For a summary

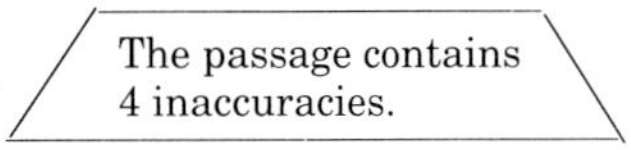

The passage contains
4 inaccuracies.

For a source

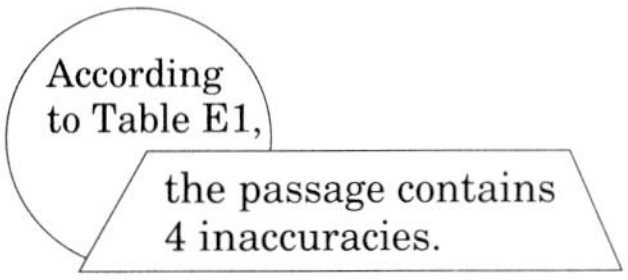

For disagreement

Mr. Jones indicated
that Alaska is in

however, Alaska is

For disagreement with source

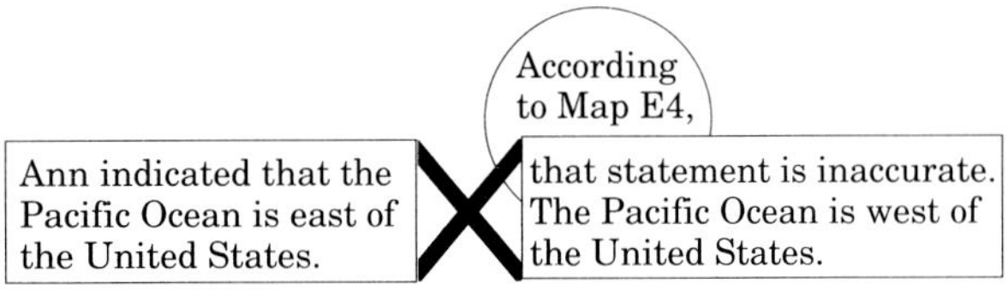

According
to Table E1,
the passage contains
4 inaccuracies.
to Table E6,
that the Gold Rush
began before 1850.
to Map E4,
Ann indicated that the
Pacific Ocean is east of
the United States.
that statement is inaccurate.
The Pacific Ocean is west of
the United States.

For agreement

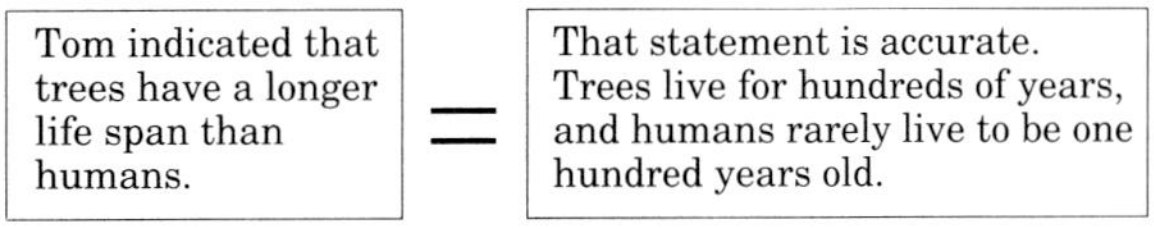

Tom indicated that
trees have a longer
life span than
humans.
That statement is accurate.
Trees live for hundreds of years,
and humans rarely live to be one
hundred years old.

For agreement with source

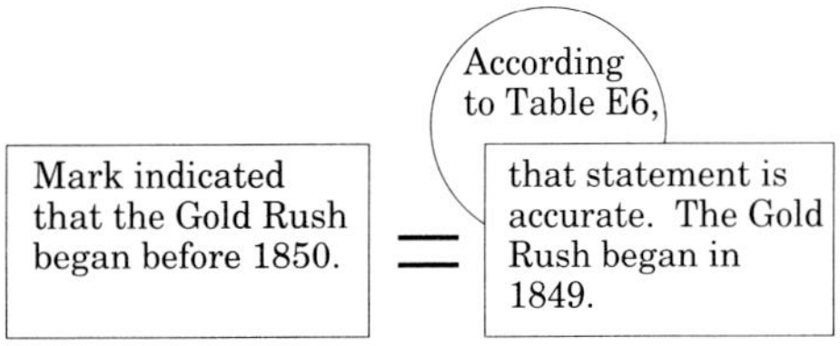

Rush began in

For expressing your personal opinion

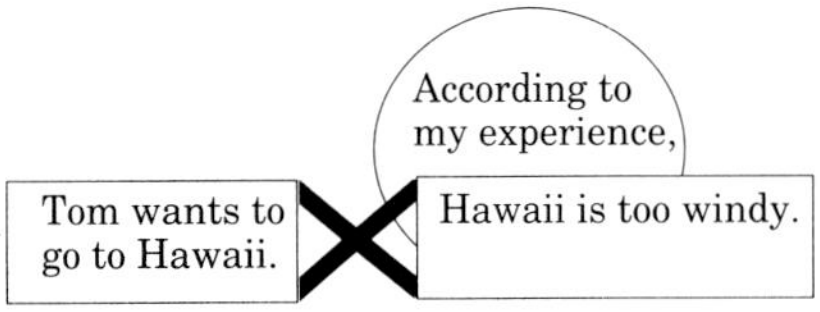

my experience,
Tom wants to
go to Hawaii.
Hawaii is too windy.

For considering one possibility at a time

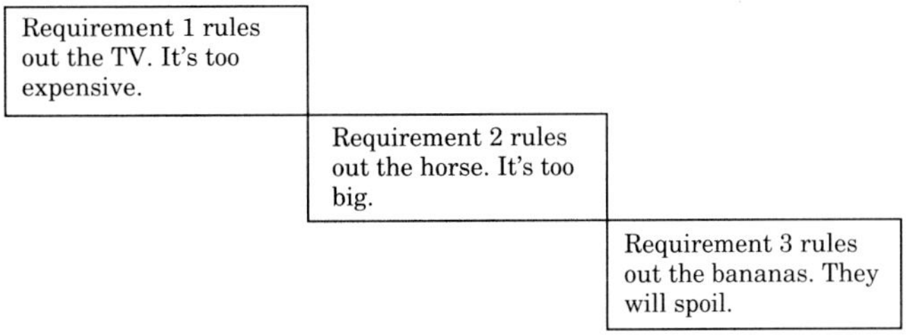

out the TV. It's too

out the horse. It's too

out the bananas. They
will spoil.

For telling more to explain a point

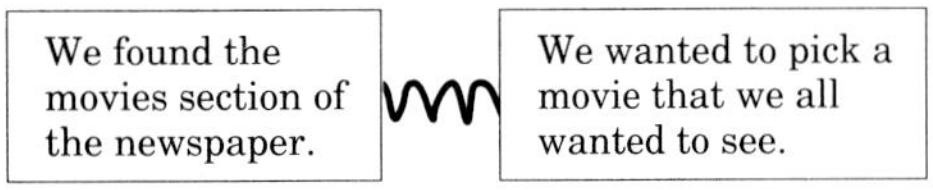

We found the
movies section of
the newspaper.
We wanted to pick a
movie that we all
wanted to see.

Statements and Claims

Supporting Accurate Statements (Lesson 6)

______________ indicates that ________________ ______________________.	=	That statement is accurate. [Give specific facts.]

Contradicting Inaccurate Statements (Lesson 6)

______________ indicates that __________________ _______________________;	X	however, that statement is inaccurate. [Give facts that contradict.]

Identifying Misleading Impressions (Lesson 35)

_______'s account gives the impressions that __ _____________________ _____________________;	X	however, that account is misleading. [Give facts.]

More Than One Requirement

Using Information to Rule Out Possibilities (Lesson 51)

The mystery object is _____________.

Clue __ rules out ____.
[Tell why.]

The only remaining possibility is _____________.

Arguments

Contradictions (Lesson 43)

_______ contradicts _______.

If ________________ ________________, would ________________ ________________.

However, ________________ ________________ ________________ ________________.

Inadequate Evidence (Lesson 43)

_______ concludes that ________________ ________________ ________________;

however, the evidence is inadequate. The specific evidence indicates only that ________________.

Possibly, ________________ ________________ ________________ ________________.

(Lesson 57)

_______ concludes that ________________ ________________ ________________.

However, the evidence does not indicate that _______ [all/only] ________________ ________________.

=

Therefore, ________________ ________________ might ________________ or ________________.

False Cause (Lesson 55)

_______ concludes that ________________ ________________ ________________;

however, the evidence is inadequate.

The evidence indicates only that when [one thing happened], [another thing happened].

The evidence doesn't indicate that _______ _______ causes ________________.

Conclusions More General Than the Evidence (Lesson 63)

_______ concludes that ________________ ________________;

however, the conclusion is more general than the evidence. Evidence about [a specific category] cannot lead to a proper conclusion about [a general category].

Improbable Inferences (Lesson 62)

_______ inferred that ________________ ________________;

however, that inference is not probable. A more probable inference is that _______ ________________.